Backpacking Washington's Alpine Lakes Wilderness

The Longer Trails

Jeff Smoot

FALCONGUIDES ®

GUILFORD, CONNECTICUT
HELENA, MONTANA

FALCONGUIDES®

Copyright © 2004 by Rowman & Littlefield

ALL RIGHTS RESERVED. No part of this book may be
reproduced or transmitted in any form by any means, elec-
tronic or mechanical, including photocopying and recording,
or by any information storage and retrieval system, except
as, may be expressly permitted in writing from the publisher.

Falcon, FalconGuides, and Outfit Your Mind are registered
trademarks of Rowman & Littlefield.

Photographs by the author unless otherwise noted. Maps
created by XNR Productions Inc. © The Globe Pequot Press

Library of Congress Cataloging-in-Publication Data
Smoot, Jeff.

   Backpacking Washington's Alpine Lakes Wilderness: the
   longer trails / Jeff Smoot. —1st ed.
      p. cm. — (A Falcon Guide)
   ISBN 978-0-7627-3098-8
    1. Hiking—Washington (State)—Alpine Lakes
   Wilderness—Guidebooks. 2. Trails—Washington
   (State)—Alpine Lakes Wilderness—Guidebooks. 3. Alpine
   Lakes Wilderness (Wash.)—Guidebooks. I. Title. II. Series.

   GV199.42.W2A465 2004
   917.97—dc22

2004040627

Printed in the United States of America

Distributed by NATIONAL BOOK NETWORK

Contents

The Hikes

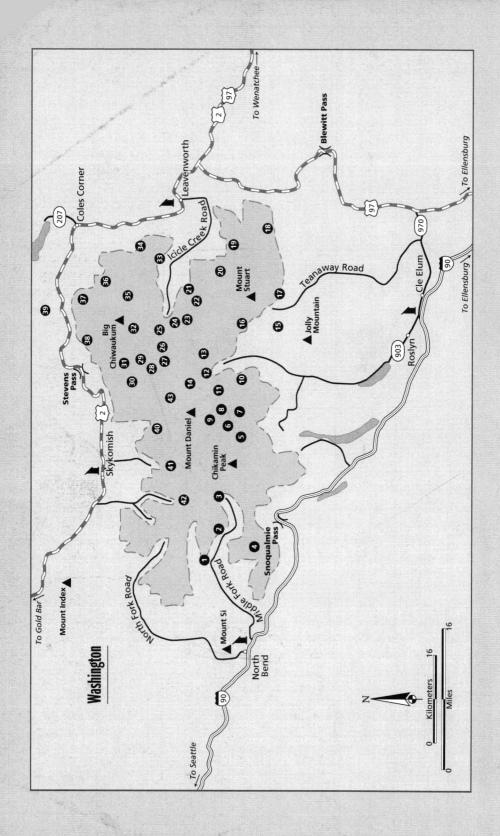

Preface

When writing guidebooks, I am constantly reminded of the need for conservancy by wilderness visitors. This project was no exception. The Alpine Lakes Wilderness is one of the most accessible wilderness areas in Washington. Almost every trail listed in this guide is within one or two hours' drive of millions of people. Because of this, it is heavily used and heavily abused. Most wilderness users—hikers, climbers, skiers, and scramblers included—do take care to minimize their impact. However, with the many thousands who come to the wilderness areas each year, and the resulting overuse and abuse of many otherwise pristine areas, there is much room for improvement.

I cannot deny that guidebooks such as this one are partly responsible for the crush of visitors to our wilderness areas. But guidebooks have been around for decades and have already lured thousands of naive visitors to the wilderness, to trample a subalpine meadow or cut a switchback. Of course, guidebooks and their authors are not solely to blame for the overuse of wilderness. With the popularity of hiking and climbing, and the influx of new residents to this state, our wilderness is shrinking at a rapid pace. In response, permit systems, quotas, and user fees are being implemented at wilderness areas throughout America. It is true what they say: We *are* loving our wilderness to death. It is my hope that this guidebook will adequately address issues of conservancy and help to educate uninitiated wilderness visitors in the ways of the "wilderness ethic."

It is not the guidebooks, really, that are to blame for abuses to our wilderness areas. It is people. In order to preserve our wilderness—or what is left of it—for future generations, each visitor must treat the wilderness with care, with love even. Those who love the wilderness do not cut switchbacks, discard trash, cut trees, harass wildlife, or foul streams and lakes; they come and go, in quiet appreciation, leaving no trace of their visit except a few dusty bootprints along the trail.

Although we won't likely wear our wilderness down with our boot soles, we may greatly detract from the beauty and serenity of the mountain environment unless we think and act in ways appropriate to preserving our wilderness areas.

A large part of the wilderness is discovery and exploration. In that spirit, this guide won't give away all of the surprises. This is not a fully illustrated instruction book for preassembled adventures; rather, it is a starting point for those who wish to discover and explore the trails of the Alpine Lakes Wilderness. While this guide follows the Falcon guidelines and provides more of a step-by-step description of many trails than some other guides, hopefully users of this guide will get where they are going without missing the best part of the outdoor experience—the adventure—in the process.

Acknowledgments

If anything is true in guidebook writing, "It's not what you know; it's who you know." Without the help of others, this guidebook would have been nearly impossible. I acknowledge those who assisted with this project, whether for providing trail information, photographs, or chapter reviews; for referring me along to someone who had information; or for chatting with me along a trail or accompanying me on a hike. Thanks to Morgan Balogh, Jim Busch, Pat Gentry, Chris and Katie Griffes, Rick Hack, Chris and Don Hanson, Darren and Ann Nelson, Michael and Kris Stanton, and Doug Weaver. Appreciation is extended to Lisa Therrell, Bill Soberoski, Lucy Schmidt, and Tom Davis of the U.S. Forest Service for providing current trail information and maintenance updates. Special thanks to Pat Gentry for driving me to distant trailheads and picking me up at others. My appreciation also to those who maintain Web sites devoted to hiking in the Cascades, which proved to be excellent sources of trail updates and information. Thanks also to the many hikers I met along the trail, who shared their experiences and told me things I never could have learned in a lifetime of hiking these trails. The list goes on and on, and I have certainly forgotten someone, whom I hope is very understanding.

Very special thanks to my wife, Karen, and daughters, Lauren and Andrea, for accompanying me on occasional hikes and for their patience and support throughout this and my many other writing projects. And as always, thanks to my parents for letting me run wild in the mountains in my youth.

Introduction

The Alpine Lakes Wilderness straddles the heart of Washington's Cascade Range. It includes a majority of the rivers, streams, lakes, old-growth forest, and mountain terrain lying between Snoqualmie Pass and Stevens Pass and is roughly bordered by Washington State's two major cross-state highways, Interstate 90 and U.S. Highway 2, stretching east to west from Leavenworth to North Bend. Unlike many of the region's better-known wilderness areas, including Mount Baker, Glacier Peak, and Mount Adams, to name only a few, this 393,000-acre wilderness area has no crowning jewel such as a high volcano. Rather, its wealth of high lakes set among the region's varied landscape—from its majestic old-growth forests to its flowery subalpine meadows, from its deeply carved river valleys to its granite ridges and glaciated peaks—makes the Alpine Lakes Wilderness a very unique, very special place. Given the fact that the wilderness lies only an hour's drive away from the state's largest metropolitan and suburban area, the Alpine Lakes Wilderness is certainly one of the most often visited wilderness areas in the western United States. People come here year-round, for recreation in all forms—hiking, backpacking, horseback riding, fishing, kayaking, climbing, skiing, and snowshoeing, to name only a few.

The uniqueness of the Alpine Lakes area was recognized by its designation as a wilderness area in 1976, although it was considered a unique place long before an Act of Congress made it official.

Geology

The Alpine Lakes Wilderness has a complex geologic history. The wilderness lies at the southern margin of the North Cascades, which are among the most complex, varied, and rugged mountains in North America. In contrast to the gentle woodland peaks and high volcanoes of the southern Cascade Range, the North Cascades are rugged beyond compare. Actually, the range has been likened to the Swiss Alps, which, although higher in elevation, are equaled if not exceeded in sheer relief and volume of ice by the peaks of the North Cascades. Uplifted by colliding continental plates and scoured and carved by glaciers, the mountains of the North Cascades rise abruptly from deep glacial valleys in steep cliffs terminating in sharp rocky points and crests. Rugged glaciers drape the highest peaks and hang menacingly from north-facing cirques and basins. Craggy granite escarpments lord over the deep valleys, while scattered volcanic and metamorphic peaks maintain a lower profile.

The Alpine Lakes Wilderness is one of the most rugged areas of the Cascade Range. Although in terms of sheer relief it does not quite compare with the North Cascades, it is still a sublime region of deep, glacier-carved valleys, pristine subalpine meadows, and craggy peaks rising to over 9,000 feet. The wilderness is varied. A few geologic features typify the wilderness. Mount Stuart and the Stuart Range are the highest and most rugged of the Alpine Lakes Wilderness mountains, a granite

Prusik Peak above Snow Creek, Enchantments

escarpment rising thousands of feet above deep glacial valleys, reminiscent of the Sierra Nevada. The Snoqualmie Crest peaks running from Snoqualmie Pass northward to Dutch Miller Gap are the Picket Range in miniature, a row of steep, craggy, glaciated peaks rising above wild basins and valleys. Gold Creek is a prototypical glacial valley, a broad U-shaped valley, deeply forested and flanked by steep cliffs and ridges. Mount Daniel, near the center of the wilderness, is an old volcanic remnant scoured by glaciers. The Wenatchee Mountains, extending nearly the length of the wilderness, are an old range of craggy peaks and ridges dotted with lakes, in wooded basins and granite cirques, weathered by snow and wind, cut deep by streams and rivers. Chiwaukum, Icicle, and Ingalls Creeks flow eastward toward the Columbia River, down deep valleys, canyons, and gorges between high ridges and stark, granite peaks. The Snoqualmie and Skykomish Rivers flow westward into Puget Sound, fed by rivers and streams flowing from glaciers and lakes down through quiet, old-growth forest valleys, some impenetrably thick with brush. Obviously, each area of the wilderness has its own unique characteristics.

Although the mountains and valleys are important geologic features, what is unique and special about the Alpine Lakes Wilderness is the lakes. There are hundreds of lakes, from tiny ponds to huge reservoirs, some deep in forested valleys, some high on barren alpine plateaus. A majority of the lakes owe their existence to glaciers, which scoured the plateaus, basins, and valleys, carving out cirques that later filled with meltwater, depositing moraines that dammed the flow of streams and rivers. Nearly every trail in the wilderness leads to a tarn, pond, or lake. Some trails follow a chain of lakes higher and higher up a wilderness valley. Beyond the trails are more lakes. And more lakes.

Flora and Fauna

Although relatively few visitors to the Alpine Lakes Wilderness come exclusively to seek out species of plants and animals—with the exception of photographers and wildflower enthusiasts, of course—the region's abundant flora and fauna is an integral part of the wilderness experience. Learning to recognize different species of plants and animals in their native environment is not always easy, but it is certainly very rewarding.

The plant life in the Alpine Lakes Wilderness is varied and abundant. The lowland forests are occupied by giants: old-growth Douglas fir, western hemlock, western red cedar, and occasional stands of sitka spruce. In their shade grow ferns, mosses, and a variety of herbs, shrubs, and small trees. Alder, maple, and salmonberry line old road grades outside the wilderness and fill in available space within the wilderness boundary. River bottoms and seeping slopes grow thick with mosses, ferns, and shrubs such as salmonberry, thimbleberry, and devil's club, with shade-tolerant hemlock starts and red huckleberry bushes shooting up from every nurse log and rotten stump. Slide alder, maple, and willow dominate avalanche slopes; mountain-ash, huckleberry, and white rhododendron on mid-elevation slopes. At higher elevations, the Douglas firs, hemlocks, and cedars are joined by Pacific silver fir, one of the predominant species of the wilderness forests. Above timberline, mountain hemlock and subalpine fir predominate, with low-lying heather, juniper, and huckleberry shrubs complimenting wide-open meadows of grasses and wildflowers. Stands of larch trees grow in high lake basins in the eastern portion of the wilderness. Above treeline, gnarled mountain hemlock and subalpine fir krummholz grow prostrate among lichen-dotted rocks. A few hardy flower species grow in high basins and meadows and on high ridges, clinging to the barren, windswept soil.

Columbine

Wildflowers are the most sought-after plants in the wilderness. The wildflower displays here are legendary: tiger lily, columbine, lupine, aster, trillium, pearly ever-lasting, valerian, skyrocket, shooting star, penstemon, lousewort, bog gentian, mon-key flower, bead lily, glacier lily, queen's cup, monkshood, bluebell, bellflower, bleeding heart, Tweedy's lewissia, balsamroot, wild orchids—too many to name. If you want to see wildflowers, come from mid-July to mid-August when the flowers are usually at their peak, especially in meadows and along stream banks. In contrast to the wildflowers, the old-growth trees are equally impressive. The contrast between the second-growth forests outside the wilderness boundary and the virgin forests within the wilderness is striking and will make a lasting impression. You'll know you've reached the wilderness boundary just by the size of the trees and by the quiet sense of wonder they inspire.

On certain summer weekends, humans might seem to be the most abundant ani-mal species in the Alpine Lakes Wilderness. With the exception of insects and birds, you will probably encounter more people on the trail than you will other wildlife. But even though you don't see them, they see you. They are everywhere. Chipmunks and ground squirrels are commonly seen scampering across the trail, as are Douglas' squir-rels, rustling in the branches overhead, scolding you as you pass or nipping off seed cones that come whizzing down all around you. Hoary marmots, the "groundhogs of the West," are abundant in talus and rocky areas at higher elevations. The marmot's shrill whistle is easily recognizable, and they can often be seen scurrying through the talus. More elusive is the pika (say PEEK-a), another talus dweller commonly heard along the trail. These guinea pig–sized members of the rabbit family (sometimes called rock rabbits) have a very shrill "eek." You'll see brown rabbits on lowland trails and forest roads and may see snowshoe hares, although you are likely to see only their tracks in the snow.

Beavers used to be abundant in lowland valleys but now are a rarity, although old beaver dams may still be encountered. Porcupines are sometimes seen along the trail and are easily identified by their lumbering gait and sharp quills. They live on tree bark, leaves, and branches, like the beaver, but they climb trees instead of cutting them down. While you rarely need to worry about porcupine encounters, dogs frequently get a little too close and end up with a bunch of quills embedded in their snout. If you leash your dog like you're supposed to, this should not happen. What hikers should worry about is porcupines eating their boots, backpack, clothing—and certain auto parts! Porcupines crave fat and salt, and will eat anything to get it. If you see a porcupine lurking about your camp, sleep close to your boots and pack straps!

Snakes and lizards are abundant in all areas; rattlesnakes are rarely encountered but may be found in lowland areas at the eastern fringe of the wilderness. You will no doubt find frogs along many lowland trails, especially near streams and boggy areas; watch your step! The lakes are full of varieties of trout, mostly too small to be keepers but not so small as to keep anglers from bothering. There are all kinds of wild birds. You are most likely to recognize the big birds—brown and bald eagles, peregrine falcons, Cooper's and red-tailed hawks, kestrels, ravens, woodpeckers, kingfishers, and owls—but the little birds are more common, especially chickadees, nuthatches, finches, jays, and juncos. Early-morning visitors to high ridges and peaks may be rewarded with close views of soaring eagles and hawks. Canadian jays, those "camp robbers" of infamy, will eat right out of your hand or your unattended bag of trail mix, if you let them.

Aside from birds, the most commonly seen animal is the black-tailed deer, abundant throughout the wilderness. Deer are most often seen early in the morning and late in the day in lowland and subalpine meadows, although a stray or small herd may be seen grazing in shady forest at midday. Elk are common in the Cascades but are only occasionally seen in the Alpine Lakes Wilderness, usually only in the Cle Elum and Teanaway regions. Mountain goats are more prevalent, especially at higher elevations east of the Cascade crest. Goats are usually wary of hikers and keep their distance, but some goats don't seem to mind. Like porcupines, mountain goats crave salt, and they don't care where they get it. For that reason, hikers are requested to urinate on rocks instead of plants or dirt in the alpine zone, so the goats don't tear up the meadows in their unabashed quest for salt.

In fall, hunters prowl the trails in and around the wilderness in search of deer, elk, and goats and their predators, bears and cougars, both of which are prevalent throughout the Alpine Lakes Wilderness. Black bears are often encountered by hikers.

Usually the bear will run away upon a hiker's approach, but occasionally a bear will stand its ground. When a bear stands up, it's trying to get a better look at you. Conventional wisdom says to stand your ground, make noise by talking or singing, and spread out your arms to make yourself "look big" to the bear. Bear attacks are rare around here; usually bears are after food, and hikers must take measures to protect their food—and themselves—from bears. How? For one, don't cook or clean up anywhere near where you camp, but at least 200 feet away. Then change out of the clothes you cooked in. Remove all food from your campsite and tent, and either store it in a bear-proof container or hang it from a tree. Bears are resourceful and can break into "bear-proof" food containers and knock down food bags that are improperly hung, so put a little thought into where and how you hang your food, lest you find your cache stolen the next morning. Bears seem to be the worst in the eastern half of the wilderness during summer and fall, especially in lowland areas near campgrounds and on the fringe of cities. Bears near Leavenworth are particularly pesky, raiding bakery garbage cans and campers' cars and coolers in broad daylight. The bears around here haven't learned all of the tricks of their national park brethren and are therefore more inclined to run away from you than bluff charge or stand their ground; some bears, though, seem remarkably unconcerned with hikers and continue pawing at rotten logs and snuffling for mushrooms right beside the trail, forcing hikers to make a wide detour. The presence of bears on hiking trails is another reason to keep your dog leashed, or leave it at home. The Washington Department of Fish and Wildlife publishes a brochure about black bears; it is available at Forest Service offices, a must-read for wilderness travelers. Grizzly bears are rumored to live in the North Cascades, and there have been reported sightings in the Alpine Lakes Wilderness, but no one I've talked to has seen one this far south. Perhaps the grizzlies sighted were just passing through; either that, or someone mistook a big black bear for a grizzly.

Less often seen but potentially more dangerous to hikers are cougars, or mountain lions, pumas, catamounts, or what have you. These wild cats have seen a growth in population since dog hunts were banned several years ago. Although very few hikers have been attacked by cougars, there have been an increasing number of encounters, mostly along lowland logging roads and trails. Don't worry too much. You probably will never see a cougar in the wild, let alone face one down on a trail. But if you do, experts recommend that you not turn and run, as that only encourages the cats to chase you. Instead, stand your ground, maintain eye contact, spread your arms to look big, and make noise to scare the cat away, and if the cat does not run away, back away slowly until well out of sight and then turn and walk quickly away. My instinct would be to pick up rocks and sticks and throw them at the cougar while yelling as loud as possible, and that is recommended as a last resort if the cat

◀ *Pika*

won't leave or gives you a menacing look or seems to be getting ready to pounce on you, fangs bared, ears back, hissing. If attacked, fight back hard to let the cat know you aren't prey. Hit it with rocks, sticks, your camera, pack, fists, whatever; grab its throat and squeeze hard. Especially keep children close, and don't try to save your dog if it happens to be attacked. There haven't been very many fatalities in cougar attacks around here. In other areas, cougars seem to have attacked solitary hikers and trail runners, especially children who have strayed too far ahead on the trail. The Washington Department of Fish and Wildlife publishes a brochure about cougars; it is available at Forest Service offices, a must-read for wilderness travelers.

To learn more about how to deal with bears and cougars or to find out about any recent sightings or problems, call or visit one of the ranger stations listed in Appendix B.

Obviously, this is a simplistic overview of plant and animal life within the Alpine Lakes Wilderness. There are so many species of plants and animals within the wilderness that to name and describe them all here would leave little room for anything else. Whole volumes have been published documenting the plant life of the Cascade mountains. Most hikers aren't interested in the minutiae of minor subspecies of moss, lichen, or rodentia, nor do they likely come only to seek out particular plant or wildlife species. Visitors interested in identifying plants should consult the list in Appendix E for topic-specific references. My favorite is *Cascade-Olympic Natural History,* an entertaining text with excellent color photos of many of the commonly seen plants and animals.

Climate

Weather is not always poor in the Pacific Northwest, even if it seems that way. The Puget Sound region bordering the Cascades on the west is considered "rainy" by most standards but has a lower average annual cumulative rainfall than many East Coast cities. However, the Pacific Northwest's reputation for precipitation is not entirely unfounded. Washington's Olympic Peninsula has one of the highest measured cumulative annual rainfalls in the nation. The slopes of Mount Rainier, Mount Baker, and Mount Olympus have hosted record snowfalls. When it rains in the Pacific Northwest, it is usually a steady drizzle lasting several days; hence the reputation for rain. If it's not raining, rejoice—and go hiking! But don't let a little rain stop you from going hiking. Rainy-day hikes may not have the inspiring views of distant peaks and valleys, but you see a lot more when you aren't always looking off in the distance.

In a nutshell, this is how Washington mountain weather works: Warm, moist air blows in off the Pacific Ocean, squeezing moisture-laden clouds against the Olympic mountains. These clouds, like large sponges, dump excessive rain on the western slopes of the mountains until, relieved of their burden, the clouds rise over the mountains and drift eastward across Puget Sound, where the process is repeated against the Cascade foothills with similar effect, although the volume of rainfall is generally less than that which falls on the rain forests of the Olympic Peninsula. Once the clouds have dumped their load on the western slopes of the Cascades, they again drift eastward over the eastern slopes of the range, which are markedly drier and less heavily vegetated. This warm, moist marine air condenses and freezes very rapidly when it hits the cold, snowy Cascades and Olympics, which accounts for high winds and the tremendous snowfalls each year. This is a bit simplistic, but it is close enough for this guide's purposes.

Wilderness Permit Requirements

Permits are required for all entry into the Alpine Lakes Wilderness, including day use and overnight visits. Self-issue permits are available at all wilderness trailheads. Sign in, attach the permit to your pack, and proceed. Your permit must be visible at all times. If you hike more than one trail during your trip, fill out a new permit for each hike. Some people don't bother, but they should. Among other things, the Forest Service uses permit data to monitor the number of hikers using a given trail, which in turn is used to determine the level of maintenance a trail receives.

Overnight visits to the Enchantments permit area require advance registration to limit the number of visitors to this beautiful but overused area, including Snow, Colchuck, Stuart, Eightmile, and Caroline Lakes, as well as the fabled Enchantment Lakes. Contact the Leavenworth Ranger District for permit details. At present, day use is still unrestricted with a trailhead day-use permit. If you get caught hiking through the Enchantments without a day-use permit or camping out in the Enchantment area without an overnight permit, you may be fined.

Northwest Forest Passes

A trailhead parking pass (presently called a Northwest Forest Pass) is required for parking at or within 0.25 mile of most trailheads included in this guide. These passes can be obtained from Forest Service district offices and most outdoor retailers. A one-day pass is presently $5.00, an annual pass $30.00. If you do a lot of hiking in Washington or Oregon, the annual pass is well worth the money. The fee is supposed to be used in part for trail maintenance and construction, and there is evidence of this in new footbridges and trailhead improvements. Many hikers resent the imposition of yet another fee for using the wilderness, but without this money the Forest Service might have to cut back on trail maintenance, which might result in roads and trails being abandoned. Some hikers think that would be just fine, since it would reduce the number of visitors to the wilderness, allowing the wilderness to become true wilderness. Politics aside, if you don't want to get a ticket, get a pass.

Sno-Park Passes

A separate parking pass—the Sno-Park Pass—is required at winter recreation trailheads. Sno-Park Pass fees are used to clear and maintain access to ski and snowshoe trailheads. Hikers planning a winter or spring hike may need to get a Sno-Park Pass.

Wilderness Regulations

In addition to permit requirements, Alpine Lakes Wilderness use is subject to certain regulations. These regulations are posted at most trailheads and are summarized on the back of your permit. They include the following:

- Maximum group size is twelve, including all people and stock. In the Enchantment Lakes, maximum group size is eight. The Forest Service refers to this as the "heartbeat rule"; count the number of heartbeats in your group, not legs. Include your dog in the count.
- No motorized or mechanized equipment is allowed. That means no motorbikes, bicycles, chainsaws, carts, or aircraft are allowed within the wilderness boundary.
- Many areas have camping restrictions such as setbacks from lakes or designated sites, usually at least 200 feet from lakes and certain meadows.
- Campfires are not allowed above 5,000 feet elevation or at popular lakes and meadows. Signs usually warn you of entry into a no-campfire area.
- Cutting switchbacks is not allowed. Stay on established trails.
- Caching of supplies for longer than forty-eight hours is prohibited.
- Do not cut trees, snags, or boughs. Do not walk or camp in areas closed for restoration.
- Pack out all litter.
- Bury human waste and pet waste well away from camps and water sources. Dispose of wash water well away from water sources.

Backcountry Safety and Hazards

Hiking Safely

All things considered, hiking on trails is probably the safest mode of wilderness travel, where usually only weather and your own or others' actions are reasons for concern. But hiking, like other modes of wilderness travel, has numerous objective dangers, and the hikes described in this guide are no exception. Hikers venturing into the wilderness subject themselves to numerous hazards. Some trails become treacherous after dark or during poor weather; losing the trail after dark is a leading cause of hiking accidents, well justifying packing a flashlight, especially given the frequency with which many overly ambitious hikers find themselves hiking out in the dark. High rainfall and snowmelt cause flooding, which can erode or undermine trails. In certain glacier-fed stream valleys, outburst floods are an infrequent but potentially serious hazard. More often, it is high streams and rivers during early-season snowmelt that cause problems; high water can wash out footlogs and bridges, making for difficult and potentially dangerous stream crossings. Falling trees and rocks have killed unfortunate hikers; these hazards are more prevalent in areas burned over by recent fires. Loose rock and gravel on trails can cause slips, falls, and sprained ankles or worse. Snow, ice, and mud on trails can be treacherous. A slip on snow, ice, wet rocks or roots, or mud can cause broken wrists and more. Snow bridges over streams easily collapse. Footlogs may be slippery; fording streams can be tricky; a plunge into an ice-cold stream can quickly lead to hypothermia. Brush covering the trail can hide rocks, roots, and holes, and can trip you up. An unseen branch can cut and scar or put an eye out. An untied bootlace can lead to a broken leg or worse. Lightning can strike anywhere but is especially frequent on the high eastern ridges and peaks during the summer months. Bears and cougars lurk in the mountains, and although animal attacks are rare, they do occur. Rattlesnakes are present in some areas on the eastern fringe of the wilderness. Insects, including bees, wasps, yellow jackets, and ticks, can cause problems for hikers, especially those with allergies. There is also the human element to consider; although rare, hikers are sometimes assaulted by other hikers.

Despite all of the obvious potential dangers, thousands of hikers make it into and out of the wilderness each year without incident or injury. However, we shouldn't be too smug about this. There are no guarantees of safety in the mountains, so proceed with caution and at your own risk. This guide will make an effort to point out obvious objective hazards. Warnings in this guide are intended to let users know of dangers that are frequently encountered on given trails. However, no guide can accurately or completely foresee every conceivable accident waiting to happen, nor point out every latent hazard along the trail. Proceed with due regard for your own safety no matter what this or any guidebook says.

This guide does not presume to know every feature of every trail or road mentioned within its pages. Mountain environments change from day to day, week to week, season to season, and year to year. Rockfalls, avalanches, floods, storms, and other occasional and seasonal changes will continue to alter the nature, course, and safety of roads and trails. Trails erode, streams and rivers flood, bridges are washed out, trees fall or are blown down, rocks freeze and thaw and tumble down, and so on. Trails may be relocated or closed. Because wilderness features can change from day to day and season to season, hiking trails may vary accordingly. A feature identified in a trail description may have changed or even disappeared between now and the time you are looking for it. Changes can and do occur overnight. Be prepared!

You should check weather conditions before each trip. Make sure you and your entire party have adequate food, water, clothing, and experience for your chosen hike. Don't be afraid to turn back if weather or trail conditions make proceeding unwise. There are plenty of days to go hiking in the future and plenty of other trails to follow.

This guide occasionally suggests a cross-country route or scramble as an option. No off-trail route is recommended for any but those with proven route-finding ability and experience. No scrambling or climbing route is recommended for any but those with proper equipment and experience in alpine scrambling and climbing.

When you venture off the trail, you subject yourself to greater risks. Leave the trail with caution, exercising good judgment, at your own risk.

Safety rules for driving to the mountains are not included in this guide, since it is assumed that all drivers on our state's highways are duly licensed to drive and therefore understand the elementary principles of auto safety. Still, there are occasional auto accidents in the mountains, usually due to inattention or unfamiliarity with driving on mountain roads. Slow down; keep your eyes on the road and your hands on the wheel. If you wish to view the scenery, pull off into a scenic turnout and then look about. Don't speed up forest roads; it is too easy to slide off the road in loose gravel, crash into oncoming traffic or wildlife crossing the road (or hikers walking up the road), or get forced off the road to avoid a collision. Most of all, pay attention to your driving.

Some may find the numerous safety suggestions and warnings in this guide to be a bit much. However, each year many inexperienced and ill-equipped visitors set off into the backcountry armed only with a water bottle and a bag of trail mix, and some wilderness visitors seem not to know any better than to walk off the edge of a cliff unless somebody tells them not to do so. Those who don't already know enough to stay out of harm's way are requested to heed this guide's warnings and to exercise a good measure of caution when traveling in the wilderness.

Mountain Weather

Of all considerations of mountain travel in Washington's mountains, weather should be among the foremost to hikers. Many a day has began calm and clear only to end in a storm. Effects of weather lead to more hiking fatalities (from hypothermia) than any other cause. The Cascade Range experiences severe storms each year, and these storms cannot always be predicted. Storms often come without any warning, sometimes with fatal consequences to unprepared hikers. But it doesn't take a big storm to create hazardous conditions. Prepare yourself for the worst, including wind, rain, and snow, no matter what the weatherman says.

Check the weather forecast and snow conditions before any hike. Although forecasters are not always right about good weather, when it comes to poor weather—considering your life may be at stake—you should give them the benefit of the doubt. Weather resources, including on-line weather reports, are listed in Appendix D.

Clothing and Equipment

Alpine Lakes Wilderness hikers should make clothing a primary consideration. It has been suggested that the only clothing modern hikers need is Gore-Tex. However, as a practical and economic matter, wool clothing is still recommended in the rainy Cascades and Olympics, as it retains some body heat even when wet. Cotton clothing is certainly more comfortable than wool, but when wet, cotton is worthless and can be deadly because it retains absolutely no body heat. Modern synthetics (e.g.,

Williams Lake ▶

polypropylene) have heat-retaining qualities similar to wool, with the comfort of cotton, making them a popular substitute for the heavy, scratchy wool garments us old-timers remember, provided rain-tight outer garments are worn in poor weather. However, these can also be expensive. Whatever you choose to wear, make sure you have warm, dry clothing available in case what you're wearing gets wet. And if you are hiking in the Alpine Lakes Wilderness, it *will* get wet.

Rain and wind-proof outer garments are a must for any mountain travel. Gore-Tex and other "waterproof" fabrics are excellent at repelling water and wind but are very expensive. A plastic poncho or less-expensive, all-weather parka may suffice for those who can't afford more high-tech, high-priced clothing. Hikers should have several light layers of clothing, which may be shed or donned as the temperature rises or falls or the wind comes up. Remember that your body temperature will rise and fall more often than the ambient temperature, depending on your level of exertion and the steepness of the trail, sun exposure, wind, and so on. A T-shirt, light wool sweater, polypropylene vest, and hooded Gore-Tex parka should cover you in almost every situation short of a full-on arctic blast. If all you have is a T-shirt and a jacket, you'll sweat or freeze all the way up the trail and never be comfortable.

Lug-soled, watertight boots are also recommended for all wilderness hikers, although modern lightweight boots and trail shoes are becoming more popular. A lightweight, multipurpose boot will do, but make sure your boots are waterproof or at least strongly water resistant unless you enjoy wet, shriveled, or frozen feet. Waterproofing is a must for whatever your footwear. Even on sunny days, you may end up with wet feet from wading through miles of dew-drenched underbrush. (Hint: Bring rain gear and an extra pair of socks even if the weatherman promises sunny skies!) Lug-soled boots provide good traction and better protection against the pounding you will receive from rocks and roots on many hikes included in this guide.

Mittens or gloves and a warm hat are important accessories for all wilderness travel, particularly if you are hiking on snow or at high elevations. Always bring sunglasses to keep out harmful light rays during any snow or high-elevation travel. Gaiters are recommended for any snow and scree travel and for wading through wet underbrush. Sunscreen is often overlooked but is as important for your skin as sunglasses are for your eyes, particularly for extended snow and high-elevation travel.

The point of bringing proper clothing is to keep warm and dry in a hostile mountain environment. While it may be possible and enjoyable to hike these trails in shorts and a T-shirt on perfect, warm, windless days, there have been many hypothermia deaths and close calls attributed to wilderness hikers wearing casual clothing. Dress properly and prepare for the worst; your very life may depend on it.

Anyone venturing onto steep snow should carry and know how to use an ice ax. Many trails have dangerous snow crossings through early summer. Crampons may be helpful on snowy trails in winter and spring. Small instep crampons are preferred by winter hikers. While a climbing rope might seem like a bit much for a mere hike, when hiking some trails in early season, you never know when you might want to belay across an avalanche gully. For most of us, though, the prospect of such a crossing is sufficient incentive to turn back and try again later in the summer, when the snow is long gone. Don't climb or cross a snow slope lacking a safe runout. Even a short slide on snow can be dangerous if there are rocks, trees, or water at the bottom of the slope.

Backpackers will need reliable shelter to provide protection from rain, wind, insects, and vermin. Some find a plastic tarp sufficient for lowland forest camps, and others are content to curl up under a stout fir or hemlock, but most bring a sturdy, lightweight tent. Figuring out where to camp is usually not a problem. There are often one or more existing bareground sites available at major trail junctions and especially at lakes, although many lakes have a 200-foot setback for overnight camping. Some of the more popular trails have designated campsites, and camping is not allowed except in those sites; other less popular hikes have few restrictions and relatively few campsites.

A lightweight sleeping bag is a must, and an insulated pad is recommended. A lightweight cookstove and fuel are not necessities unless you are one of those hikers who is content eating veggies, crackers, energy bars, and gorp all weekend. Speaking of food, it is necessary to store food out of reach of bears and other critters. A bear-resistant container is recommended for food storage, and bring along a length of cord to hang food from a tree well away from your camp. Remove all food and food-smelling stuff from your tent at night, and don't forget about that Snickers bar at the bottom of your backpack, or you might have unwelcome visitors chewing holes in your tent and backpack or slashing your tent open in search of a snack. The Forest Service publishes information about how best to bear-proof your campsite; read it.

Other gear can be brought along, although one of the "secrets" of successful backpacking trips is keeping the weight down. The more gadgets you bring along, the heavier your backpack. Seasoned hikers know just what to bring and how much. The rest of us have to learn through trial and error what is and isn't necessary to bring along.

Ten Essentials

Everyone hiking in the Cascades should know the "ten essentials" by heart, but if not, here they are:

1. Map (in a waterproof cover)
2. Compass
3. Flashlight (with extra bulb and batteries)
4. Extra food (at least enough for an extra day)
5. Extra clothing (in a waterproof container)
6. Matches (in a waterproof container)
7. Candle or other fire starter
8. Knife
9. Sunglasses
10. First-aid kit

These items have, through time and experience, proven to be lifesavers when things go bad, even on short hikes. Of course, water, a water filter, and sunblock are very important to bring along, too. On long day hikes, a bivouac sac or plastic tarp could be a lifesaver in the event of a forced bivouac in the rain or wind. Some hikers eschew the ten essentials, or at least some of them. But then, a map carried in a waterproof container can do double duty as fire starter if an emergency arises. Each individual hiker will have his or her preferences as to what is really necessary and what is optional. Don't limit yourself only to these ten items.

Hypothermia

Hypothermia is a genuine risk for all backcountry travelers, especially hikers in the Cascade Mountains. This often fatal lowering of the body temperature is brought on by continued exposure to low temperatures, winds, and rain soaking, usually a combination of all three. Hikers venturing too far from the safety and comfort of shelter with inadequate clothing risk hypothermia. Wool clothing and some synthetics, such as polypropylene, insulate even when wet and are recommended. However, without a weather-resistant shell, any insulating clothing has limitations. It doesn't have to be cold, wet, and miserable for hypothermia to set in. At high elevation, even a sunny day can be cool and breezy enough to bring on hypothermia. Do everything possible to stay warm and dry, particularly during rain and windy conditions. Heed the wind even on sunny summer days. At high elevations, a prevailing cold breeze may blow all day, lowering your body temperature little by little. Have a sweater handy, and put it on whenever you feel a chill.

Hypothermia's symptoms include fatigue, awkwardness, chills, lethargy, irritability, clumsiness, uncontrolled shivering, and slurred speech. Most victims don't realize they are hypothermic and will deny it up to the end. Act quickly to save them. Stop, find or make shelter, get the victim's wet clothes off, and get him or her into a sleeping bag (with somebody undressed and warm if they appear to be seriously hypothermic, although decency permits wearing underwear for you modest would-be rescuers). If you can't stop where you are, get down the trail fast! Warm liquids should be given to conscious victims but not to comatose victims. If the victim does not appear to recover, send someone for help immediately. The faster the victim's body temperature is raised, the better his or her chance of survival.

Like altitude sickness, prevention of hypothermia is easier than the cure. If you suspect you or one of your partners is becoming hypothermic, don't delay—get to shelter quickly and get the victim warm and dry. Don't hesitate to call for emergency assistance.

Altitude Sickness

Altitude sickness is not an uncommon malady in the mountains. Although it is usually suffered by climbers on the Cascade volcanoes and other high peaks, people have died from its symptoms at modest elevations. Trails in this guide lead up to more than 7,000 feet elevation, high enough to suffer altitude sickness. Hikers who rush into the mountains from sea level and hit the high trails may suffer some symptoms of altitude sickness, including headache, dizziness, nausea, vomiting, weakness, shortness of breath, blueness of lips, chills, insomnia, increased pulse and respiration, blurred vision, confusion, and disorientation. If you or any of your party experience or exhibit any of these symptoms, descend immediately, slow down to reduce demand for oxygen, and breathe deeper and faster (which may cause nausea and dizziness, but keep at it). Usually, all you will notice is a bad headache, which is common enough on sunny summer days, especially when hiking on snow or in high granite basins. If the headache doesn't go away, you may want to consider heading down soon. The sooner you get to lower elevation, the faster you will recover from mountain sickness.

Like almost any other mountain hazard, prevention is easier than treatment: acclimatize, increase fluid intake and carbohydrate consumption, decrease fats in your diet, avoid alcohol prior to your hike, and don't smoke, drink carbonated beverages, or take antidepressants.

Preparation

Although even the most sedentary among us can manage some of the hikes in this guide, hikers should be in good physical condition when hiking a majority of these trails. Fatigue is a leading cause of accidents on the trail; if your legs are tired, you are more likely to trip or stumble over rocks and roots. Tired legs cramp easily. Repetitive strain injuries are easier to suffer if your legs are weak. Although you don't need to train like a marathon runner to go hiking, it's a good idea to stay active during the "off season," taking walks whenever possible and visiting lowland trails through the winter so you're ready to go when spring and summer hikes open up.

Winter and Spring Hiking

Despite inherent hazards, winter and spring hiking are popular. Winter hikes can sometimes be made under perfect conditions with little more risk than a late spring or late fall hike. With snowshoes, you can plod right along atop the snow. With instep crampons, you can walk along slippery trails with impunity. Ice and hard snow on trails is a hazard; ask anyone who has slipped on a winter trail and broken a wrist or tailbone.

The major considerations for winter hiking are weather and snow conditions. Cascade weather is unpredictable enough during the summer; during the winter, storms lasting several days at a time are common. Rain, snowfall, and high winds mean trouble for hikers. Whiteout conditions are frequent, particularly above timberline. Winter hikers have become lost or pinned down for days by storms, unable to find their way out or unable to move because of severe avalanche risk caused by several feet of new, wet snow.

Although foul weather is the major hazard for winter hikers, avalanches are more feared. This is not a snow hiking guide, so an extensive discussion of avalanche safety is not included. If you're going to venture into the mountains during winter and spring, you should have training and experience with spotting and avoiding dangerous avalanche conditions and with avalanche rescue techniques. Avoiding potential avalanche slopes is the best way to avoid getting caught in an avalanche.

Frostbite is also a risk during winter hikes. Keeping your extremities warm, dry, and unconstricted is important. Overly tight boots (which reduce circulation) are a leading cause of frostbite.

This guide, being a hiking guide, cannot provide a thorough lesson on avalanche safety, snow travel, navigation, or winter safety and survival strategies. Winter and spring hikers should learn about preventing frostbite, hypothermia, and avalanche prediction and rescue and should know how to prepare for winter travel before they find themselves lost in a blizzard or sunk in up to their necks (or worse) in wet snow.

Zero Impact

Because of the popularity of the Alpine Lakes Wilderness, many popular trails, campsites, and high routes are showing signs of overuse. Zero-impact use of the wilderness areas of the Cascade Range is urged by the Forest Service. Here are some simple suggestions to help minimize your impact on the mountain environment:

- Travel in small groups to do less damage to meadows and campsites.
- Stay on trails, even when muddy, to avoid sidecutting or erosion; do not take shortcuts or cut switchbacks.
- Tread gently if you stray off the trail to avoid trampling fragile vegetation.
- Use a stove for cooking, and bring a tent rather than rely on scarce natural resources. Do not cut trees or boughs for any reason.
- Use existing campsites rather than create new ones.
- Choose stable sites for camps and rest stops, not areas with fragile vegetation.
- Don't construct rock windbreaks or clear bare-ground areas of rocks or vegetation for any reason.
- Camp on snow instead of bare ground whenever possible.
- Avoid having leftover food, so as not to attract wildlife to your camp.
- Use pit toilets or practice accepted human waste disposal practices (such as not eliminating waste near water sources, burying your waste at least 200 feet from water sources, or packing it out in plastic bags).
- Don't bring your pets with you. If you do bring them with you, keep them under control or leashed and clean up after them.
- Pack out your trash and any other trash you find.
- Plan your actions so as to make the least impact on the environment.

Water

Long gone are the days when hikers could dip their tin Sierra cups into a stream or lake and drink freely. These days, many streams and lakes are contaminated with bacteria and microorganisms that can make a hiker quite ill. Hikers must now bring water from home or the grocery store on day hikes and either filter or purify drinking water in the wild. Boiling is the best way to purify water; boil for five minutes to be safe. Most hikers bring a filter, which weighs less than a stove and fuel. Check with the experts to find out which filter is right for you. Some filters filter out everything but are very expensive. Since your health is on the line, though, maybe money isn't the most important thing to consider.

Camping

Although some of the hikes included in this volume are day hikes that can be done in a day without the necessity of camping, most of these hikes are popular as overnight or weekend backpacks. Nearly all of the trails in this guide have campsites. The longer the trail, the more campsites—at trail junctions, in meadows, and beside rivers and lakes. A few considerations for those who will be camping out: Many areas are overused and often crowded; please limit your use to day visits to avoid further impacts to already abused areas. If camping at a popular lake, don't just drop your pack and set up camp at the first bare-ground site you come to. Take the time to explore first, to find the designated camps or a camp away from the lake. Always camp at least 200 feet away from a lake, unless a designated campsite is closer to the water or camping farther away is impossible due to terrain. Use existing sites only; don't clear rocks, logs, or vegetation to create a new campsite or stack rocks or logs to create a windbreak. Camp on snow, rock, or gravel when possible to avoid adverse impacts. Don't dig trenches or create new fire pits. Spread out to do less damage. If an existing path to the water source exists, use it so a new path isn't created. Be sure to do your cooking and cleaning well away from your tent, to avoid attracting bears, and don't wash up in the lake. Try not to camp right next to the trail, for your sake and the sake of other hikers on the trail; nobody likes tripping over your tent lines or backpack any more than you'll like the invasion of privacy. No campfires above 4,000 feet elevation west of the crest, above 5,000 feet elevation east of the crest, or at any of the "popular" lakes. Don't cut live trees for firewood; find deadfall in the woods well away from camp. Police your campsite before you leave to make sure you've left nothing behind. Protect your food from bears and other wildlife in a bear-resistant container or by properly hanging it from a tree. Don't keep any food in your tent.

Human Waste Disposal

Litter and human waste disposal are major problems on many Alpine Lakes Wilderness trails. Use pit toilets and trash containers where available or else pack it out, particularly in high-use areas. Pit toilets are available at many lakes and high-country campsites; side trails leading to toilets are usually well marked. In and above the subalpine zone, do your business well away from lakes and streams, and don't dig "cat holes" in fragile meadows and tundra. For a thorough discourse on proper human waste disposal in the wilderness, please read *How to Shit in the Woods* (see the "Selected References" section of the Appendix).

In Case of Emergency

To report a hiking accident or any other life-threatening emergency, dial 911. If the situation is less critical or you don't feel it is an emergency worthy of dialing 911, contact the nearest Park Service or Forest Service district office, campground ranger or host, or the local sheriff or police department. See Appendix B for a list of Forest Service phone numbers. Also, consider carrying a cellular phone, just in case of an emergency. A cellular phone can aid rescue personnel in locating your exact position if you are lost or injured. Just make sure your battery is fully charged before you leave home. And when you get through, be sure to state your location and the nature of your emergency right away in case you lose the connection and can't get it back. Also, don't expect to get cellular service everywhere in the wilderness. Your phone may get a signal from a high ridge, but in most valleys and basins service is spotty to nonexistent. Even with a cell phone, you still have to rely on yourself.

How to Use This Guide

This is a guide to several of the longer overnight hikes in the Alpine Lakes Wilderness. Originally intended to cover only trails in the Alpine Lakes Wilderness, this guide was expanded to include trails outside the wilderness, including many of the popular hikes across the highway. Those who enjoy hiking in the Alpine Lakes Wilderness region will appreciate the inclusion of these other hikes and the fact that they do not have to buy three separate guidebooks to read about them.

This guide is intended to assist hikers and wilderness visitors in locating and following the many, varied hiking trails in the Alpine Lakes Wilderness. To that end, each chapter of this guide includes written descriptions with driving directions, trailhead and permit information, mileage and elevation charts, a description of the hike including scenic highlights, and a map showing the approximate route of the trail. Trail descriptions and maps are deemed accurate, based on in-field observations and other information, but may vary from season to season and year to year. Maps are approximate only and should not be relied upon except to the extent that they will help get you to your chosen hike and on the right trail. Although these descriptions and maps will be helpful in choosing and following a given trail, they are not exact and cannot substitute for wilderness experience. Use your best judgment on each hike, based on what you see when you arrive, regardless of the written descriptions, illustrations, and photographs contained in hiking guides. Basically, this guide will show you what's there and approximately where to go; from there it's up to you.

All route descriptions and directions assume you are facing your objective or your direction of travel, unless otherwise stated. Whenever there is apparent confusion in the directions given, an approximate compass direction will be provided for clarity. All distances, including road and trail mileages, elevation gain and loss figures, and elevations of points along the trail, are approximate only.

Each hike chapter begins with a list of particulars about the hike, including a description, mileage, a difficulty rating, elevation gain, maps, and so on, following the Falcon guidelines.

Overview

The hike description begins with an overview, a one-sentence summary of where you're going and how you're going to get there. It will let you know whether you are going to a lake or summit, whether the trail loops, and so on.

Distance

The mileage given for each hike is for a round-trip from the trailhead to the primary destination and back or for the loop hike, where applicable. Mileage listed for some hikes will differ slightly from the "official" mileage published by the Forest Service or other sources. Since nearly every source of information lists a different mileage and the author did not take a measuring wheel to each trail, mileage given is approximate only. Your actual mileage may vary.

Difficulty

Each hike's overall difficulty is given as easy, moderate, or strenuous. No particular formula was used to determine a hike's difficulty. Elevation gain and distance factored in but were not necessarily determinative. For instance, a 10-mile hike with little elevation gain could be called easy, while a 10-mile hike with steady elevation gain might be moderate, and a 10-mile hike with 9 miles of level hiking and 1 mile of steep hiking could be strenuous. Likewise, a short hike with lots of elevation gain might be strenuous. In general, if the hike gains less than 500 feet per mile average, it will be easy or moderate. If the hike gains between 500 and 1,000 feet per mile, it will be moderate or strenuous. And if the hike gains 1,000 feet per mile or more, or has any segment where elevation gain is over 1,000 feet in a mile, it will most likely be strenuous or possibly very strenuous. This is a subjective rating, which really just depends on the hike. Your fitness level will also play a large part in determining whether a hike seems easy or strenuous on a given day.

Some hikes are also described as difficult, which usually means those hikes follow trails that are either unmaintained or difficult to follow due to overgrowth, fallen trees, washouts, rocky tread, risky stream crossings, and the like.

Best Season

The best season for backpacking in the Alpine Lakes Wilderness is midsummer through early fall. Some of the lower elevation trails are snow-free almost all year, but many high-elevation trails are impassable to a majority of hikers until August or even September, depending on the previous winter's snowpack. Some years you can hike in the high country until early November; other years, it starts snowing in late September. Some hikers are willing to brave snow-covered trails; some even prefer it. Conditions vary from year to year, so the "best season" given in this guide may not be the best season if the winter snowpack is deep or the spring was unusually rainy. It is always best to check trail conditions before your hike, so you aren't disappointed to find your trail buried under feet of snow or the access road washed out. When hiking in early season, carry an ice ax and know how to use it to self-arrest, since you will probably be crossing snowfields as you venture into the high country.

Traffic

All trails are open for foot traffic. Some are open for stock (horses, llamas, and the like). A few are open to mountain bikes, at least to a certain point. No hike in this guide is open for motorbike use except the last 6 miles of Nason Ridge Trail, which can be bypassed. All allowed trail uses will be noted in the introduction to each hike.

The volume of traffic on each trail is described as light, moderate, or heavy. Again, this is not based on any set formula but was based on typical weekend volume, which is when a majority of us go hiking. Light traffic means you are likely to encounter only a few other hikers on the trail during a summer weekend. Moderate traffic means you may encounter several hikers and groups of hikers on the trail. Heavy traffic means you'll be running into hikers and their dogs all along the trail. If you want some solitude, come on a weekday when the trails are much less crowded.

Dogs are not allowed on any trails in the Enchantment Lakes area, including Snow Lakes, Colchuck and Stuart Lakes, and Eightmile and Caroline Lakes, nor at Ingalls Lake. For the most part, dogs are allowed on other trails in the wilderness, except as noted in particular hike chapters. Some hikers are annoyed by dogs and get angry about them being on the trail. Most hikers don't mind a dog or two on a hike, as long as they are leashed and under control.

High Point

An approximate high point of each hike is provided because most hikers like to know how high the trail leads. In some cases, the high point is estimated and rounded to the nearest 100 feet. When the high point is a summit, an official elevation is given.

Maps

USGS (United States Geological Survey) and Green Trails maps are listed for each hike. The USGS maps tend to be outdated; Green Trails maps include trail mileage and elevation data and are popular with hikers. A good but somewhat dated topographic map of the entire Alpine Lakes Wilderness is published by the Alpine Lakes Protection Society. Other maps covering the Alpine Lakes Wilderness are listed in Appendix C, along with several outdoor retailers who carry them. Please note that none of these maps is entirely accurate, so check with the Forest Service before setting out on a hike, especially a long hike, in case trails have been rerouted, closed, or abandoned.

Elevation Profiles

This book uses elevation profiles to provide an idea of the length and elevation of hills you will encounter along each hike. In each of the profiles, the vertical axes of the graphs show the total distance climbed in feet. In contrast, the horizontal axes show the distance traveled in miles. It is important to understand that the vertical (feet) and horizontal (miles) scales can differ between hikes. Read each profile carefully making sure you read both the height and distance shown. This will help you interpret what you see in each profile. Some elevation profiles may show gradual hills to be steep and steep hills to be gradual.

For More Information

Because road and trail conditions change throughout the season, it is highly recommended that you check road and trail conditions and current regulations regarding trail use, camping setbacks, and other information before each hike by calling the local Forest Service office or other agency managing the trail listed for each hike. Additional phone numbers and addresses are listed in the Appendix.

Dogs and Stock Animals

Dogs are allowed on most hikes included in this guide but must be leashed on all hikes off Interstate 90 west of Rachel Lake Trail and off U.S. Highway 2 west of Stevens Pass. Although dogs are not required to be leashed on all trails, as a matter of trail etiquette it is suggested that dogs be leashed so they don't scare off wildlife, spook horses, attack other dogs, or annoy hikers. Some hikers are offended by dogs on the trail, leashed or not, but most hikers are at least tolerant of dogs as long as the dogs and their owners are not a nuisance. Dogs are not permitted in the Enchantments permit area including Nada and Snow Lakes, the Enchantments, Colchuck and Stuart Lakes, and Eightmile and Caroline Lakes, or at Ingalls Lake.

Stock, including horses, llamas, and other pack animals, are permitted on many trails in the Alpine Lakes Wilderness. Hikes open for stock animals are noted in each hike chapter. Stock must be contained at least 200 feet from all lakes. If hobbled, stock can be tied to trees larger than 6 inches in diameter for up to four hours. When using highlines, hobble stock standing within 8 feet of trees. Use only processed stock feed to avoid introducing exotic grasses and other plants into the wilderness. This is not a guide to horse packing or stock trails; for specific information about where and how to hike with stock, contact the Forest Service.

When encountering horses and other stock animals along the trail, hikers should yield the right of way. Step off the trail on the downhill side. Horses tend to shy away from hikers, and their riders get mad when you stand uphill, since the horses get close to the trail's edge and have occasionally stumbled, dumping their riders and provisions.

Map Legend

═══84═══	Interstate
═26═	U.S. highway
──①──	State highway
──549──	Forest road
──────	Paved road
═ ═ ═ ═ ═	Unimproved road
▬▬▬▬▬▬	Featured trail
- - - - - - -	Other trail
⬚	National Land/Wilderness
⸻	Swamp
⋈	Bridge
⛺	Campground
∘	City
•━○	Gate
🚶	Other trailhead
◻	Overlook/Viewpoint
)(	Pass/Gap
▲	Peak/elevation
■	Point of interest
─•─	Powerline
▶	Ranger station
START 🚶	Trailhead
∥	Waterfall

The Hikes

1 Taylor River to Lake Dorothy

A one-way hike up Taylor River to Lake Dorothy, or an out-and-back hike to Sno-qualmie Lake.

Start: Trailhead for Taylor River Trail 1002.
Distance: 15 miles one way to Dorothy Lake trailhead or out and back to Snoqualmie Lake.
Difficulty: Easy for the first 6 miles, strenuous to Snoqualmie Lake, then easier to Dorothy Lake trailhead.
Best season: All year for most of lower Taylor River trail; summer through fall to lakes.
Traffic: Foot traffic only past wilderness boundary; moderate use.
Total climbing: About 1,900 feet to Sno-qualmie Lake.

High point: About 3,150 feet.
Fees and permits: A Northwest Forest Pass is required.
Maps: USGS Lake Philippa and Snoqualmie Lake; Green Trails No. 174 (Mount Si) and 175 (Skykomish).
Trail contacts: Mt. Baker-Snoqualmie National Forest, Snoqualmie Ranger District, North Bend Office, 42404 SE North Bend Way, North Bend, WA 98045; (425) 888-1421; www.fs.fed.us/r6/mbs.

Finding the trailhead: Taylor River Trail 1002 is approached from North Bend via Middle Fork Road. Drive I-90 to North Bend exit 34 (Edgwick Road/468th). Head north from the exit on 468th Avenue SE, past the truck stops, 0.6 mile to SE Middle Fork Road. Turn right and continue 0.9 mile to a fork. Stay right, taking the high road (marked Lake Dorothy Road), and continue another 1.6 miles to pavement's end, where the road becomes Forest Road 56. Continue on FR 56 another 9.5 miles, past the Middle Fork trailhead and across a bridge over Taylor River to a junction. Stay left, along the river, and proceed 0.2 mile to the trailhead parking lot at road's end. The trailhead used to be several miles up the road, but a bridge washout many years ago closed the road, forcing hikers to start here. Park your car at the gate, or back at the river if the parking lot is full, and start hiking.

The Hike

Snoqualmie Lake used to be an easy day hike of just a few miles, but during the 1980s the Taylor River bridge washed out and the Forest Service did not repair it, thus adding about 12 miles to the round trip. Now most hikers access Snoqualmie Lake via Lake Dorothy Trail, a more enjoyable 14-mile round trip that gets you to lake country in a scant 1.5 miles instead of 7.5 miles via Taylor River. But the lakes are not the only worthwhile aspect of this hike. The first 5.7 miles along Taylor River is flat and easy hiking through shady forest, with several waterfalls including the spectacular Otter Falls. But the high lake country is less visited, more serene, a worthy destination for an overnight hike.

Otter Falls ▶
Photo: Matt Robertson

Taylor River to Lake Dorothy

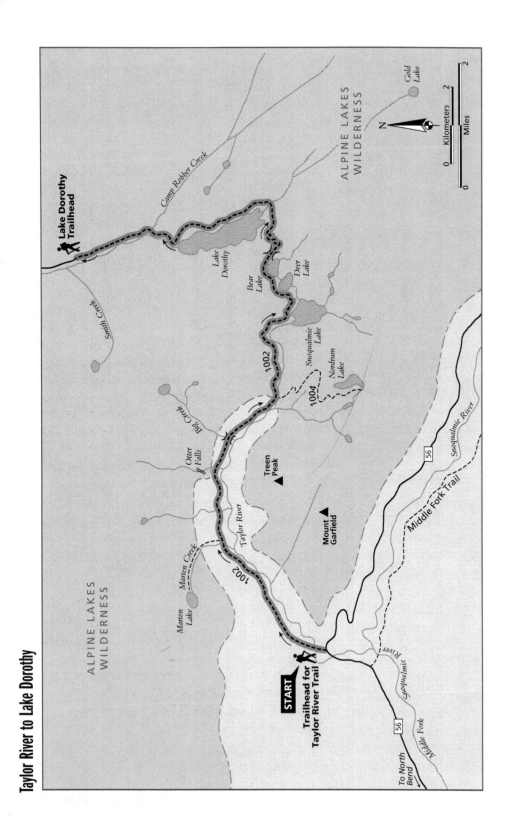

Get your permit and start hiking up the old road grade, then find the hiker trail that drops down into woods and leads to a footbridge over Taylor River, then climbs up to rejoin the old road grade, staying right at a road fork in another 0.2 mile. The trail leads along the road on the western side of the river, through deep, mossy forest, barely gaining elevation, crossing several creeks. At 2.8 miles is Marten Creek and a small waterfall. Tread lightly across the bridge and continue up the trail, which becomes more trail-like, narrowing down and weaving in and out of forest and talus and across several streams, which can be difficult to cross during early season, especially after winters with high snowfall. At 4.3 miles is Otter Creek and Otter Falls, a 700-foot-high waterfall down granite slabs, cascading into Lipsy Lake, a good rest spot. At 5 miles is Big Creek, which is crossed on an oversized concrete bridge left over from the days when you could drive this far. The hike to Big Creek has only about 600 feet of elevation gain, making it a popular winter and spring warm-up, but the best hiking is above and beyond.

In another 0.7 mile from Big Creek, the old road ends and the trail begins at the old Snoqualmie Lake trailhead. The trail soon forks. The right fork leads to Nordrum Lake in 2.6 miles, with 1,820 feet of elevation gain. To get to Snoqualmie Lake, take the left fork. The trail climbs, gaining some 1,300 feet in the next 1.4 miles, to reach Snoqualmie Lake, elevation 3,147 feet. The lake is set in a quiet forest basin thick with fir and hemlock, heather and huckleberry brush. There are several campsites near the lakeshore. Deer Lake and Bear Lake, two smaller lakes nestled in quiet hemlock and silver fir forest, are just 1.1 and 1.5 miles beyond Snoqualmie Lake, respectively. There are a few campsites at these lakes, although you might have to thrash around in the bushes to find them.

From Bear Lake, continue up through open hemlock and silver fir forest and mossy talus. About 0.5 mile beyond is the high point of the hike, 3,820 feet, at a wooded divide. From here, the trail descends about 1.5 miles to the south shore of Lake Dorothy. As you descend, you catch glimpses of the upper end of Lake Dorothy, including the several forested rock islands rising out of the deep blue water. At the south shore, cross the inlet stream via a narrow, leaning footlog, anchored by a cable but a little insecure nonetheless, then hike up the eastern lake shore. The trail climbs and drops, through boulders and hemlock forest, then down to the rocky shore. A few campsites present themselves, but the designated sites are near the north end of the lake. If you want to stop and enjoy the lake, do so at the first good spot, because later on the trail veers away from the lake, and there is no good lake access at the far end.

From the north end of the lake, the trail descends in rock and root steps and switchbacks. In a short mile, cross Camp Robber Creek just above its confluence with East Fork Miller River, then descend the final 0.5 mile along the noisy river splashing down granite slabs and out to Lake Dorothy trailhead.

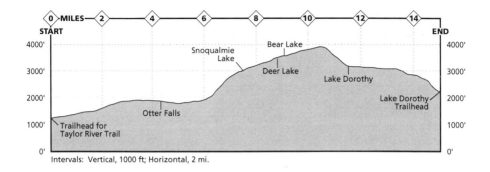

Intervals: Vertical, 1000 ft; Horizontal, 2 mi.

Options

Of course, you can do this hike in the opposite direction, starting from Lake Dorothy and ending at Taylor River, or as a round-trip overnight hike to Snoqualmie, Deer, or Bear Lake. From that direction, a round-trip overnight hike to Snoqualmie Lake is also about 15 miles. To approach from this direction, drive U.S. Highway 2 to the Money Creek Campground turnoff (about 2.9 miles west of Skykomish), follow the Old Cascade Highway 1 mile to Miller River Road (FR 6410), then follow that road 9.1 miles to the trailhead at road's end. Neither approach is recommended over the other. One-way hikers must, of course, arrange for transportation at each trailhead.

The 2.6-mile trail to Nordrum Lake is mostly overlooked. Nordrum Lake offers a bit more solitude than Snoqualmie Lake. Unlike Snoqualmie Lake, there is no back way in to Nordrum Lake, and the steeper, scarcely maintained trail tends to deter less motivated hikers from going this way.

Key Points

0.0 Trailhead for Taylor River Trail 1002.

0.2 Trail fork; stay right.

2.8 Marten Creek.

4.3 Otter Creek and Otter Falls.

5.0 Big Creek bridge.

5.7 The old road grade ends and trail begins.

6.2 Nordrum Lake Trail junction. Take the left fork to Snoqualmie Lake.

7.5 Snoqualmie Lake.

8.6 Deer Lake.

9.0 Bear Lake.

11.5 Lake Dorothy.

15.0 Lake Dorothy trailhead.

2 Dingford Creek to Myrtle Lakes

A day hike or backpack up Dingford Creek to Myrtle Lakes.

Start: Dingford Creek trailhead.
Distance: 12.6 miles out and back.
Difficulty: Moderate.
Best season: Midsummer through fall.
Traffic: Foot traffic only; moderate use.
Total climbing: About 3,450 feet.
High point: About 4,000 feet.
Fees and permits: A Northwest Forest Pass is required.

Maps: USGS Big Snow Mountain; Green Trails No. 175 (Skykomish).
Trail contacts: Mt. Baker-Snoqualmie National Forest, Snoqualmie Ranger District, North Bend Office, 42404 SE North Bend Way, North Bend, WA 98045; (425) 888-1421; www.fs.fed.us/r6/mbs.

Finding the trailhead: Dingford Creek Trail 1005 is approached from North Bend via Middle Fork Snoqualmie Road. Drive I-90 to North Bend exit 34 (Edgewick Road/468th). Head north from the exit on 468th Avenue SE, past the truck stops, 0.6 mile to SE Middle Fork Road. Turn right and continue 0.9 mile to a fork. Stay right, taking the high road (marked Lake Dorothy Road), and continue another 1.6 miles to the pavement's end, where the road becomes Forest Road 56. Follow FR 56 some 16 miles to the Taylor River fork. Turn right and follow FR 56 (may be marked 5620 or 5640, but the Forest Service says it's really FR 56) another 5.5 miles or so to the Dingford Creek trailhead on the left. Parking on the right side of the road is limited; please leave room for other vehicles. This road is very rugged and not recommended for most passenger cars; a high-clearance, four-wheel-drive vehicle is suggested.

The Hike

Dingford Creek Trail climbs alongside its namesake creek to its source, the Myrtle Lakes, two of several quiet lakes set in a high basin above the Middle Fork Snoqualmie River in the shadow of Big Snow Mountain. This is frequently done as a day hike, but the rough approach drive deters many from visiting this trail, making it a good choice if you want to get away from the crowds. There is a lot to explore here, including high lakes, vistas, and summits.

Get your permit and start hiking, following the trail up Dingford Creek. The trail climbs steadily through old-growth silver fir and hemlock forest, gaining 1,420 feet in the first 3.5 miles. At about 2 miles the trail crosses the many rivulets of Goat Creek. Consider taking a snack break here on one of the islands between the stream branches, amid old-growth hemlocks. A fishermen's trail leads upstream from here to Horseshoe and Goat Lakes; it is a rough, brushy trail, not for the casual hiker.

From Goat Creek, continue along Dingford Creek another 1.3 miles to a fork. The left fork goes to Myrtle Lake; the right fork to Hester Lakes. Take the left fork and climb along the western bank of Dingford Creek through open fir and hemlock forest. In about a mile the trail crosses a stream flowing from Nimue Lake, one

Dingford Creek to Myrtle Lakes

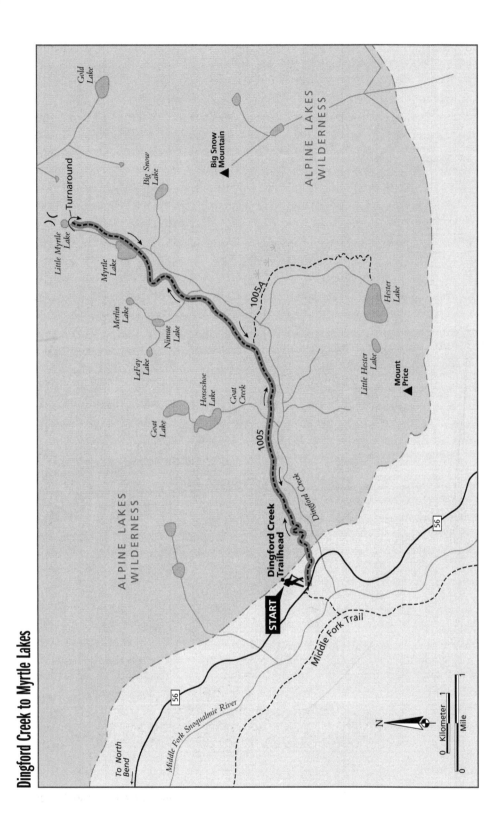

of the many small lakes hidden in a basin above Myrtle Lake. Continue up Dingford Creek, soon coming right to the edge of the creek, then away, climbing up a sub-alpine slope before traversing gentle parkland to the outlet of Myrtle Lake. There are campsites near the lakeshore.

To get away from the crowds at Myrtle Lake, follow the diminishing trail up the lake's eastern shore, then continue up a talus basin, through brushy forest, climbing a final mile to Little Myrtle Lake, elevation 4,220 feet. There is a pass just above the lake that offers views, including a look down to Lake Dorothy and the Miller River valley.

Options

From the fork at 3.3 miles, the trail on the right (Trail 1005A) leads another 2.7 miles to Hester Lake. This trail is notoriously muddy and buggy, leading through marshes and streambeds to the less popular but less crowded of the lakes.

There are lots of small lakes in the cirques and basins hereabouts, reached via boot-beaten fishermen's trails and cross-country over talus and across brushy mead-ows. At about 2 miles up the trail, a fishermen's trail leads northward to Goat Lake and Horseshoe Lake. West from Myrtle Lake are Merlin, Nimue, and LeFay Lakes, small lakes tucked into the woods, popular with fishermen and adventuresome hik-ers. More rugged cross-country hiking leads to Big Snow Lake perched on the shoulder of 6,680-foot Big Snow Mountain, which is a popular climb from Myrtle Lake, although route-finding challenges and a bit of rock scrambling near the top make it unsuitable for hikers without scrambling experience.

Experienced cross-country hikers can find a route from Bear Lake to Little Myr-tle Lake. This is a bit rugged and requires precise route-finding skills, but it offers the adventuresome wilderness traveler a "back door" into this high lake country.

There is talk that the Forest Service might someday close the Middle Fork Road at Taylor River and convert the road to a trail, which would add about 11 miles to a round-trip hike to Myrtle Lakes, either via the road when converted to trail or via the Middle Fork Trail.

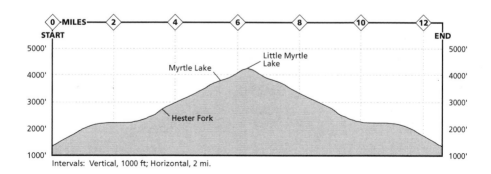

Intervals: Vertical, 1000 ft; Horizontal, 2 mi.

Key Points

0.0   Dingford Creek trailhead.

2.0   Goat Creek.

3.3   Trail fork; go left to Myrtle Lake.

5.3   Myrtle Lake.

6.3   Little Myrtle Lake, turn around.

12.6   Dingford Creek trailhead.

3 Dutch Miller Gap

A long, scenic hike up the enchanting Middle Fork Snoqualmie River to Dutch Miller Gap and Williams Lake.

Start: Dutch Miller trailhead.
Distance: 15 miles out and back to Dutch Miller Gap.
Difficulty: Long but generally easy going.
Best season: Midsummer to fall.
Traffic: Foot traffic only; light to moderate use.
Total climbing: About 2,000 feet.
High point: About 5,000 feet.
Fees and permits: A Northwest Forest Pass is required.

Maps: USGS Big Snow Mountain and Mount Daniel; Green Trails No. 175 and 176 (Skykomish and Stevens Pass).
Trail contacts: Mt. Baker-Snoqualmie National Forest, Snoqualmie Ranger District, North Bend Office, 42404 SE North Bend Way, North Bend, WA 98045; (425) 888-1421; www.fs.fed.us/r6/mbs.

Finding the trailhead: Dutch Miller Trail 1030 begins up the Middle Fork Snoqualmie River, about 35 miles northeast of North Bend. Drive I-90 to North Bend exit 34 (Edgewick Road/468th). Head north from the exit on 468th Avenue SE, past the truck stops, 0.6 mile to SE Middle Fork Road. Turn right and continue 0.9 mile to a fork. Stay right, taking the high road (marked Lake Dorothy Road), and continue another 1.6 miles to the pavement's end, where the road becomes Forest Road 56. Continue on FR 56 another 9.5 miles, past the Middle Fork trail-head and across a bridge over Taylor River to a junction. Turn right on FR 56 (may be marked 5640; consult your map), and continue 13.2 rough miles, past the Dingford Creek trailhead, staying on the main road to the Dutch Miller trailhead at road's end. The Middle Fork Road is very rough; it takes about two hours to drive the 25 miles from North Bend to the trailhead. A high-clearance, four-wheel-drive vehicle is recommended.

The Hike

Dutch Miller Gap is one of the high passes of the Alpine Lakes Wilderness, dividing the Middle Fork Snoqualmie and Waptus Rivers. The trail leading up the river to the gap is part of the old Cascade Crest Trail, a fairly long, wondrously scenic hike up the Middle Fork Snoqualmie River valley to the rugged 5,000-foot-high gap. Despite a difficult approach drive, this is a fairly popular hike best done over two or three days with camps at Williams Lake or Lake Ivanhoe, or both.

Assuming your car survived the drive up here, get your permit and start up the trail, which soon crosses Hardscrabble Creek via a footlog below where the old bridge washed out, then contours through a stand of old-growth cedars. The trail drops, then climbs, then drops and climbs again through hemlock and silver fir forest, a pattern often repeated during the first few miles of the hike. Just past the 1-mile marker, the trail crosses a rocky streambed and climbs past the wilderness

boundary marker, then drops toward the river, passing a side trail leading down to a large riverside camp at 1.5 miles. The trail continues contouring above the river, with views of several craggy peaks across the valley. There is some brushy going, easier after the trail crews have passed through, as the trail traverses overgrown talus slopes, through slide alder and bracken ferns and wildflowers—columbine and tiger lilies prominent among them. The trail descends abruptly through a talus slide, levels out near the river bottom, then climbs and drops again before crossing Crawford Creek and a small trailside campsite at 2.7 miles.

After crossing Crawford Creek and two other creeks in quick succession, the trail climbs away from the river. This section of the trail was recently rerouted to bypass a dangerous section of trail undercut by the river, which has probably caved in by now. It's just as well, since the old trail was a boggy mess. After crossing another creek and passing an ugly, seldom-used campsite, the trail climbs a bit more, then levels out and squeezes through a broad stand of bristly subalpine fir, mountain hemlock, and cedar close to the river. In early morning or after rain, this section can seem like walking through a car wash. Expect a good scrubbing; have rain gear ready even on a nice day. This claustrophobic trail section ends abruptly in wondrously broad, grassy meadows below the imposing cliffs and talus slides of 6,347-foot Iron Cap Mountain. Meander through the meadows, amid giant boulders and subalpine firs, marveling at the complex vertical and overhanging granite walls, and across the river at the higher peaks along the crest. Wildflowers bloom in the meadows; pika scurry in the talus. The trail is boggy here and there, and in a couple of places you need to be careful where you step lest your boots get sucked into the mess. The Forest Service has been restoring several sections of trail here, installing or replacing puncheon to bridge the worst of the muck.

The trail climbs a bit from the meadows, staying near the river, which cascades down a series of slabby falls. Just before the 5-mile marker, the trail reaches the river at an inviting spot, where flat boulders provide a good place to sit and rest. In another 0.4 mile, after a short climb, the trail reaches Pedro Camp, where a fork of the river slows and pools amid wide, marshy, talus-lined meadows before meandering beneath a footbridge and dropping noisily down to join the other river fork. This is one of the prettiest spots on the hike, a popular spot to take a break. Not surprisingly, there are several campsites here, as well as a few too many eroded side trails. Do the meadows a favor and stay on the trail.

Past Pedro Camp, the trail climbs gradually through increasingly subalpine meadows. The trail is boggy and eroded badly in places; do your best to stay on the trail to avoid additional erosion, but be careful not to slip in the mud. At 6.2 miles, the trail forks. Stay right if you're headed to Dutch Miller Gap. Boulder-hop or ford

◀ *Meadow, lake, and talus along Dutch Miller Trail*

Dutch Miller Gap

across the river, a mere stream now, and wade through wildflowers—lupine, valerian, aster—and up switchbacks, soon passing the 7-mile marker. The trail recrosses the stream higher up at a rocky spot where the trail is easy to lose for a moment, but it is soon found on the other side. After a few more switchbacks, the trail enters rocky heather meadows in a high basin. At the head of the basin is Dutch Miller Gap, overlooking Lake Ivanhoe, a deep, narrow lake set in a rocky basin to the east, easily reached in another 0.5 mile, descending several switchbacks down the rocky slope and passing close below a waterfall. There are a few campsites at Lake Ivanhoe, which is a bit less crowded than Williams Lake.

Options

If you want to hike to Williams Lake, backtrack to the trail fork and head up the left fork, fording or boulder-hopping across a small stream and ascending the heavily eroded trail (a muddy ditch in places) into a heather and talus basin. Stay on the trail to avoid more erosion. The trail crosses two more streams and swings westward through a thick grove of mountain hemlocks before descending to Williams Lake. You'll find great views here of the peaks of the Snoqualmie Crest and down the valley, assuming you have the good fortune of arriving on a clear day. Finding a campsite may be trouble; on a sunny summer weekend, tents spring up everywhere, as colorful and plentiful as wildflowers.

An old miners' trail continues up the inlet stream from Williams Lake to Chain Lakes, several small tarns set in a rocky basin below La Bohn Gap. Mining relics, shafts, and debris lie scattered here and there in the basin. From Chain Lakes, it's an easy hike up to La Bohn Gap and over to La Bohn Lakes, although an ice ax may be helpful in early season. Experienced scramblers can head up 6,852-foot La Bohn Peak, a relatively easy climb west from the gap, or 7,492-foot Mount Hinman, a long and more difficult rocky ridge scramble to the east. A high route down to Necklace Valley is possible, but it is too risky to be recommended for any but the most experienced off-trail travelers equipped for steep snow and rock scrambling.

A one-way hike can be made across Dutch Miller Gap and down past Lake Ivanhoe to Waptus Lake, a good three-day, 21-mile traverse following a segment of the

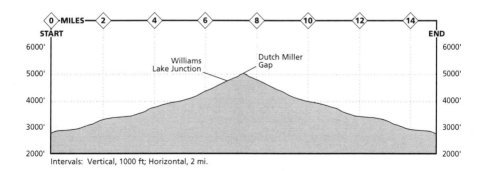

Intervals: Vertical, 1000 ft; Horizontal, 2 mi.

old Cascade Crest Trail. Adventuresome backpackers can retrace the entire Cascade Crest Trail from Snoqualmie Pass to Stevens Pass, although some sections are abandoned; most now opt for the Pacific Crest Trail.

There is talk that the Middle Fork Road might be closed someday at the Taylor River junction, or possibly at Dingford Creek, with the road being converted to trail. This would add between 8 and 13 miles to the one-way hike distance. Those who want to get a feel for what such a hike might be like can hike the Middle Fork Trail now; it leads about 16 miles up the river from the trailhead just before Taylor River bridge all the way to the Dutch Miller trailhead, for a 23.5-mile, one-way hike to Dutch Miller Gap.

Key Points

0.0 Dutch Miller trailhead.

0.1 Footlog across Hardscrabble Creek.

1.1 Alpine Lakes Wilderness boundary.

1.5 Side trail to riverside campsite.

2.7 Crawford Creek crossing.

4.3 Boulder meadows below Iron Cap Mountain.

5.5 Pedro Camp.

6.9 Williams Lake Trail junction. Take the right fork to Dutch Miller Gap.

7.2 Heather basin below Dutch Miller Gap.

7.5 Dutch Miller Gap, turnaround.

15.0 Back to Dutch Miller trailhead.

4 Kaleetan Lake

An out-and-back hike to remote Kaleetan Lake.

Start: Pratt Lake trailhead.
Distance: 20 miles out and back.
Difficulty: Moderate to strenuous.
Best season: Summer through fall.
Traffic: Foot traffic only; heavy use to Pratt Lake, light use beyond.
Total climbing: About 4,130 feet gain, 2,160 feet loss one way to Kaleetan Lake.
High point: About 4,850 feet.

Fees and permits: A Northwest Forest Pass is required.
Maps: USGS Bandera, Snoqualmie Pass; Green Trails No. 207 (Snoqualmie Pass).
Trail contacts: Mt. Baker-Snoqualmie National Forest, Snoqualmie Ranger District, North Bend Office, 42404 SE North Bend Way, North Bend, WA 98045; (425) 888-1421; www.fs.fed.us/r6/mbs.

Finding the trailhead: The hike to Kaleetan Lake begins from the Pratt Lake trailhead, just west of Snoqualmie Pass. Drive I-90 to the Denny Creek/Asahel Curtis exit 47. Head north to a junction, turn left, and follow the paved road about 0.3 mile to the Pratt Lake trailhead. The parking lot is often very crowded on sunny weekends. Come early to find a parking space. This is a high car-prowl trailhead, so lock up and leave no valuables behind.

The Hike

Kaleetan Lake, nestled in a basin below its namesake peak, is one of the more remote alpine lakes despite its close proximity to Snoqualmie Pass. The hike to Kaleetan Lake passes other lakes, some popular, some hardly visited. The farther you hike along this trail, the greater your sense of solitude, unless you pick a weekend when a scout troop has chosen to make Kaleetan Lake their destination.

Get your permit and start hiking up Pratt Lake Trail 1007. The trail begins gradually in an eastward arc through shady second-growth hemlock and fir forest. In about 0.5 mile, the trail abruptly reverses direction and climbs, still gradually, along the steepening slopes of Granite Mountain. Just short of 1 mile is the junction with Granite Mountain Trail 1016. Pratt Lake Trail continues westward, still traversing the slope and climbing gradually, here crossing a stream below a small waterfall, there contouring a steep slope bordered by hemlocks, firs, and cedar, and eventually climbing a forested ridge before crossing a marshy section that used to be a boggy nightmare before a wooden walkway was built in the late 1980s. Once past this, the trail reaches the junction with Talapus Lake Trail and a side trail to Olallie Lake. This is far enough for most hikers, who swarm to Olallie Lake on sunny summer weekends but rarely venture farther. Camping at these lakes is popular and not a private affair by any means.

Olallie Lake

The trail beyond Olallie Lake is noticeably less crowded. It ascends a wide arc above the lake. Silver firs give way to subalpine, western hemlock to mountain hemlock. Beargrass, lupine, and paintbrush bloom alongside the trail. The trail soon reaches the Talapus-Pratt divide, from where Mount Defiance Trail 1009 leads westward to Rainbow and Mason Lakes. Pratt Lake Trail descends over the divide another 1.4 miles to Pratt Lake. This section of trail is scenically unremarkable, just quiet forest hiking down to the lake. There are several campsites at Pratt Lake, but they are taken fast on most summer weekends.

From Pratt Lake, continue 0.9 mile through quiet timber to Lower Tuscohatchie Lake. A shelter cabin by the lakeshore offers a mouse-infested night's sleep for those inclined to stay there. There are other campsites nearby.

A scant 0.2 mile beyond the shelter is the junction with Kaleetan Lake Trail 1010. Take a left and follow the trail 0.5 mile down through dense forest to Pratt River, crossed via a footlog. Once across the river, the trail begins climbing in long switchbacks, gaining 1,850 feet in 1.5 miles to a high ridge overlooking the Kaleetan Creek drainage. From the ridge the trail plunges to tiny Windy Lake, nestled in

Kaleetan Lake

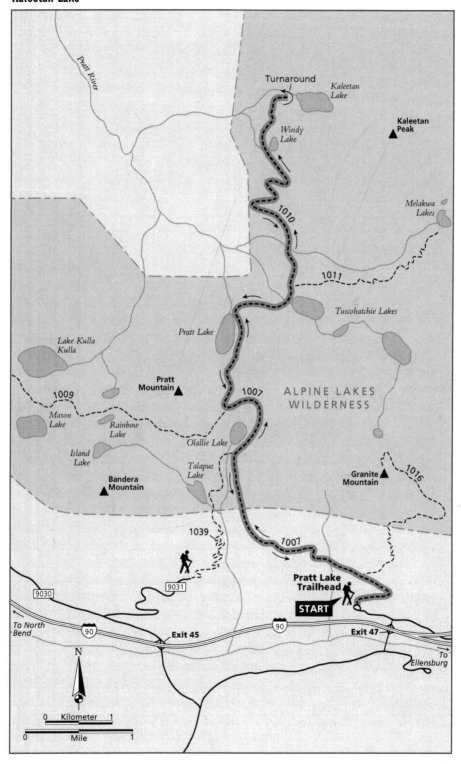

a wooded basin. The trail continues down to Kaleetan Creek, then follows the creek shortly to Kaleetan Lake, tucked into a talus-strewn basin on the west side of Kaleetan Peak.

Options

Pratt Lake Trail provides access to several other trails in this part of the Alpine Lakes Wilderness. Granite Mountain Trail 1016 climbs 3.2 steep miles from the trail junction to a summit lookout. Mount Defiance Trail 1009 leads off from the Talapus-Pratt divide and traverses a lovely, lake-strewn table set in between Pratt and Bandera Mountains to Mason Lake. Rainbow Lake, the largest of the trailside lakes, is only about 1.5 miles beyond the divide, but Island Lake, the largest and most popular of the group, is hidden off the trail, nestled in the shadows of Bandera Mountain. This is a much more scenic hike than to Pratt Lake, and is a popular day hike and overnight destination in its own right. Popular side trips from here include a talus scramble up 5,099-foot Pratt Mountain or 5,241-foot Bandera Mountain, or both, for experienced off-trail travelers.

A favorite of adventuresome hikers is to continue on from Pratt Lake via Tuscohatchie Lakes Trail 1011 to Melakwa Lakes, then cross-country across Melakwa Pass and out via Snow Lake Trail. This is a rugged traverse of some 16-plus miles, including a few miles of off-trail hiking and scrambling. This is definitely not for casual hikers; it will put your route-finding skills to the test. Come prepared for snow; definitely bring an ice ax. An easier loop option is to exit from Melakwa Lakes via Denny Creek Trail 1014. Both of these loops can be made more feasible by stashing a mountain bike at trail's end so you can coast back to the car when you finish your hike.

Key Points

0.0   Pratt Lake trailhead.

0.9   Granite Mountain Trail junction; stay left.

2.9   Talapus Lake Trail junction and side trail to Olallie Lake; stay right.

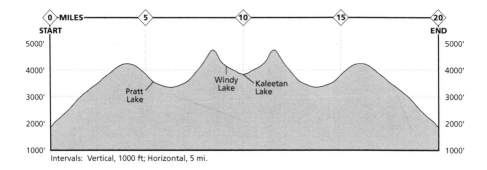

4.0	Talapus-Pratt divide; Mount Defiance Trail junction. Take the right fork, staying on Pratt Lake Trail.
5.4	Pratt Lake.
6.3	Lower Tuscohatchie Lake.
6.5	Kaleetan Lake Trail junction; take the left fork to Kaleetan Lake.
7.0	Pratt River crossing.
9.1	Windy Lake.
10.0	Kaleetan Lake, turn around.
20.0	Back to Pratt Lake trailhead.

5 Spectacle Lake

A strenuous hike to spectacular Spectacle Lake.

Start: Pete Lake trailhead.
Distance: About 18.2 miles out and back.
Difficulty: Mostly easy, but strenuous to the lake.
Best season: Midsummer through fall.
Traffic: Foot and stock traffic; heavy use.
Total climbing: About 1,500 feet.
High point: About 4,300 feet.

Fees and permits: A Northwest Forest Pass is required.
Maps: USGS Polallie Ridge; Green Trails No. 208 (Kachess Lake).
Trail contacts: Wenatchee National Forest, Cle Elum Ranger District, 803 West Second Street, Cle Elum, WA 98922; (509) 674-4411; www.fs.fed.us/r6/wenatchee.

Finding the trailhead: The hike to Spectacle Lake follows Pete Lake Trail 1323 and the Pacific Crest Trail (PCT). It begins from the western end of Cooper Lake. Drive I-90 to Roslyn/Salmon la Sac exit 82. Drive north 2.8 miles to the State Route 903 junction. Turn left and follow SR 903 through the towns of Roslyn and Ronald and along the east shore of Cle Elum Lake to Cooper Lake Road (Forest Road 46). Turn left and follow Cooper Lake Road 4.6 paved miles to the Cooper Lake turnoff, then turn right on FR 4616 and follow the gravel road 1.6 miles down across the river and up along the lakeshore to the Pete Lake Trail turnoff. A spur road leads 0.2 mile down to the trailhead.

The Hike

Spectacle Lake is a large alpine lake nestled in a rocky basin below Chikamin Peak, one of the 7,000-foot peaks that lord over this section of the Alpine Lakes Wilderness. It is one of the most spectacular of the alpine lakes, a jewel among the high subalpine meadows of the Cascade Crest.

The hike begins up Cooper River Trail 1323, flat and easy, hiking directly up Cooper River valley from the northwest shore of Cooper Lake, through deep old-growth forest. Just past the 1-mile mark the trail crosses Tired Creek, and just beyond the creek reaches the Tired Creek Trail junction, elevation 2,850 feet. From this junction, the trail continues straight ahead along the river bottom, crossing another creek and reaching another trail junction in the next mile. In another 0.5 mile, the trail crosses the Alpine Lakes Wilderness boundary at the first of three streams. The next mile is much the same—flat forest hiking along the river bottom. At 3.5 miles, the trail crosses Cooper River, then a tributary of Lemah Creek in another 0.3 mile. Pete Lake is reached in another 0.3 mile. There are several campsites at Pete Lake, although the lake is often overcrowded on summer weekends.

From Pete Lake, follow the trail around the lake shore and up the valley another 1.3 miles to a fork. Take the left fork, staying on trail 1323, and follow 1.2 miles to

Spectacle Lake

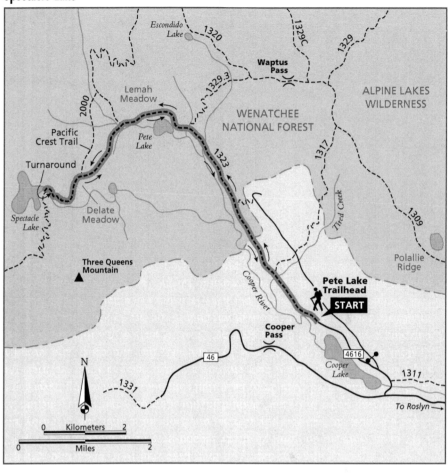

the PCT junction at Delate Meadow, a lovely meadow basin with campsites. No campfires are allowed here. From here, follow the PCT southward, climbing a steep and strenuous 2.5 miles to a side trail that leads to Spectacle Lake, elevation 4,300 feet. This large lake, set in a glacier-polished granite basin, is surrounded by subalpine meadows and 7,000-foot peaks. The lake is often crowded on sunny summer weekends, despite the 9-mile hike to get there. No campfires are allowed at Spectacle Lake or beyond.

Options

One may visit Spectacle Lake while hiking the Pacific Crest Trail from Stevens Pass to Snoqualmie Pass. It is also possible to approach via Mineral Creek Trail 1331 and Park Lakes but with greater elevation gain and distance. If you are camped at Park Lakes, you can make a day trip to Spectacle Lake.

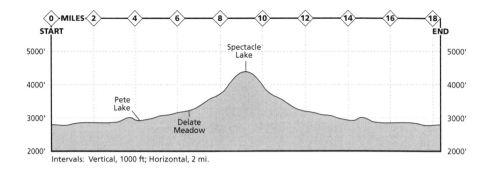

Intervals: Vertical, 1000 ft; Horizontal, 2 mi.

There are many off-trail destinations in the vicinity of Spectacle Lake. Glacier Lake is a short jaunt to the southwest, and Chikamin Lake is nestled in the basin between Chikamin Peak and Lemah Mountain. Reaching these lakes requires some rugged cross-country hiking over talus, polished granite slabs, and rocky subalpine slopes, and it is not recommended for those without scrambling experience. The summits of Chikamin Peak and Lemah Mountain's south peak are moderately difficult alpine scrambles; refer to *Climbing Washington's Mountains* (Falcon, 2001) for route information. *Cascade Alpine Guide* (The Mountaineers, 2003) shows cross-country routes to various lakes in this area.

Key Points

0.0 Pete Lake trailhead.

1.2 Tired Creek Trail junction; stay straight on Pete Lake Trail.

2.1 Cutoff trail junction; stay left on Pete Lake Trail.

2.6 Alpine Lakes Wilderness boundary.

3.5 Cooper River crossing.

3.8 Lemah Creek Fork crossing.

4.0 Waptus Burn Trail junction; stay left.

4.1 Pete Lake.

5.4 Lemah-Delate fork; take the left fork.

6.6 Delate Meadow and Pacific Crest Trail junction; go left (south) on the PCT.

9.1 Spectacle Lake.

18.2 Back to Pete Lake trailhead.

6 Waptus-Escondido Loop

A loop hike over a high pass and along a scenic subalpine ridge below the spectacular Snoqualmie Crest peaks.

Start: Pete Lake trailhead.
Distance: About 22 miles.
Difficulty: Strenuous.
Best season: Summer through fall.
Traffic: Foot and stock traffic; light to moderate use.
Total climbing: About 2,800 feet.
High point: About 5,600 feet.

Fees and permits: A Northwest Forest Pass is required.
Maps: USGS Polallie Ridge; Green Trails No. 208 (Kachess Lake).
Trail contacts: Wenatchee National Forest, Cle Elum Ranger District, 803 West Second Street, Cle Elum, WA 98922; (509) 674-4411; www.fs.fed.us/r6/wenatchee.

Finding the trailhead: The Waptus-Escondido Loop hike begins via Cooper River/Pete Lake Trail 1323. The trailhead is located at the western end of Cooper Lake. Drive I-90 to Roslyn/Salmon la Sac exit 82. Drive north 2.8 miles to the State Route 903 junction. Turn left and follow SR 903 through the towns of Roslyn and Ronald and along the east shore of Cle Elum Lake to Cooper Lake Road (Forest Road 46). Turn left and follow Cooper Lake Road 4.6 paved miles to the Cooper Lake turnoff, then turn right on FR 4616 and follow the gravel road 1.6 miles down across the river and up along the lakeshore to the Pete Lake Trail turnoff. A spur road leads 0.2 mile down to the trailhead.

The Hike

The Waptus-Escondido Loop hike combines segments of several trails in the vicinity of Pete Lake and Waptus Pass for an excellent three- or four-day backpacking trip. It is one of many options for overnight hikes in this area.

The hike begins up Cooper River/Pete Lake Trail 1323, flat and easy, hiking directly up Cooper River Valley from the northwest shore of Cooper Lake, through deep old-growth forest. Just past the 1-mile mark the trail crosses Tired Creek, and just beyond the creek reaches the Tired Creek Trail junction, elevation 2,850 feet. From this junction, the trail continues straight ahead along the river bottom, crossing another creek and reaching another trail junction in the next mile. In another 0.5 mile, the trail crosses the Alpine Lakes Wilderness boundary at the first of three streams. The next mile is much the same—flat forest hiking along the river bottom. At 3.5 miles, the trail crosses Cooper River, then a tributary of Lemah Creek in another 0.3 mile. Pete Lake is reached in another 0.3 mile. There are several campsites at Pete Lake, although the lake is often overcrowded on summer weekends.

From Pete Lake, follow Quick Creek Trail 1329 about 1.9 miles to a junction with Escondido Lake Trail 1320. The first bit of trail climbs steeply along a creek, then levels out a bit as it traverses eastward through pine and fir forest, crossing Escondido Creek and meandering to the junction. Tiny Escondido Lake is a short 1.2 miles up the trail, an option for a first night's camp.

From the junction, the trail traverses lovely subalpine meadows 0.5 mile to Waptus Pass, a broad col dividing Cooper and Waptus River valleys. Wildflowers bloom everywhere here in season. There is a campsite at the junction, and another 0.4 mile to the east at the Quick Creek Trail junction.

From Waptus Pass, follow trail 1329.3, which leads 2.5 miles through the meadows to a broad forested ridge, then up the ridge to a junction with the Pacific Crest Trail (PCT). Take a left and follow the PCT southward, traversing subalpine slopes 1.2 miles to a saddle overlooking Escondido Lake, then contour southward to a subalpine meadow bench dotted with tarns, the so-called Escondido Tarns. The trail continues around a ridge to near a saddle, over which lie Vista Lakes, a few more tiny subalpine lakes set on a high shelf below Summit Chief Mountain. The entire traverse of Escondido Ridge is fantastically scenic, through lovely subalpine meadows with views of mountains near and far, especially as you turn the corner and behold the Snoqualmie Crest peaks up close in all their sublime glory. Truly, this is one of the most beautiful spots in the Alpine Lakes Wilderness; take your time here. Some hikers camp in the vicinity of the tarns and lakes; please use existing sites only, away from the lakes. Campfires are not allowed.

From here, the trail descends rapidly, losing 2,400 feet of elevation in the next 4 miles before leveling out at Lemah Meadow, a broad, grassy meadow. There are campsites here; no campfires are allowed. At the south end of the meadow is a junction with Lemah Creek Trail 1323.1. Follow that trail 0.8 mile to its junction with Cooper River Trail 1323. In 1.2 miles, you are back at Pete Lake, with 4 miles of easy hiking down Cooper River back to the trailhead.

Options

There are many loop options in this area, combining Cooper River Trail, Tired Creek Trail, Waptus Pass Trail, Quick Creek Trail, and the Pacific Crest Trail. The more time you have, the more trails you can follow. This is a good area to "get lost" in for a couple of days. Consult your map, plot a course, and see where it leads.

Summit Chief Mountain is a popular alpine scramble approached via the PCT from Vista Lakes. There are also several small lakes in the cirques and basins hereabouts. For more information, consult *Climbing Washington's Mountains* (Falcon, 2002) or *Cascade Alpine Guide* (The Mountaineers Books, 2000).

◀ *Waptus Pass meadow*

Waptus-Escondido Loop

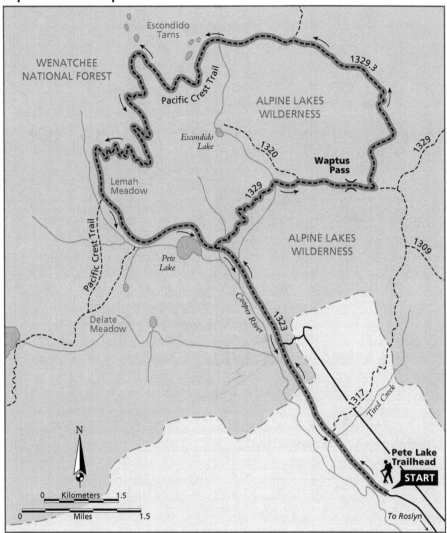

Key Points

0.0 Pete Lake trailhead.

1.2 Tired Creek Trail junction.

2.1 Cutoff trail junction.

2.6 Alpine Lakes Wilderness boundary.

3.5 Cooper River crossing.

4.0 Waptus Burn Trail junction; take a right (north) on Waptus Burn Trail.

5.9 Waptus Pass; take the left fork on trail 1329.3.

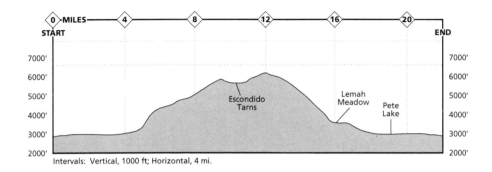

Intervals: Vertical, 1000 ft; Horizontal, 4 mi.

8.4 Pacific Crest Trail junction; turn left (south) on the PCT.

10.1 Escondido Tarns.

16.0 Lemah Meadow; take the left fork to Pete Lake.

18.0 Pete Lake.

22.0 Pete Lake trailhead.

7 Polallie Ridge

A long ridge and meadow hike with close views of the Snoqualmie Crest peaks.

Start: Salmon la Sac trailhead.
Distance: 15.2 miles out and back to high point.
Difficulty: Strenuous.
Best season: Midsummer through fall.
Traffic: Foot and stock traffic; moderate use to Diamond Lake, light beyond.
Total climbing: About 3,900 feet.
High point: 5,570 feet.

Fees and permits: A Northwest Forest Pass is required.
Maps: USGS Polallie Ridge; Green Trails No. 208 (Kachess Lake).
Trail contacts: Wenatchee National Forest, Cle Elum Ranger District, 803 West Second Street, Cle Elum, WA 98922; (509) 674-4411; www.fs.fed.us/r6/wenatchee.

Finding the trailhead: Polallie Ridge Trail 1309 begins from the Salmon la Sac trailhead. To get there, drive I-90 to Roslyn/Salmon la Sac exit 80. From the exit, drive north 2.8 miles to the State Route 903 junction. Turn left and follow SR 903 past Roslyn, Ronald, and Cle Elum Lake, 16.5 miles to pavement's end just past the Salmon la Sac guard station. The road forks here; take the left fork and follow across the river, then turn right onto spur road 111 and follow 0.6 mile to the trailhead loop.

The Hike

Polallie means "dust" in the Chinook jargon, and the name is partly apt. Polallie Ridge Trail is a long, sometimes dry, dusty ridge hike on the high divide between Waptus and Cooper Rivers. But the trail also leads to a sparkling lake and through verdant meadows to a high ridge with spectacular views. This is not as popular as many other nearby hikes, since it is long and strenuous and takes its sweet time getting to the views, but the little bit of suffering is worth it in the long run. The views are that good, and the trail has a wilderness flavor that is unmatched by other, more accessible trails.

Get your permit at the trailhead and start hiking up the dusty trail that serves as the start to three hikes, Cooper River Trail 1311, Polallie Ridge Trail 1309, and Waptus River Trail 1310. In a dusty 0.1 mile, Cooper River Trail forks off to the left. Stay right a short distance to another junction, where Waptus River Trail breaks off to the right. Stick to the middle path, which leads through open fir and pine forest with some views down the valley as you climb higher. In late summer and fall, Douglas' squirrels scamper high overhead, breaking off seed cones that sometimes land disconcertingly near, making you wonder if they aren't purposely trying to hit you. The trail climbs steadily up a rocky slope, then tapers off slightly in forest, with vanilla leaf, wintergreen, and Oregon grape growing in the shady spots. More climbing

Lemah Peak from Pollalie Ridge Trail ▶

Polallie Ridge

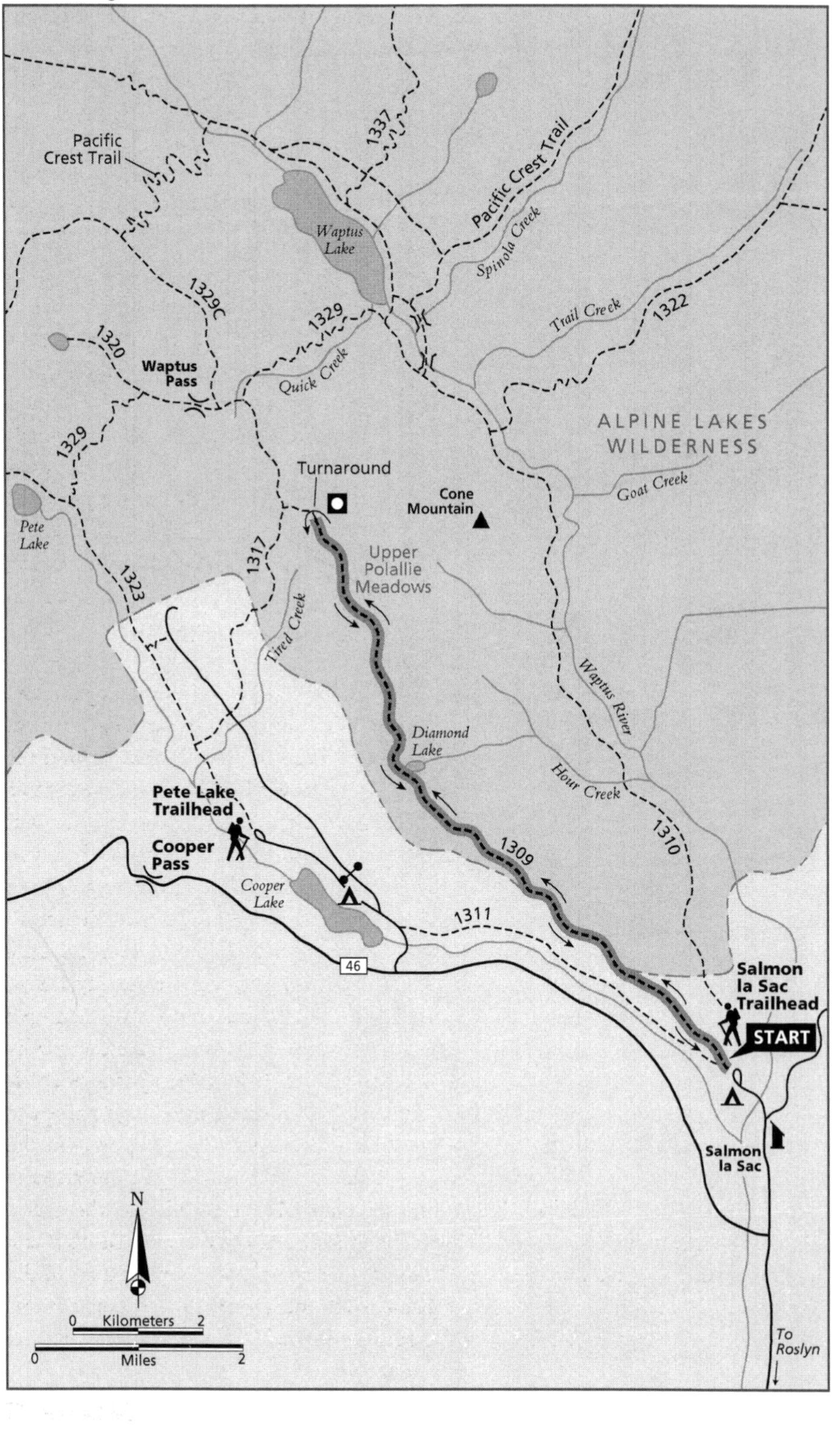

Pacific Crest Trail

1337

Pacific Crest Trail

Spinola Creek

Waptus Lake

1329C

1329

1320

Waptus Pass

Quick Creek

Trail Creek

1322

Goat Creek

ALPINE LAKES WILDERNESS

1329

Pete Lake

1323

1317

Turnaround

Cone Mountain

Upper Polallie Meadows

Tired Creek

Diamond Lake

Waptus River

Hour Creek

1310

Pete Lake Trailhead

Cooper Pass

Cooper Lake

46

1311

1309

Salmon la Sac Trailhead

START

Salmon la Sac

To Roslyn

N

0   Kilometers   2

0   Miles   2

follows, up rocky benches and steep forest, eventually along a defined ridge and through little meadows fringed with wildflowers. The trail dips briefly and passes a big, mossy boulder, seemingly out of place on the wooded ridge crest. Past the boulder, the trail flattens out, traversing quiet montane forest benches, passing a grove of lodgepole pines, and too soon starts climbing again. Just over an hour up the trail is a rocky viewpoint, a great spot to take a deserved break and enjoy the views, including a glimpse of Mount Stuart poking up over the intervening ridges. By this point, having hiked up a hot, dusty ridge for an hour or so, you may be having doubts about having picked this hike. Don't worry, it gets better.

The trail crosses a rock rib and passes over a divide onto the northeast slope of Polallie Ridge, then descends into a basin. The trail skirts under a talus bowl, then climbs up over a ridge to the Alpine Lakes Wilderness boundary and the first good views to the north, including Cone Mountain, Mount Daniel, and Granite Mountain. Past the boundary, the trail traverses a series of ups and downs through shady fir and hemlock forest, with lupine and aster bursting amid the heather and rhododendron. After a bit more traversing, the trail crosses a little meadow basin and an explosion of wildflowers in season. The trail climbs a bit up a narrow meadow gully to a 5,140-foot-high gap, then drops through delightful heather and huckleberry meadows to Diamond Lake, elevation 4,880 feet. A round trip to Diamond Lake is about 9 miles, making it a good day hike. There is a large campsite near the lake's southern shore, and more along the western shoreline.

Continuing from the lake, hike left up the rocky trail at an indistinct junction. It's easy to miss the trail here; if you find yourself hiking along the western shore of Diamond Lake, you've missed the turn. The trail becomes less distinct beyond the lake, but is not difficult to follow as it leads up and over a saddle and down into a broad meadow at the head of Hour Creek. The trail disappears in the meadow, but is picked up again if you skirt the lower fringe of the meadow. A cairn may help you find the trail if it's still standing. From the other side of the meadow, the trail climbs steeply from the basin, gaining 600 feet in 0.6 mile to another saddle, then descends again into another wide meadow with a marshy stream. The trail vanishes once more, but it is easily found on the far side. Start climbing once more, steeply at first, before traversing a subalpine meadow slope with wildflowers and views, then up a short, absurdly steep section leading directly to the ridge crest. Traverse woodsy huckleberry meadows along the gentle crest to the 5,570-foot-high point of Polallie Ridge, and continue along the crest another 0.4 mile to a bald ridge point, site of a former fire lookout and one of the best hiker-accessible viewpoints in the Alpine Lakes Wilderness. Plan on spending some time here, soaking in the views of the multitude of peaks in all directions, including Mount Rainier to the south, Lemah Peak, Chimney Rock and Summit Chief Mountain to the west, Bear's Breast Mountain and Mounts Hinman and Daniel to the north, and Mount Stuart to the east, to name only a few. The lookout point would be a great spot to enjoy a sunrise, but it isn't a recommended campsite because of the broken glass, rusty nails, and other debris from the lookout cabin. Luckily, there's a campsite a short distance down the trail, near the Tired Creek Trail junction. The site's not quite as scenic, but it's close enough that you can enjoy the sunset from the lookout point, then hike down the trail by flashlight to your camp.

Options

A more direct route up to Polallie Ridge viewpoint is Tired Creek Trail 1371, leading 5.4 miles up from the Pete Lake trailhead. This trail is shorter and a bit more popular than the ridge trail, but it is unrelentingly steep and strenuous and not especially wonderful.

Once atop Polallie Ridge, you may loop out via Tired Creek and Cooper River Trails instead of backtracking along the ridge; this is more conveniently done if you can arrange to have a ride waiting at Pete Lake trailhead. Or you may continue on Polallie Ridge Trail some 1.2 miles north down a ridge and forested slopes to its end at the Quick Creek Trail junction of Waptus Pass Trail 1329, then loop down Quick Creek Trail to Waptus Lake and out via Waptus River Trail. This is an excellent three- or four-day loop hike of some 22 miles, providing a sampler of this area's ridge, lake, and river trails.

There are many more options for loop and one-way hikes, too many to list here. Take any trail; it will lead you somewhere.

Key Points

0.0 Salmon la Sac trailhead.

0.1 Cooper River Trail junction to left, Waptus River Trail junction to right; stay on the middle trail.

2.8 Alpine Lakes Wilderness boundary.

4.5 Diamond Lake.

5.2 Hour Creek basin.

6.5 Upper Polallie Meadows.

7.6 Polallie Ridge viewpoint.

15.2 Back to Salmon la Sac trailhead.

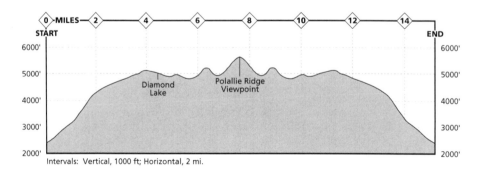

8 Waptus River to Waptus Lake

A long hike up Waptus River to Waptus Lake, one of the largest lakes in the Alpine Lakes Wilderness.

Start: Salmon la Sac trailhead.
Distance: 18.8 miles out and back to Waptus Lake.
Difficulty: Moderate.
Best season: Early summer through fall.
Traffic: Foot and stock traffic; heavy use.
Total climbing: About 600 feet.
High point: About 3,100 feet.
Fees and permits: A Northwest Forest Pass is required.

Maps: USGS Davis Peak, Polallie Ridge, Mount Daniel; Green Trails No. 208 (Kachess Lake).
Trail contacts: Wenatchee National Forest, Cle Elum Ranger District, 803 West Second Street, Cle Elum, WA 98922; (509) 674-4411; www.fs.fed.us/r6/wenatchee.

Finding the trailhead: Waptus River Trail 1310 is approached from Roslyn via Cle Elum River Road. Drive I-90 to Roslyn/Salmon le Sac exit 80. From the exit, drive north 2.8 miles to the State Route 903 junction. Turn left and follow SR 903 past Roslyn, Ronald, and Cle Elum Lake, 16.5 miles to the pavement's end just past the Salmon le Sac guard station. The road forks here; take the left fork and follow across the river, then turn right onto spur road 111 and follow 0.6 mile to the trailhead loop.

The Hike

The hike up Waptus River to Waptus Lake is one of the longer lowland river hikes in the Alpine Lakes Wilderness. Unlike most other river valleys (the nearby Cooper and Cle Elum Rivers being prime examples), no road was pushed up Waptus River by miners or loggers, which has allowed the river valley and lake to maintain a wilderness aspect unmatched by other big lakes in the region. The only thing missing is solitude; this hike, although long, gets a lot of traffic, especially horses. The going is mostly flat and easy, but with the usual ups and downs of Cascades river valley hiking. Waptus Lake, one of the largest lakes in the Alpine Lakes Wilderness, is very popular with fishermen and horse packers, yet it is large enough that you can find a secluded spot.

Get your permit at the trailhead register, then start up the trail, which serves three trails, including Cooper River Trail 1311, Polallie Ridge Trail 1309, and Waptus River Trail 1310. The trail contours above Cooper River briefly to a junction, where Cooper River Trail forks off to the left. A few paces farther, Waptus River Trail forks off to the right. Follow it and continue on a winding course through dusty pine and fir forest 0.7 mile to the old trail junction. Forge ahead, ignoring the wide path leading off to the right. In late summer and fall, Douglas' squirrels will be

busy harvesting seed cones here; watch out below! You soon pass the Alpine Lakes Wilderness boundary marker. The trail climbs a bit, then levels off some and passes a big pond, lily pads and all, below a little rock cliff, then proceeds past several marshes and a grove of lovely cedars. Watch for frogs hopping underfoot and mosquitoes attacking every bit of exposed skin in early season. The trail curves to the right and traverses around a rocky ridge, then cuts sharply upriver and contours along some distance above the river's south bank, descending gradually through dusty silver fir and hemlock forest and a few stands of lodgepole pine. You can hear the river, which keeps its distance for a few miles yet, a murmur in the valley below.

At about 3 miles and just over an hour from the trailhead for most hikers, the trail crosses Hour Creek and soon comes to within a stone's throw of Waptus River. Crossing this and other creeks may be challenging in early season due to high water; look for a footlog just downstream. There are a few riverside camps just beyond the creek crossing, used mostly by stragglers who started too late in the day. The trail continues up Hour Creek for about 0.7 mile, traversing the slope of a quiet basin thick with old-growth fir and cedar, with Douglas maple and wild rose along the trail, to a divide, then dropping back to the river's edge. The trail stays there for a while, passing a slot canyon with noisy rapids and a couple of campsites, then climbing and dropping again to the river. Here is a little granite dome beside the river, a great spot to take a break. Shortly beyond, the trail passes several giant boulders that tumbled down from the granite cliffs of Cone Mountain. The trail climbs yet again, this time to a rocky shelf far above the river, then drops steeply and follows the river a bit farther, passing several more campsites, then climbs again across a brushy avalanche slope to enter shady old-growth hemlock and fir forest with some big cedars. Luxuriant ferns, devil's club, bead lily, and bunchberry line the trail, and grass-of-Parnasus can be found beside the marshy streams. Soon comes the junction with Trail Creek Trail 1322, and beyond, more climbing as the trail leads up alongside a babbling brook, crosses it, then heads up over a rise and down a dusty ravine. After crossing a little stream, the trail reaches the junction with Quick Creek Trail 1329, just a holler from the lake, where you have a couple of options.

Those who want the full effect of Waptus Lake should take the right fork, which leads down a dusty path to the Waptus River footbridge, a wide bridge spanning the river where it drops through a little rock canyon. The trail leads another 0.4 mile through quiet pine forest to Spinola Creek, also crossed via a sturdy footbridge. Once across the bridge, the trails fork. If you stay right, you reach Spinola Creek Trail junction; to the left, staying alongside the creek, is a bypass that connects with the main trail in a short distance. Either way, continue along a wooded flat another 0.4 mile to Waptus Lake, then as far as you like up the lakeshore. The "official" turnaround point of this hike is Spade Lake Trail junction, at 9.4 miles, making this an 18.8-mile round trip. There are several campsites along the lakeshore.

◀ *Reeds, Waptus Lake*

Waptus River to Waptus Lake

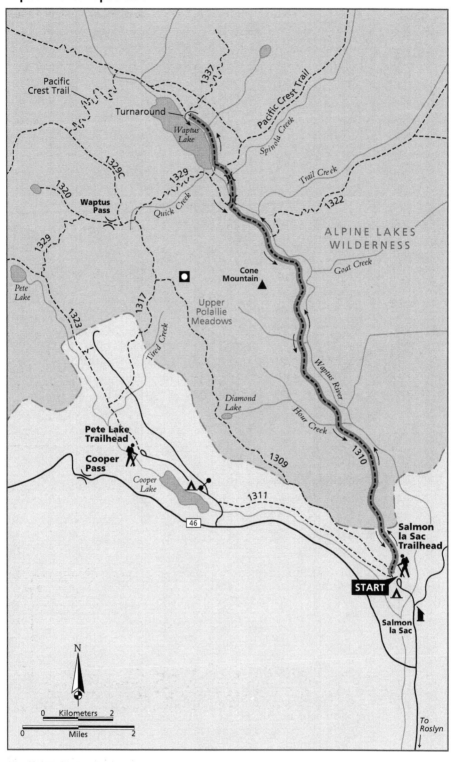

Pacific
Crest Trail

1337

Pacific Crest Trail

Turnaround

Waptus
Lake

Spinola Creek

1329

Trail Creek

1329C

1320

Waptus
Pass

Quick Creek

1322

1329

ALPINE LAKES
WILDERNESS

Goat Creek

Pete
Lake

Cone
Mountain

1317

Upper
Polallie
Meadows

1323

Tired Creek

Waptus River

Diamond
Lake

Hour Creek

1310

Pete Lake
Trailhead

Cooper
Pass

Cooper
Lake

1309

1311

46

Salmon
la Sac
Trailhead

START

Salmon
la Sac

N

0   Kilometers   2

0   Miles   2

To
Roslyn

An alternative is to stay left at the Quick Creek junction and follow Quick Creek Trail another 0.6 mile, beyond the Waptus River horse ford trail junction. This trail leads along the southeastern shoreline. You can leave the trail in several places to access the reedy lakeshore, which is quiet and scenic and actually less crowded than the main trail. Going this way saves a mile or so off your round-trip distance, although you won't get the best views of the lake. There is a horse camp down a side trail from Quick Creek Trail, another place to access the lakeshore.

If you need to filter water on this hike, you are advised to do so on the uphill side of streams feeding into Waptus River, not from the river or lake or any stream in a horse trail drainage, for reasons that will be obvious as you hike up the trail.

Options

Trails lead off in several directions from Waptus Lake. You can continue another 5-plus miles up Waptus River to Lake Ivanhoe and Dutch Miller Gap, and continue out via Dutch Miller Trail if you have arranged transportation. Spade Lake is 4.5 miles from Waptus Lake via Spade Lake Trail. Deep Lake is 5 miles up Spinola Creek Trail and the Pacific Crest Trail (PCT); a long but interesting loop can be made via Deep Lake and Cathedral Pass, then back down Trail Creek Trail and out. A side trail to Lake Vicente offers more high-lake wandering. Another loop option is to hike up Quick Creek Trail to Waptus Pass, then hike down Polallie Ridge Trail for a total of 22 miles round trip; this loop is better done starting with Polallie Ridge. The PCT can be hiked in either direction from Waptus Lake. There are plenty of other options; if you want to fully explore this area, plan on spending several days.

Key Points

0.0 Salmon la Sac trailhead.

0.1 Polallie Ridge-Waptus River junction; stay right.

0.6 Alpine Lakes Wilderness boundary.

3.0 Crossing of Hour Creek.

4.4 Crossing of Cone Mountain Creek.

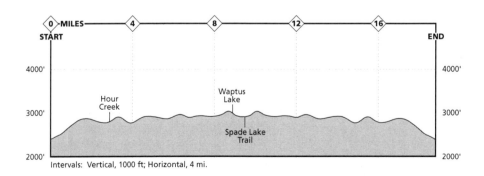

Intervals: Vertical, 1000 ft; Horizontal, 4 mi.

6.7 Junction with Trail Creek Trail; stay left.

7.8 Junction with Quick Creek Trail; stay right.

8.0 Footbridge crossing Waptus River.

8.4 Footbridge crossing Spinola Creek; turn left to Waptus Lake.

8.8 Waptus Lake.

9.4 Junction with Spade Lake Trail.

18.8 Back to Salmon la Sac trailhead.

$\mathcal{9}$ Spade Lake

A spur trail from Waptus Lake leading to this remote, lovely alpine lake.

Start: Salmon la Sac trailhead.
Distance: 6.8 miles out and back from Waptus Lake; 25.6 miles out and back from Salmon la Sac trailhead.
Difficulty: Very strenuous.
Best season: Late summer to early fall.
Traffic: Foot traffic only; light use.
Total climbing: About 2,300 feet from Waptus Lake.

High point: About 5,400 feet.
Fees and permits: A Northwest Forest Pass is required.
Maps: USGS Mount Daniel; Green Trails No. 176 (Stevens Pass).
Trail contacts: Wenatchee National Forest, Cle Elum Ranger District, 803 West Second Street, Cle Elum, WA 98922; (509) 674-4411; www.fs.fed.us/r6/wenatchee.

Finding the trailhead: Spade Lake Trail 1337 begins from the northern shore of Waptus Lake. Drive I-90 to Roslyn/Salmon le Sac exit 80. From the exit, drive north 2.8 miles to the State Route 903 junction. Turn left and follow SR 903 past Roslyn, Ronald, and Cle Elum Lake, 16.5 miles to the pavement's end just past the Salmon le Sac guard station. The road forks here; take the left fork and follow across the river, then turn right onto spur road 111 and follow 0.6 mile to the trailhead loop.

The Hike

Spade Lake is a lovely, lonesome lake nestled in a rocky cirque high on Mount Daniel. It is one of the most remote lakes in the Alpine Lakes Wilderness. The shortest path to the lake is some 13 miles one way, with plenty of elevation gain up a rugged trail. This hike is best done as a three-day backpack, with a base camp at Waptus Lake, allowing a full day to hike up to Spade Lake and explore. Backpackers who venture to Spade Lake will enjoy a profound sense of solitude unknown to most wilderness visitors, interrupted only by jets flying overhead and the occasional day-trippers up from Waptus Lake.

From Salmon la Sac trailhead, follow Waptus River Trail 1310. Stay right at the Polallie Ridge–Waptus River junction at 0.1 mile. Stay left at the junction with Trail Creek Trail 1322 at 6.7 miles, and left at the junction with Quick Creek Trail 1329 at 7.8 miles. At the footbridge Spinola Creek, turn left toward Waptus Lake. Spade Lake Trail is at 9.4 miles. Turn right and start climbing up from the lake, through tall timber, 0.3 mile to the Pacific Crest Trail (PCT) junction. Cross the PCT and continue up the relentlessly steep path, which climbs switchbacks when the going is too steep, but mostly just up and up. This slope is south facing, making for hot, sweaty hiking on sunny summer days; start early. The firs and hemlocks provide some shade,

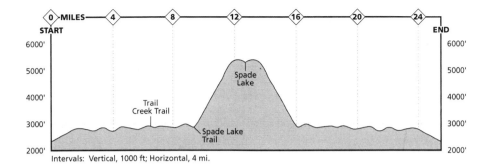

Intervals: Vertical, 1000 ft; Horizontal, 4 mi.

but in the heat of the day you'll suffer. After about 2 miles, gaining 2,000 feet of elevation, the switchbacks end and the trail angles westward, contouring subalpine slopes and crossing an unnamed creek, then rounding a ridge and traversing into a craggy basin just below the lake. The upper trail has expansive views down to Waptus Lake, across to Polallie Ridge, Waptus Pass, and the Summit Chief peaks, and across a craggy ridge to the peak of Bear's Breast Mountain. A waterfall drops down cliffs on the far side of the basin. The trail barely enters the basin, then climbs steeply up the eastern slope, through talus and brush, with views down to Waptus Lake and across to the Snoqualmie Crest peaks and south to Mount Rainier, then drops over a rocky rib to Spade Lake, elevation 5,210.

Hikers who come to Spade Lake early in the summer should bring an ice ax and be prepared for snow camping. Although the south-facing slope climbed on the hike is usually snow free much earlier, the lake does not melt out until late July of most years, August in years of heavy snowpack.

Options

A short cross-country hike up glacier-scoured rocks leads to Venus Lake, a tiny, snowbound lake cupped between the upper ridges of Mount Daniel. The lake melts out by late summer most years. A climber's route up Mount Daniel begins here, but it is rocky, steep, loose, and fairly hazardous to the uninitiated; this route is not popular with climbers (mostly because of the long approach hike), and is not at all recommended for hikers. Those wishing to climb Mount Daniel should approach via Cathedral Pass and Peggy's Pond; refer to *Climbing Washington's Mountains* (Falcon, 2001) for details.

◀ *Spade and Venus Lakes from Mount Daniel*

Spade Lake

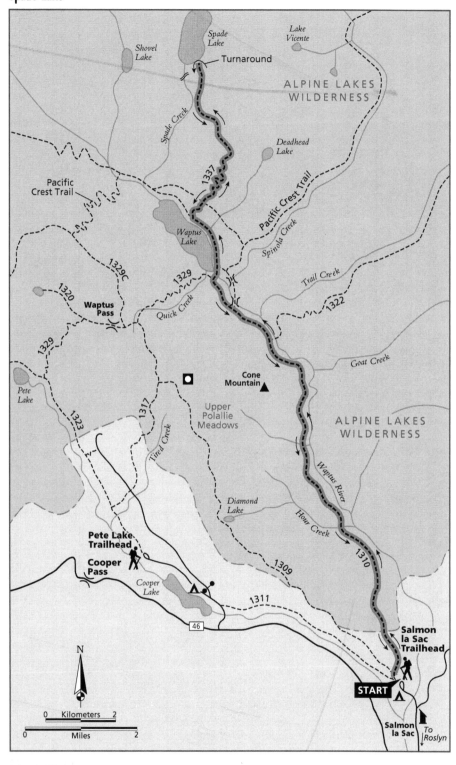

- Spade Lake
- Shovel Lake
- Lake Vicente
- *Turnaround*
- ALPINE LAKES WILDERNESS
- *Spade Creek*
- Deadhead Lake
- 1337
- Pacific Crest Trail
- *Waptus Lake*
- Pacific Crest Trail
- *Spinola Creek*
- 1329C
- 1329
- *Quick Creek*
- *Trail Creek*
- 1320
- **Waptus Pass**
- 1322
- 1329
- *Goat Creek*
- Pete Lake
- 1323
- 1317
- Cone Mountain ▲
- Upper Polallie Meadows
- *Tired Creek*
- ALPINE LAKES WILDERNESS
- *Waptus River*
- Diamond Lake
- **Pete Lake Trailhead**
- **Cooper Pass**
- *Hour Creek*
- 1310
- *Cooper Lake* △
- 1309
- 1311
- 46
- N
- **Salmon la Sac Trailhead**
- **START** △
- **Salmon la Sac**
- *To Roslyn*
- 0 Kilometers 2
- 0 Miles 2

Key Points

0.0   Salmon la Sac trailhead.

0.1   Polallie Ridge–Waptus River junction; stay right.

6.7   Junction with Trail Creek Trail; stay left.

7.8   Junction with Quick Creek Trail; stay right.

8.4   Footbridge crossing Spinola Creek; turn left to Waptus Lake.

9.4   Spade Lake Trail junction.

9.7   Pacific Crest Trail crossing.

11.9   Switchbacks end.

12.8   Spade Lake.

25.6   Back to Salmon la Sac trailhead.

10 Lake Michael

Backpack to a remote lake nestled on the western slopes of Goat Mountain.

Start: Cathedral Pass trailhead.
Distance: 19 miles out and back.
Difficulty: Moderate.
Best season: Summer through fall.
Traffic: Foot and stock traffic; light hiker use.
Total climbing: About 3,300 feet gain, 500 feet loss one way to Lake Michael.
High point: About 5,100 feet.

Fees and permits: A Northwest Forest Pass is required.
Maps: USGS Mount Daniel, The Cradle; Green Trails No. 176 (Stevens Pass).
Trail contacts: Wenatchee National Forest, Cle Elum Ranger District, 803 West Second Street, Cle Elum, WA 98922; (509) 674-4411; www.fs.fed.us/r6/wenatchee.

Finding the trailhead: Lake Michael Trail 1366 is approached via Cathedral Pass Trail 1345 and Trail Creek Trail 1332 from Cathedral Pass trailhead, near the end of Cle Elum River Road (Forest Road 4330). To get there, drive I-90 to Roslyn/Salmon la Sac exit 80. From the exit, drive north 2.8 miles to the State Route 903 junction. Turn left and follow SR 903 through Roslyn and Ronald and along Cle Elum Lake, 16.5 miles to pavement's end. The road forks here; take the right fork and continue another 12.3 miles on FR 4330 to the Cathedral Pass trailhead on the left just before road's end. The road crosses two streams, which run high in early season. If you don't have a high-clearance vehicle, consider parking, fording the creeks, then walking or riding your bike up the road to the trailhead.

The Hike

Lake Michael is a small alpine lake lying in a rocky basin just north of Davis Peak. The hike to Lake Michael follows a horse-trodden trail through quiet old-growth forest. The lake is a popular horse-packing trip, and hikers seem to prefer the more scenic hike to Deep Lake and Lake Vicente. If you don't need spectacular views and get along well with horses, you might enjoy this hike. There's a good chance you'll have it all to yourself.

The hike begins via Cathedral Pass Trail 1345. The trail starts from the Cle Elum River valley bottom, crosses the river via a sturdy footbridge, then climbs, switching back several times through deep silver fir and hemlock forest, vanilla leaf, twinflower and bunchberry lining the trail, and devil's club and ferns in the many streambeds. This portion of the trail is cool in the morning and late afternoon but can be hot by midday. The slope angle tapers off noticeably as you near the ridge crest, and at 1.8 miles, just across a rocky divide, is the Trail Creek Trail junction. Take a left on Trail Creek Trail 1322 and soon pass the marshy remains of Squitch Lake. There is a campsite here, but it is buggy and not popular. Continue southward, down a gentle vale at the head of Trail Creek, through hemlock and fir forest, soon contouring the western bank of the creek. The trail is wide and easy, losing little more than 100 feet of

Trail Creek Valley from Pollalie Ridge

Lake Michael

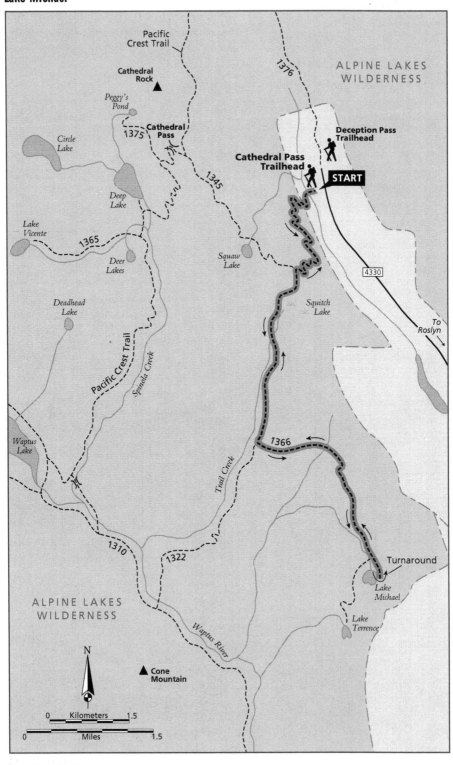

Pacific
Crest Trail

1376

ALPINE LAKES
WILDERNESS

Cathedral
Rock

Peggy's
Pond

Cathedral
Pass

Deception Pass
Trailhead

1375

Circle
Lake

1345

Cathedral Pass
Trailhead

START

Deep
Lake

Lake
Vicente

1365

Squaw
Lake

4330

Deer
Lakes

Squitch
Lake

Deadhead
Lake

To
Roslyn

Pacific Crest Trail

Spinola Creek

Trail Creek

Waptus
Lake

1366

1310

1322

Turnaround

Lake
Michael

ALPINE LAKES
WILDERNESS

Waptus River

Lake
Terrence

N

Cone
Mountain

0   Kilometers   1.5

0   Miles   1.5

elevation in the next mile. After crossing Trail Creek, the trail contours the east bank of the creek, climbing gradually as it traverses the steepening forested slopes.

In a mile from the creek crossing is the Lake Michael Trail junction. Take a left up Trail 1366, and climb up and away from Trail Creek, then across a gentle divide into Goat Creek Basin. The trail swings across the upper basin slopes below the craggy west face of Goat Mountain, through open, dusty fir and hemlock forest, crossing several streams. Finally, the trail contours southward and traverses the slopes of Goat Mountain, descending 2 miles into a basin, then climbing a final 0.5 mile to Lake Michael, elevation 5,100 feet. A trail leads along the lake's eastern shore, and a way trail continues around the lake. There are several campsites here, including a horse camp.

Options

The trail continues another 1.5 miles beyond Lake Michael to Lake Terrence, elevation 5,550 feet, a teardrop-shaped lake perched on a shelf just north of Davis Peak. There aren't many crowds to get away from at Lake Michael, but if you're camped there, this is a good side trip. That's about all there is to do other than hang around the lake swatting flies and mosquitos. Experienced scramblers might find a route up to tiny Opal Lake or one of the other small lakes scattered about, or even to the summit of Davis Peak, but the terrain is steep and rocky, definitely not recommended for hikers without alpine scrambling experience.

Key Points

0.0 Cathedral Pass trailhead.
0.1 Cle Elum River crossing.
1.8 Trail Creek Trail junction; take the left fork.
2.2 Squitch Lake.
3.9 Trail Creek crossing.
5.0 Lake Michael Trail junction; take the left fork.
9.5 Lake Michael, turn around.
19.0 Back to Cathedral Pass trailhead.

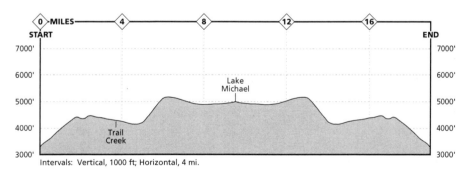

Intervals: Vertical, 1000 ft; Horizontal, 4 mi.

11 Deep Lake and Lake Vicente

A hike over Cathedral Pass to the lush meadow basin of Deep Lake and beyond.

Start: Cathedral Pass trailhead.
Distance: 13.8 miles out and back to Deep Lake; 18.4 miles out and back to Lake Vicente.
Difficulty: Moderate to strenuous.
Best season: Late summer through fall.
Traffic: Foot and stock traffic; moderate to heavy use.
Total climbing: About 3,350 feet gain, 1,200 feet loss one way to Lake Vicente.

High point: About 5,600 feet.
Fees and permits: A Northwest Forest Pass is required.
Maps: USGS Mount Daniel; Green Trails No. 176 (Stevens Pass).
Trail contacts: Wenatchee National Forest, Cle Elum Ranger District, 803 West Second Street, Cle Elum, WA 98922; (509) 674-4411; www.fs.fed.us/r6/wenatchee.

Finding the trailhead: The hike to Deep Lake and Lake Vicente begins via Cathedral Pass Trail 1345. To get there, drive I-90 to exit 80, marked Roslyn and Salmon la Sac. From the exit, drive north 2.8 miles to the State Route 903 junction. Turn left and follow SR 903 through Roslyn and Ronald and along Cle Elum Lake, 16.5 miles to pavement's end. The road forks here; take the right fork and continue another 12.3 miles on Forest Road 4330 to the Cathedral Pass trailhead, on the left just 0.1 mile from road's end. This road has two stream crossings that can be difficult when water is running high. Those with low-clearance vehicles sometimes park at the stream crossings and hike or bike up to the trailhead.

The Hike

Deep Lake is one of the jewels of the Alpine Lakes Wilderness, a striking blue lake set in lush green meadows in a remote cirque below Mount Daniel in the heart of the wilderness. It is a popular destination of day hikers and backpackers. By contrast, Lake Vicente is a small lake set in a higher cirque that doesn't melt out until late summer and is rarely visited.

Get your permit and start hiking down the trail, which begins from the Cle Elum River valley bottom, crosses the river via a footbridge, then climbs, switching back several times through silver fir and hemlock forest, vanilla leaf, twinflower and bunchberry lining the trail, and devil's club and ferns in the streambeds. This portion of the trail is cool in the morning and late afternoon but can be hot by midday. The slope tapers off noticeably as you near the ridge crest, and at 1.8 miles, just across a rocky divide, is the junction with Trail Creek Trail 1322, the turnoff for Lake Michael.

Stay on the Cathedral Pass Trail, continuing northward, level at first but soon climbing through subalpine forest, with rhododendron, huckleberry, and mountain

Pond along Cathedral Pass Trail

Deep Lake and Lake Vicente

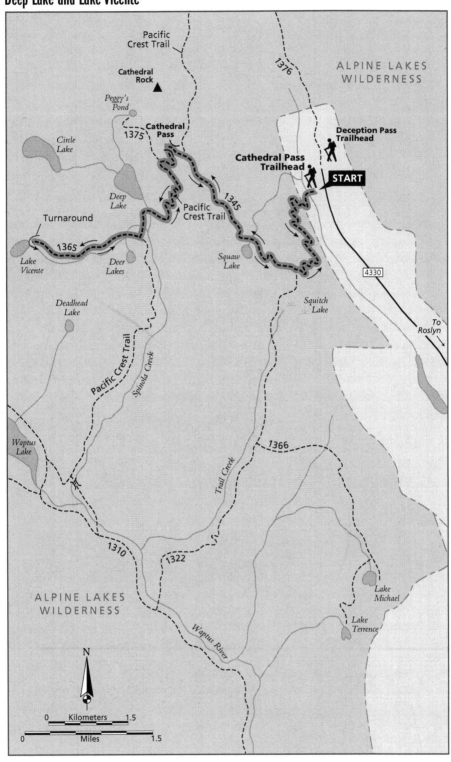

ash lining the trail. The trail levels off again, and just 0.5 mile from the junction it reaches Squaw Lake, elevation 4,841 feet, a nice lake set on a talus- and cliff-rimmed shelf. There are several campsites here, none very private. From the lake, the trail climbs a bit, then crosses a divide and levels off, traversing a grassy meadow, then a subalpine bench dotted with tarns, with views across the valley to the Wenatchee Mountains and ahead to Cathedral Rock. There are campsites hidden among the trees here; don't camp on the meadows, please. Look for lupine, lousewort, and shooting star among the many flowers growing here. Once past the biggest tarn, the trail climbs briefly to the Pacific Crest Trail (PCT) junction. Go left from the junction, climbing a couple of switchbacks to Cathedral Pass, a rocky divide, elevation 5,600 feet. There are several places to sit and enjoy the view.

From the pass, Deep Lake glistens invitingly, like a sparkling sapphire set among emerald meadows. The trail continues down from the divide 2.9 miles, switching back forever down the rocky slope. Finally, the trail levels out amid broad meadows, crosses Spinola Creek, and reaches a junction with the lakeshore trail. Follow this trail 0.5 mile northward along Deep Lake's western shore; there are plenty of campsites.

To get to Lake Vicente, continue south from the junction and follow the PCT another 0.5 mile to the Lake Vicente Trail 1365 junction. This trail leads into a narrow meadow basin, soon passing tiny Deer Lakes, then climbing gradually along Vicente Creek for a short mile before climbing 400 feet in a final 0.5 mile to Lake Vicente, elevation 5,503 feet. Most parties make a base camp at Deep Lake and make a day jaunt up to Lake Vicente. The trail becomes less distinct on the final climb to the lake, a bit rough for horses but an easy scramble for hikers.

Options

Two switchbacks down from Cathedral Pass is the Peggy's Pond Trail junction. This 0.5-mile trail leads to Peggy's Pond, a small lake set below Cathedral Rock. There are several campsites near the lake, as well as others in the vicinity. This is a popular destination, as well as a traditional base camp for climbers on their way up Mount Daniel, and is often crowded.

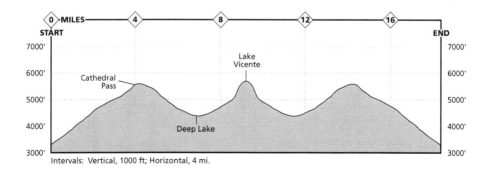

Intervals: Vertical, 1000 ft; Horizontal, 4 mi.

Adventuresome off-trail hikers can scramble up from Deep Lake to Circle Lake, an icebound lake set in a cirque at 6,000-feet elevation. A high route can be found from Deep Lake or Lake Vicente to Spade and Venus Lakes. Off-trail travel in this area involves steep snow and rock scrambling and is not recommended for any but experienced alpine scramblers.

A longer loop hike option of some 23 miles is to continue down the PCT from Deep Lake to Waptus Lake, then down Waptus River Trail to Trail Creek Trail, and up Trail Creek to the junction with Cathedral Pass Trail and out. This loop can be done in three or four days.

Key Points

0.0 Cathedral Pass trailhead.

0.1 Bridge crossing Cle Elum River.

1.8 Trail Creek junction; take a right (north).

2.3 Squaw Lake.

3.8 Pacific Crest Trail junction; turn left onto the PCT.

4.0 Cathedral Pass.

4.2 Peggy's Pond Trail junction; stay left.

6.9 Deep Lake.

7.4 Lake Vicente Trail junction; turn right (west).

7.6 Deer Lakes.

9.2 Lake Vicente.

18.4 Back to Cathedral Pass trailhead.

12 Deception Pass Loop

A loop hike connecting Deception Pass and Cathedral Pass, with several options.

Start: Deception Pass trailhead.
Distance: 14.4 miles.
Difficulty: Moderate.
Best season: Late summer through fall.
Traffic: Foot and stock traffic; moderate to heavy use.
Total climbing: About 2,400 feet.
High point: About 5,600 feet.

Fees and permits: A Northwest Forest Pass is required.
Maps: USGS Mount Daniel; Green Trails No. 176 (Stevens Pass).
Trail contacts: Wenatchee National Forest, Cle Elum Ranger District, 803 West Second Street, Cle Elum, WA 98922; (509) 674-4411; www.fs.fed.us/r6/wenatchee.

Finding the trailhead: The Deception Pass Loop hike begins from either Deception Pass or Cathedral Pass trailheads at the end of Cle Elum River Road (Forest Road 4330). To get there, take I-90 to Roslyn/Salmon la Sac exit 80. From the exit, drive north 2.8 miles to the State Route 903 junction. Turn left and follow SR 903 through Roslyn and Ronald and along Cle Elum Lake, 16.5 miles to pavement's end. The road forks here; take the right fork and continue another 12.4 miles on FR 4330 to the Deception Pass trailhead at road's end. The road crosses two streams, which run high in early season. If you don't have a high-clearance vehicle, consider parking and fording the creeks on your walk or bike ride up the road to the trailhead.

The Hike

The Deception Pass Loop hike connects several trails in a 14.4-mile loop, a popular long day hike or a two- or three-day backpack. The hike can be made longer with side trips to the many lakes along the way, including Tuck and Robin Lakes, Marmot Lake, and Peggy's Pond.

The loop is traditionally begun from the Deception Pass trailhead at the end of Cle Elum River Road. Register at the trailhead, then start hiking northward along the Cle Elum River bottom. The trail is fairly flat and wide, leading at first through lush meadows, then through silver fir and cedar forest. In 0.2 mile, the trail crosses the Alpine Lakes Wilderness boundary at Skeeter Creek. In early summer, there's no mystery how the creek got its name. Splash the bug juice liberally, or suffer the consequences! Continue up the trail, which climbs and drops a little, but fails to gain even 100 feet of elevation in the first mile, then actually loses a few feet of elevation in the second mile, where it reaches Hyas Lake, a mile-long lake near the headwaters of Cle Elum River. The hike this far is a pleasant one-hour walk through shady forest and grassy meadows. There are several campsites along the lakeshore, none very private.

Keep hiking up the lakeshore to the north end of Hyas Lake. In another 0.2 mile is upper Hyas Lake, a tiny marsh by comparison, invisible from the trail. A few unmarked side trails lead to the lakeshore and a few more campsites. About 0.5 mile past Upper Hyas Lake, the trail crosses a creek and then crosses Cle Elum River, a mere stream here, just before leaving the river basin and climbing steep forest slopes to Deception Pass. The trail climbs steadily and steeply for 0.5 mile, switching back most of the way, then crosses a creek and curves into a brushy basin, where the angle abates. The trail to Tuck and Robin Lakes departs here. Continue gradually upward through brushy open forest and increasingly subalpine meadows to Deception Pass, elevation 4,470 feet. The pass is a low, broad wooded bench, with trails leading off in all directions, including to Marmot and Deception Lakes.

From Deception Pass, follow the Pacific Crest Trail (PCT) southward, first through meadow flats, then along the rocky slopes above Hyas Lakes, with views down Cle Elum River valley and across to Granite and Trico Mountains. At about 1.8 miles from Deception Pass is Daniel Creek, a notoriously difficult stream to cross at times. In early season, the volume of water may make this crossing too dangerous to risk; the Forest Service usually posts a warning sign at Deception and Cathedral Passes advising PCT hikers to detour to avoid this hazard. By late season, the crossing is safer, but cross with care, and if it is too risky, turn back.

If you make it across Daniel Creek, continue contouring above Hyas Lakes toward Cathedral Rock, entering meadows as you near this landmark. The trail traverses subalpine meadows, climbing to the Cathedral Pass Trail junction just a few steps below Cathedral Pass. Take a left at the junction, and descend Cathedral Pass Trail through lovely tarn-dotted meadows, then down through subalpine forest to Squaw Lake, with several campsites.

From Squaw Lake, the Trail Creek Trail junction is just 0.5 mile along. Hang a left and descend quiet forest slopes to Cle Elum River and the Cathedral Pass trailhead. A short walk up the road finishes the loop.

Options

You can make this loop longer by taking side trails to the many lakes along the path. At 4 miles is the Tuck and Robin Lakes Trail 1376.1, which leads 2 miles up to Tuck Lake. From Deception Pass, you can follow the PCT about 3.5 miles northward to Deception Lakes, or take another trail 3.4 miles to Marmot Lake. From Cathedral Pass, you can hike 0.7 mile to Peggy's Pond. Although the Deception Pass Loop can be hiked in a single day, it would be easy to spend a week hiking this loop, following every side trail to each sparkling jewel at trail's end.

◀ *Cathedral Rock, Deception Pass Loop*

Deception Pass Loop

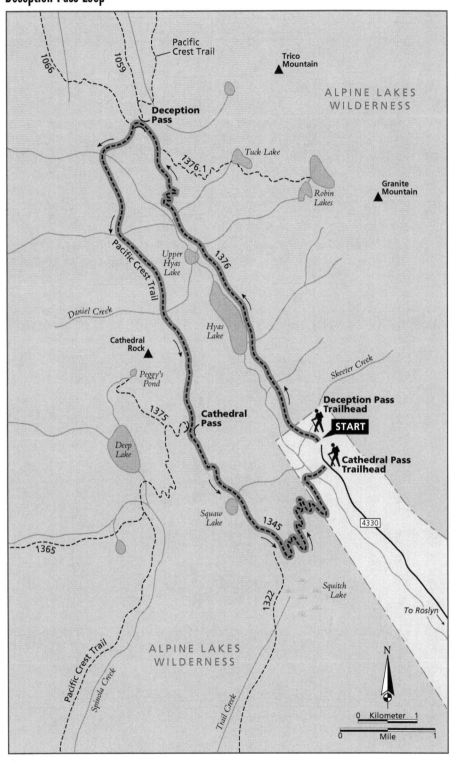

Pacific
Crest Trail

1066

1059

Tuck Lake

**Deception
Pass**

1376.1

Trico
Mountain ▲

ALPINE LAKES
WILDERNESS

*Robin
Lakes*

Granite
Mountain ▲

Pacific Crest Trail

*Upper
Hyas
Lake*

1376

Daniel Creek

*Hyas
Lake*

Cathedral
Rock ▲

*Peggy's
Pond*

1375

Skeeter Creek

**Deception Pass
Trailhead**

START

**Cathedral
Pass**

*Deep
Lake*

**Cathedral Pass
Trailhead**

1365

*Squaw
Lake*

1345

4330

1322

*Squitch
Lake*

To Roslyn

ALPINE LAKES
WILDERNESS

Pacific Crest Trail

Spinola Creek

Trail Creek

N

0   Kilometer   1

0   Mile   1

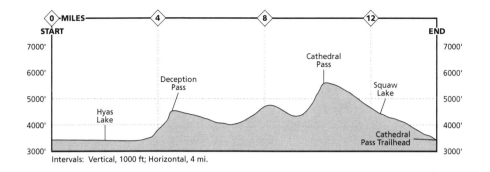

Intervals: Vertical, 1000 ft; Horizontal, 4 mi.

Key Points

0.0   Deception Pass trailhead.

0.2   Alpine Lakes Wilderness boundary.

2.0   Hyas Lake.

3.2   Side trail to Upper Hyas Lake.

3.7   Cle Elum River crossing.

4.2   Tuck Lake Trail junction; stay left to Deception Pass.

4.4   Deception Pass; turn left (south) onto the Pacific Coast Trail.

6.2   Daniel Creek crossing.

9.6   Cathedral Pass junction; turn left (south) onto Cathedral Pass Trail.

12.3   Squaw Lake.

12.8   Trail Creek Trail junction; stay left.

14.3   Bridge crossing Cle Elum River.

14.4   Cathedral Pass and Deception Pass trailheads.

13 Tuck and Robin Lakes

A steep day hike or backpack to Tuck and Robin Lakes.

Start: Deception Pass trailhead.
Distance: 15.6 miles out and back from Deception Pass trailhead.
Difficulty: Strenuous.
Best season: Midsummer through fall.
Traffic: Foot traffic only; heavy use.
Total climbing: About 3,700 feet.
High point: About 6,330 feet.

Fees and permits: A Northwest Forest Pass is required.
Maps: USGS Deception Pass; Green Trails No. 176 (Stevens Pass).
Trail contacts: Wenatchee National Forest, Cle Elum Ranger District, 803 West Second Street, Cle Elum, WA 98922; (509) 674-4411; www.fs.fed.us/r6/wenatchee.

Finding the trailhead: The hike to Tuck Lake and Robin Lakes begins from Deception Pass trailhead at the end of the Cle Elum River Road (Forest Road 4330). To get there, take I-90 to Roslyn/Salmon la Sac exit 80. From the exit, drive north 2.8 miles to the State Route 903 junction. Turn left and follow SR 903 through Roslyn and Ronald and along Cle Elum Lake, 16.5 miles to pavement's end. The road forks here; take the right fork and continue another 12.4 miles on FR 4330 to the Deception Pass trailhead at road's end. The road crosses two streams, which run high in early season. If you don't have a high-clearance vehicle, consider parking and fording the creeks on your walk or bike ride up the road to the trailhead.

The Hike

Tuck and Robin Lakes are among the most revered by Alpine Lakes Wilderness hikers. These lovely lakes and the several granite-rimmed ponds scattered nearby have been called a little version of the Enchantments. This means, of course, that they are very popular and often overcrowded on summer and autumn weekends. The countless bare-ground campsites and crisscrossing trails bear witness to the annual onslaught of hikers. But then, inexplicably, on a midweek summer day, one can find complete solitude here. Almost.

From Deception Pass trailhead, follow Deception Pass Trail 1376 past Hyas Lake to the Robin Lakes Trail junction. From the junction, hike downhill briefly before leveling out and crossing a stream. The trail begins climbing soon, up through thinning silver fir, cedar, and pine forest, and doesn't stop until just before Tuck Lake. The trail isn't what you might expect; it's a narrow, steep, rocky trail in places, with odd switchbacks. The trail wasn't built for hikers, but for fire crews, which may explain why at times it seems in a hurry to get somewhere. The trail is dry and dusty, and on a sunny summer afternoon it can be almost insufferable. Save yourself some

A frozen Robin Lake

Tuck and Robin Lakes

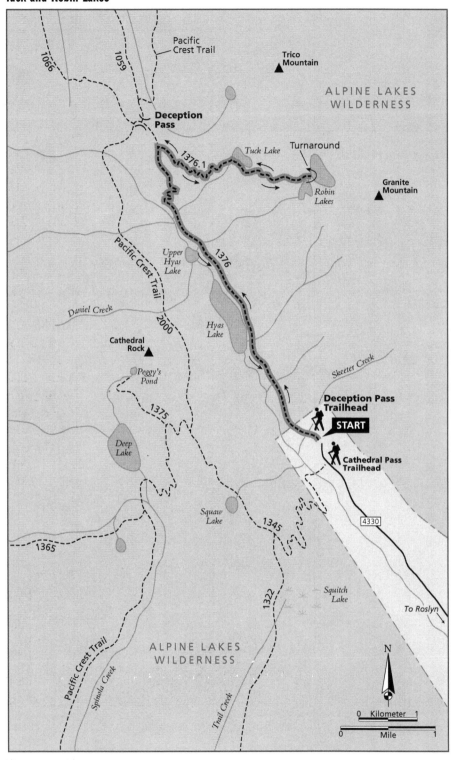

sweating, and come early in the morning before the day's heat bakes the slope, or later after the day's heat has abated. After almost 2 miles, the trail crests a knoll amid penstemon and phlox, with mesmerizing views across the valley to Mount Daniel and Cathedral Rock, then descends briefly to Tuck Lake, passing several campsites. There is much exploring to do at Tuck Lake, as the myriad side trails attest. Hike over a granite dome to Tuck's Pot, a large pond just southwest of the lake, or swim out to the lovely rock island.

The trail continues another 1.8 miles to Robin Lakes, but it's not your typical trail. It leads rightward and up from the lakeshore, over a small granite dome, then down to the outlet stream, which is crossed at the logjam. From there, the trail is little more than a rut scraped out by boots in places, nonexistent in others. Scramble up granite slabs and through granite boulders; occasional cairns mark the path, but it is easily lost if you are not diligent. The trail can be easily lost in poor visibility; get a compass bearing to save yourself some aimless wandering in case clouds drift in. Side trails, dead ends, and drop-offs await those who stray from the true path. Early season snow can complicate the ascent to Robin Lakes; bring an ice ax before August of most years. After 1.7 miles or so, the trail crests a granite knoll, and you behold Robin Lakes, two of the loveliest of the alpine lakes outside of the Enchantments, nestled in granite-walled basins. Watch for goats gamboling among the rocks above the lake. The lakes melt out by August of most years. There are several campsites around the lakes; stick to snow, rock, and existing bare ground, please.

Tuck and Robin Lakes are typically an overnight destination, but strong hikers can make a day hike of it with an early start. The fewer people who camp here on weekends, the better. If you must, be sure to mitigate your impact by camping on existing bare-ground sites, rock, or snow, and by using toilets or doing your business at least 200 feet away from the lakes, preferably downhill from the lakes, and consider packing it out. There is no permit system in place here yet, but like the Enchantment Lakes, if hikers don't take care of this area, access could someday be limited.

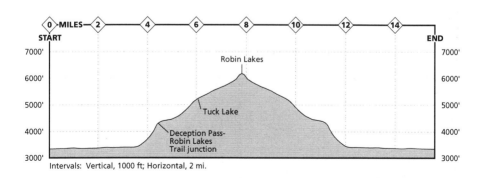

Intervals: Vertical, 1000 ft; Horizontal, 2 mi.

Rock island, Tuck Lake

Options

Explorations abound at Tuck and Robin Lakes. Experienced scramblers can climb 7,144-foot Granite Mountain, which offers panoramic views, including Mounts Rainier, Stuart, and Daniel, to name only a few. Or cross over the divide and explore the Granite Potholes, a cluster of ponds perched on a shelf just over the ridge. An ascent of 6,640-foot Trico Mountain can be made from the divide, or by scrambling leftward and up from the Tuck Lake shoreline, but it is not recommended for casual hikers.

Key Points

0.0 Deception Pass trailhead.

0.2 Alpine Lakes Wilderness boundary.

2.0 Hyas Lake.

3.7 Cle Elum River crossing.

4.2 Deception Pass–Robin Lakes Trail junction; turn right (east).

6.0 Tuck Lake and Tuck's Pot.

7.8 Robin Lakes.

15.6 Back to Deception Pass trailhead.

14 Marmot Lake

A long day hike or backpack to remote Marmot Lake.

Start: Deception Pass trailhead or Forest Road 6830 and Tonga Ridge Trail.
Distance: 7 miles out and back from Deception Pass; 16.4 miles out and back from Deception Pass trailhead; 18.4 miles from FR 6830.
Difficulty: Moderate.
Best season: Summer through fall.
Traffic: Foot and stock traffic; light use.
Total climbing: About 1,800 feet gain and

600 feet loss one way.
High point: About 4,940 feet.
Fees and permits: A Northwest Forest Pass is required at each trailhead.
Maps: USGS Mount Daniel; Green Trails No. 176 (Stevens Pass).
Trail contacts: Wenatchee National Forest, Cle Elum Ranger District, 803 West Second Street, Cle Elum, WA 98922; (509) 674-4411; www.fs.fed.us/r6/wenatchee.

Finding the trailhead: Marmot Lake Trail 1066 can be approached either via Deception Pass Trail from the Cle Elum River via Tonga Ridge Road (Forest Road 6830), or via Deception Creek Trail from Stevens Pass Highway.

To reach Deception Pass trailhead at the end of the Cle Elum River Road (FR 4330), take I-90 to Roslyn/Salmon la Sac exit 80. From the exit, drive north 2.8 miles to the State Route 903 junction. Turn left and follow SR 903 through Roslyn and Ronald and along Cle Elum Lake, 16.5 miles to pavement's end. The road forks here; take the right fork and continue another 12.4 miles on FR 4330 to the Deception Pass trailhead at road's end. The road crosses two streams, which run high in early season. If you don't have a high-clearance vehicle, consider parking and fording the creeks on your walk or bike ride up the road to the trailhead.

To reach the Tonga Ridge Road trailhead for Deception Creek Trail, drive U.S. Highway 2 to Foss River Road (FR 68), about 2 miles east of Skykomish. Follow Foss River Road 1.1 miles to a fork, where a sign points the way to various trailheads. Take the right fork, continuing 2.4 miles on FR 68 to a well-signed fork. Take the left fork and follow FR 6830 11 miles to the end. The trailhead is on the left just before the end of the road. The Key Points lists the mileage from Deception Pass trailhead through the Marmot Lake Trail junction at Deception Pass, the usual approach.

The Hike

Marmot Lake is a remote lake lying about 3 miles north of Mount Daniel. Geographically, the lake is not all that remote; it lies only a few miles north of Mount Sawyer and would be easily accessible via Tonga Ridge Trail if there was a trail leading directly from Sawyer Pass. However, the trail to Marmot Lake begins from Deception Pass, which is about 5 miles in from the nearest trailhead, making this a long day hike best done as an overnight trip.

Begin by hiking to Deception Pass via your choice of approach hikes. The shortest approach to Marmot Lake Trail is 4.7 miles via Deception Pass Trail, although it

Marmot Lake

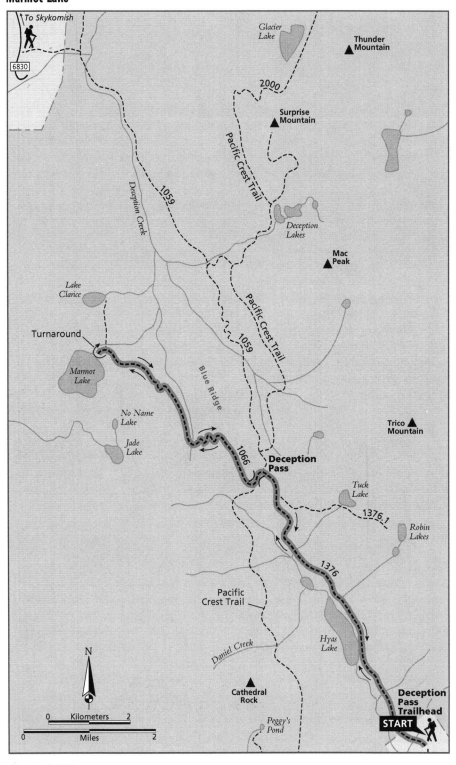

may also be reached in 5.7 miles from Deception Creek, as described in Options below. The entire round-trip distance is about 16 miles from Deception Pass trailhead, 18 miles via Deception Creek cutoff.

However you get there, from Deception Pass hike briefly southward on the Pacific Crest Trail (PCT) to the Marmot Lake Trail junction, then turn northward and traverse a subalpine bench, through meadows and past ponds, to the Blue Ridge divide. Drop down into a broad meadow basin, passing a small lake, cross Blue Ridge Creek, then parallel the creek on the west side, descending directly downstream 0.7 mile through shady old-growth silver fir and hemlock forest to the low point of the trail. The trail starts climbing and gains elevation steadily as it traverses a steep wooded slope above the creek. In a mile from the creek bottom, the trail forks; the right fork leads 0.8 mile to Lake Clarice. Stay left and keep climbing along a splashy stream into the quiet lake basin. The final 0.4 mile is the steepest, but soon the trail levels out and drops to Marmot Lake's eastern shore. There are campsites near the lakeshore, usually vacant.

Options

Marmot Lake may be approached from the north via Forest Road 6830 and the Tonga Ridge Trail spur connecting FR 6830 and Deception Creek Trail. Follow FR 6830 about 11 miles past the Tonga Ridge turnoff to the "upper" Tonga Ridge trailhead. Hike down the trail 0.6 mile to join Deception Creek Trail, and follow that trail another 5.1 miles up to Deception Pass. This approach adds about 2 miles to the round-trip distance, but it takes slightly less time for those approaching via U.S. Highway 2.

The 0.8-mile side trail to Lake Clarice is obligatory. It's only a little out of the way, but since you're here, you must go see. This lake offers more private camping than Marmot Lake, although both lakes are fairly quiet, even on sunny summer weekends.

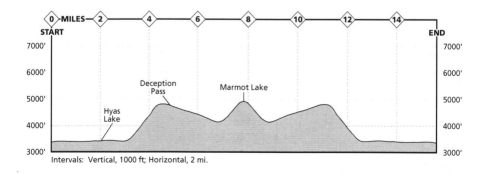

Intervals: Vertical, 1000 ft; Horizontal, 2 mi.

Key Points

0.0 Deception Pass trailhead.

0.2 Alpine Lakes Wilderness boundary.

2.0 Hyas Lake.

4.2 Tuck Lake Trail junction; stay left to Deception Pass.

4.7 Marmot Lake Trail junction at Deception Pass; take Marmot Lake Trail north.

5.7 Blue Ridge meadows.

7.2 Blue Ridge basin.

7.9 Lake Clarice Trail junction; stay left to Marmot Lake.

8.2 Marmot Lake.

16.4 Back to Deception Pass trailhead.

15 Esmerelda Loop

A semi-loop through Esmerelda Basin and down De Roux Creek.

Start: Esmerelda trailhead.
Distance: 12.2-mile loop.
Difficulty: Moderate.
Best season: Summer through fall.
Traffic: Moderate.
Total climbing: About 3,400 gain and loss for entire loop.
High point: About 6,020 feet.

Fees and permits: A Northwest Forest Pass is required.
Maps: USGS Mount Stuart; Green Trails No. 209 (Mount Stuart).
Trail contacts: Wenatchee National Forest, Cle Elum Ranger District, 803 West Second Street, Cle Elum, WA 98922; (509) 674-4411; www.fs.fed.us/r6/wenatchee.

Finding the trailhead: Esmerelda Basin Trail 1394 is approached from near Cle Elum via Teanaway Road, which begins from State Route 970 (the highway linking I-5 and State Route 97 just east of Cle Elum) about 6.8 miles east of Cle Elum exit 85. Turn up Teanaway Road and follow 13 miles to pavement's end, where the road forks. Take the right fork and follow Forest Road 9737 about 9.5 miles to the Esmerelda trailhead at road's end.

The Hike

The Esmerelda Loop combines several trails in a convenient 12-mile loop around the Esmerelda Peaks in the upper Teanaway River region, just outside the Alpine Lakes Wilderness. As described here, the loop begins from the Esmerelda trailhead, but one may also begin the hike from the De Roux Creek trailhead. Most hikers do only the first few miles of the loop, hiking through Esmerelda Basin to Fortune Pass or Lake Ann and back, a reasonable and popular day hike. Determined hikers can complete the entire loop in a day, but most will do it as a two-day backpack with a camp at Gallagher Head Lake or thereabouts.

From the trailhead, hike up a rocky mining road alongside the North Fork Teanaway River, an ebullient stream here. At 0.3 mile is the Ingalls Way Trail junction; this trail, which leads to Ingalls Lake and Longs Pass, siphons off its share of day hikers. Esmerelda Basin Trail continues straight ahead, following the river up into the namesake basin, passing through grassy meadows and pine and fir groves, with close views of the Esmerelda Peaks. Wildflowers grow in abundance, too many to name here. There are several campsites in the basin.

The main trail leads up the northern slope of the basin, switching back a few times as it climbs through meadows and dusty open slopes. In just over a mile is the County Line Trail junction; this trail leads up over an unnamed pass to Lake Ann. There is an excellent campsite at this pass overlooking Lake Ann. The Esmerelda Loop continues 0.3 mile from the Lake Ann junction to the high point at Fortune

Creek Pass, elevation 6,020 feet. Most hikers stop at the pass, enjoy the views, then hike back down to the trailhead for a 6.6-mile round-trip day hike.

Beyond Fortune Creek Pass, the trail descends steeply down a long series of switchbacks, losing 1,000 feet of elevation in just over a mile to the Fortune Creek jeep road junction. Hike up the road, hopefully without the company of motorbikes and off-road vehicles, a long mile up Fortune Creek and over a slight divide to Gallagher Head Lake, a pretty lake tucked high in De Roux Creek basin between Esmerelda Peaks and Hawkins Mountain. This is about the halfway point of the loop hike; if you're backpacking, Gallagher Head Lake is the obvious place to camp. If you come early enough in the season, you can spend a quiet night here without the intrusion of motorized vehicles, but the best season is summer when the meadows are abloom with wildflowers and, alas, the jeep road is snow-free.

At the southwest shore of the lake is the De Roux Creek Trail junction, and it's nearly all downhill from here. The trail descends gradually into De Roux Creek basin, a lovely meadow basin, then crosses the creek and drops more steeply down a series of switchbacks, losing 800 feet in a mile before reaching the Koppen Mountain Trail junction. This 2.5-mile side trail leads to the 6,031-foot summit of Koppen Mountain, a grand viewpoint that is a worthy destination in its own right. Just below the junction, the trail crosses back to the north side of De Roux Creek and continues another long mile to the North Fork Teanaway River, then climbs a brief 0.3 mile to the De Roux Creek trailhead. The old footbridge was washed out several years back but was recently replaced. For those who wonder what the Forest Service does with the parking pass money, here's a good for instance.

The final segment of the trail leads 1.5 miles up the North Fork Teanaway River back to the Beverly trailhead. There is an old trail segment close to the river, but it is abandoned and brushy, so the final bit of hiking is along the road. One could avoid this by hiking the trail in the reverse direction, starting at De Roux Creek and looping down through Esmerelda Basin to the upper trailhead, then riding a mountain bike down the road to the car.

Options

A hike up the old Koppen Mountain Trail 1225 is a popular side trip, and a good day hike in its own right. The trail, faint in places but not too hard to follow, leads 2.5 miles up from De Roux Creek to the 6,031-foot summit, a worthy objective in its own right, best approached via De Roux Creek Trail for a 7.6-mile round-trip summit hike. One can continue along the trail from Koppen Mountain down to Medra Pass and out via Johnson Creek Trail 1383, another 6 miles one way. Doing this hike in the reverse direction would probably be best, an 8.5-mile one-way hike

Koppen Mountain and De Roux Creek from Esmerelda Loop

Esmerelda Loop

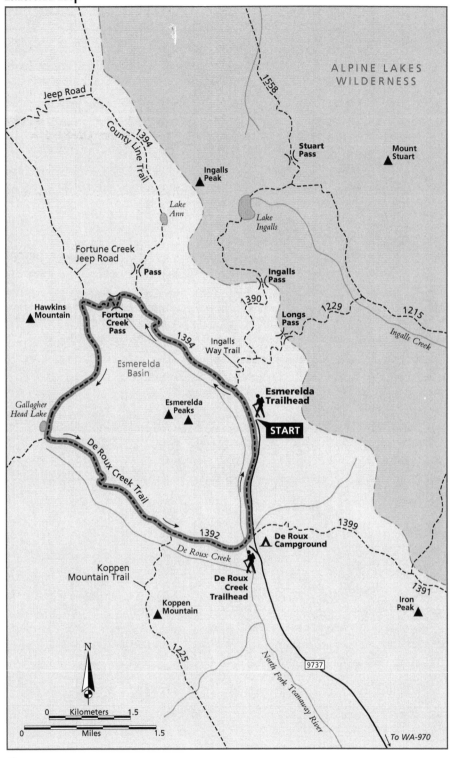

Jeep Road

County Line Trail

1394

1558

ALPINE LAKES
WILDERNESS

Stuart
Pass

Mount
Stuart

Ingalls
Peak

Lake
Ann

Lake
Ingalls

Fortune Creek
Jeep Road

Pass

Ingalls
Pass

Hawkins
Mountain

Fortune
Creek
Pass

1390

1229

1215

1394

Longs
Pass

Ingalls Creek

Esmerelda
Basin

Ingalls
Way Trail

Esmerelda
Trailhead

Gallagher
Head Lake

Esmerelda
Peaks

START

De Roux Creek Trail

De Roux
Campground

1399

1392

De Roux Creek

Koppen
Mountain Trail

De Roux
Creek
Trailhead

1391

Iron
Peak

Koppen
Mountain

1225

9737

North Fork Teanaway River

N

1.5
Kilometers 1.5

0
Miles 1.5

To WA-970

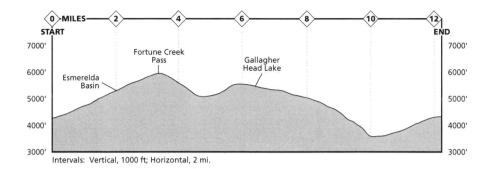

Intervals: Vertical, 1000 ft; Horizontal, 2 mi.

with a long, mostly downhill mountain bike ride back to the Johnson Creek trail-head, better if you have a ride waiting at the opposite end.

Key Points

0.0   Esmerelda trailhead.

0.3   Ingalls Way Trail junction; stay left.

2.0   Esmerelda Basin.

3.0   County Line Trail junction; stay left.

3.4   Fortune Creek Pass.

5.1   Fortune Creek jeep road junction; turn left (south).

6.3   Gallagher Head Lake and De Roux Creek trail junction; turn left.

8.8   Koppen Mountain Trail junction; stay left.

10.1   Footbridge over Teanaway River.

10.4   De Roux Creek trailhead; hike road left (north).

12.2   Loop's end at Esmerelda trailhead.

16 Lake Ann-Ingalls Peak Loop

A long, seldom-traveled loop hike around Ingalls Peak.

Start: Esmerelda trailhead.
Distance: 19-mile loop.
Difficulty: Overgrown in places; hard to follow.
Best season: Summer through fall.
Traffic: Foot and stock traffic; light use.
Total climbing: About 4,500 feet gain, 4,500 feet loss.
High point: About 6,500 feet.

Fees and permits: A Northwest Forest Pass is required.
Maps: Green Trails No. 209 (Mount Stuart).
Trail contacts: Wenatchee National Forest, Cle Elum Ranger District, 803 West Second Street, Cle Elum, WA 98922; (509) 674-4411; www.fs.fed.us/r6/wenatchee.

Finding the trailhead: This loop hike begins from the Esmerelda trailhead, which is approached from near Cle Elum via Teanaway Road, which begins from State Route 970 (the highway linking I-5 and State Route 97 just east of Cle Elum) about 6.8 miles east of Cle Elum exit 85. Turn up Teanaway Road and follow Forest Road 9737 about 9.5 miles to the Esmerelda trailhead at road's end.

The Hike

A day hike or overnight trip to Lake Ann is a reasonable 9.2-mile round trip. However, Lake Ann can be just the first stop on a 19-mile loop hike through some of the least traveled landscape in the Alpine Lakes wilderness. This loop is not often done, as parts are not well maintained. Routefinding may be necessary.

From the trailhead, hike up a rocky mining road alongside the North Fork Teanaway River into Esmerelda Basin, by staying left at the Ingalls Way Trail junction at 0.3 mile. The trail leads up the northern slope of the basin, switching back a few times as it climbs through meadows and dusty open slopes. In just over a mile is the County Line Trail junction. Follow this trail, which leads about 1.3 miles up the basin to a high pass overlooking Lake Ann. There is an excellent campsite at this pass, although water must be fetched from the lake 0.3 mile distant.

From Lake Ann, the trail contours a broad talus basin below the rocky spine of Ingalls Peak, losing about 300 feet of elevation in 1.7 miles to Van Epps Pass. Like other portions of the County Line Trail and other less traveled trails in this area, the trail is faint in places, though not hard to follow. At the pass, the trail comes into contact with a jeep road, and you may encounter trail bikes or off-road vehicles here, making this a poor choice for a campsite. Thankfully, you can leave them behind at the pass. From the pass, the trail contours the head of Van Epps Creek

Hiker on Ingalls Peak Loop ▶

Lake Ann–Ingalls Peak Loop

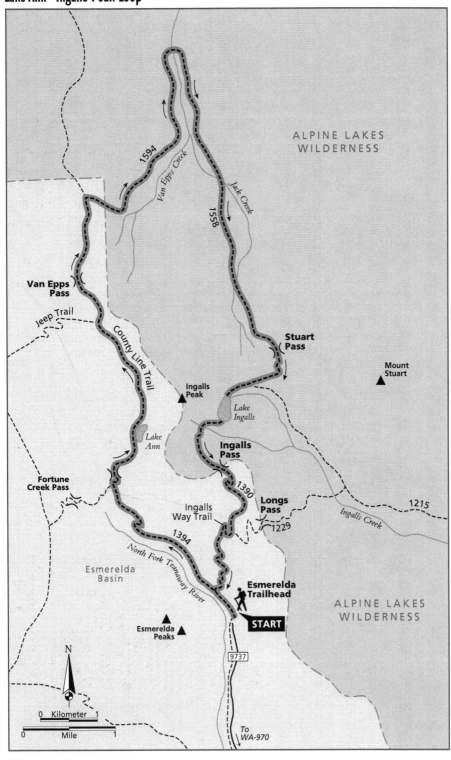

Basin and in 1 mile reaches the remnants of mining operations. The trail descends along Van Epps Creek, dropping into shady pine and fir forest for another 3 miles to Jack Creek. Like several trails in this area, this segment of the loop is not well maintained and may be difficult to follow in places

Once across Jack Creek, the trail climbs 3.9 miles up Jack Creek Trail to Stuart Pass. From the pass, the trail descends 0.4 mile to a junction, where a side trail leads another 0.4 mile to Lake Ingalls, one of the scenic high points of the hike. No camping at Lake Ingalls; camp at Stuart Pass or another mile or so along the trail at Ingalls Pass. From the lake, scramble down a rocky gully and contour across Headlight Basin. The trail can be easily lost here; look for cairns to help guide you through the talus. Once across Headlight Creek, the trail climbs to a lovely meadow basin with meandering streams, wildflowers, and larch trees. Shortly beyond is Ingalls Pass, then it's all downhill 1.5 miles to Longs Pass Trail junction, 1 mile to Esmerelda Trail junction, and 0.3 mile back to the Esmerelda trailhead via Ingalls Way Trail.

Key Points

0.0   Esmerelda trailhead.

0.3   Ingalls Way Trail junction; stay left.

2.0   Esmerelda Basin.

3.0   County Line Trail junction; turn right.

4.6   Lake Ann.

6.3   Van Epps Pass; turn right (north).

10.1 Jack Creek Trail; turn right (east).

14.2 Stuart Pass.

15.0 Lake Ingalls.

16.2 Ingalls Pass.

17.7 Longs Pass Trail junction; stay right (south).

18.7 Esmerelda Trail junction; turn left (south).

19.0 Esmerelda trailhead.

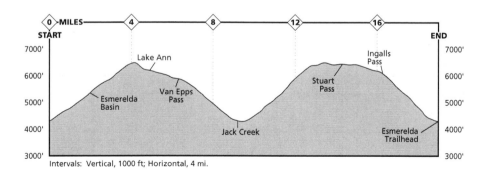

17 Forgotten Trail Loop

A rugged loop trip along a segment of the abandoned County Line Trail.

Start: Beverly Creek trailhead.
Distance: 15.7-mile loop via Beverly-Turnpike Trail.
Difficulty: Strenuous and hard to follow.
Best season: Summer through fall.
Traffic: Foot and stock traffic only; light use.
Total climbing: About 5,000 feet gain, 5,000 feet loss.
High point: About 6,500 feet.

Fees and permits: A Northwest Forest Pass is required.
Maps: USGS Mount Stuart, Enchantment Lakes; Green Trails No. 209 (Mount Stuart).
Trail contacts: Wenatchee National Forest, Cle Elum Ranger District, 803 West Second Street, Cle Elum, WA 98922; (509) 674-4411; www.fs.fed.us/r6/wenatchee.

Finding the trailhead: This hike follows a segment of County Line Trail 1226.1 and is best begun from the Beverly Creek trailhead, just off North Fork Teanaway Road (Forest Road 9737) north of Cle Elum. Beverly-Turnpike Trail 1391 is approached via North Fork Teanaway Road (FR 9737) north of Cle Elum. If approaching via I-90, turn off at exit 85 and follow State Route 970 east 6.8 miles to Teanaway Road. If approaching via U.S. Highway 97, follow to the 97-970 junction, and drive west on SR 970 just 3.4 miles to the Teanaway River Road turnoff. Follow Teanaway Road about 13 miles to pavement's end, where two dirt roads fork off. Take the right fork (FR 9737), and follow 3.6 miles to the Beverly Creek spur road (FR 9737-112), then take the right fork and follow 1.1 miles to the Beverly Creek trailhead at road's end.

The Hike

The Forgotten Trail Loop is a high traverse of the so-called County Line Peaks, a subrange of rocky mountains dividing the Teanaway River and Ingalls Creek drainages, which also form the boundary between Chelan and Kittitas Counties as well as the Alpine Lakes Wilderness boundary. The loop follows portions of the old, abandoned County Line Trail, a segment of which is called the Forgotten Trail. This is a high loop, averaging over 5,000 feet of elevation, which provides excellent close-up views of the entire Stuart Range. The hike is feasible as a long day hike for conditioned hikers, but it makes for a more reasonable backpack that is far less crowded than many nearby trails.

The loop can be done in either direction; here, it is presented in a clockwise direction starting from Beverly-Turnpike trailhead, the shortest option with the least climbing. Get your permit and start hiking up Beverly-Turnpike Trail 1392, crossing Bean Creek in 0.4 mile and continuing up Beverly Creek. The trail climbs steadily through grassy pine and fir forest and a rocky basin another 2.4 miles to the

Along the Forgotten Trail

Forgotten Trail Loop

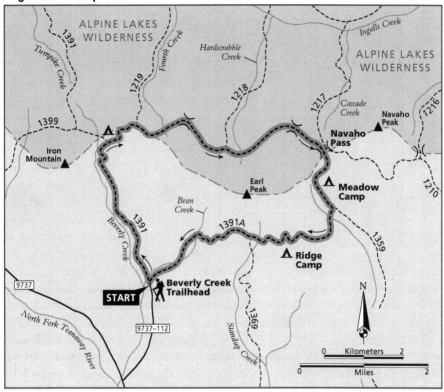

Fourth Creek Trail junction. Take a right and follow Fourth Creek Trail 1218, which leads abruptly up from Beverly Creek to a 5,560-foot pass overlooking Fourth Creek basin and the craggy Stuart Range. County Line Trail 1226.1 forks off to the east, contouring lovely, occasionally boggy subalpine meadows along the north slope of Bean Peak, crossing Fourth Creek in about a mile, then climbing up rocky meadow slopes toward a craggy ridge. There are several big whitebark pines here, surrounded by clusters of subalpine fir and an occasional spruce. The trail is faint in places but not too hard to follow just yet.

Just below the first ridge is a rocky overlook not far off the trail, a good spot for a break and to get out the camera and shoot a roll of film of the spectacular peaks rising across Ingalls Creek. A short climb up a gravelly slope leads to a saddle and even better views of Mount Stuart and the Enchantment Peaks. This is a good turn-around point for day hikers, making for a 9-mile round trip that covers most of the scenic highlights.

Experienced backcountry travelers can continue beyond. From this ridge, you can see the trail far across Hardscrabble Creek basin where it climbs a scree slope to a pass. Make a mental note of the landscape, because the trail getting there is faint to nonexistent and easily lost. Descend steeply from the ridge into the basin, down a gravelly slope, then traverse subalpine meadows 0.7 mile to Hardscrabble Creek Trail junction. Cairns helpfully keep you on course where the trail vanishes; when the cairns vanish, you're on your own. Continue on the ever fading trail, contouring across the basin, crossing Hardscrabble Creek and traversing along the foot of tawny talus slides, then climb a steep scree slope to a 6,500-foot saddle at the Hardscrabble-Stafford Creek divide, the high point of the loop hike, a most scenic spot. The trail between Hardscrabble junction and the divide is extremely hard to follow and very easily lost. If you lose the trail, as you probably will, stay close to the foot of the talus slides, and you'll pick it up again at the scree slope. When ascending to the divide, stay on the established path to avoid creating an unsightly mess of little trails in the gravelly scree.

From the divide, descend a rocky slope into Stafford Creek Basin about 0.6 mile to a junction with Stafford Creek Trail 1359, just below Navaho Pass. The trail disappears in several places; occasional cairns may be helpful. From the junction, you can hike up to Navaho Pass for views down Cascade Creek and across to the Enchantment Peaks, including Dragontail Peak, Little Annapurna, and McClellan Peak. The County Line Trail continues eastward here, traversing the southern slope of Navaho Peak; Cascade Creek Trail 1217 descends 4.1 miles down to Ingalls Creek Trail.

To complete the loop from Navaho Pass, descend Stafford Creek Trail southward, crossing a rocky shelf above subalpine meadows, then descending open forest to a wide, grassy meadow. There are a couple of good campsites here, in the trees bordering the meadow. Beyond the meadow, the trail descends steep, wooded slopes a short mile to Standup Creek Trail junction. Proceed up Standup Creek Trail 1369, which crosses Stafford Creek and climbs into a lovely meadow basin. The trail crosses and climbs along several small streams and pocket meadows, all bursting with wildflowers, including bog gentian, Indian paintbrush, and the ubiquitous lupine and aster. Above the upper meadow, the trail climbs a wide-open rocky slope, hot going by late morning, then tops out at a flat, wooded ridge with a large campsite. Take one last look across Stafford Creek Basin to Navaho Pass, Navaho Peak, the Three Brothers, and the Stuart Range, then descend westward through cool forest into Standup Creek Basin. After a few switchbacks in the trees, the trail traverses steep, open meadow slopes below Earl Peak and soon crosses Standup Creek, which flows from a perennial spring. A narrow swath of lush herbage grows up alongside the trickling creek, in stark contrast to the pale grass and hardy wildflowers eking out an existence in the dusty, rocky soil everywhere around.

Shortly past the creek is the Bean Creek Trail junction, which marks the beginning of the end of the loop. Stay high, following Bean Creek Trail 1391A across the steep meadow slopes to a rocky gully and an easily missed turnoff. It is confusing here because an obvious trail keeps going straight ahead across the slope and into the trees. Keep a lookout on the uphill side of the trail for a row of cairns, which mark the "path" to the upper trail. If you miss the turn, you'll end up scrambling up scree and steep, dusty meadows to rejoin the trail, not too difficult, but a waste of time and energy. Once on the upper trail, continue up to a ridge saddle below Earl Peak, then plunge into Bean Creek Basin. The trail descends a steep, wooded slope via a series of switchbacks, losing over 1,000 feet of elevation in the next mile before leveling out, crossing the basin, and fording Bean Creek. Take care on the downhill section; the trail is narrow in places, and a misstep could result in a tumble down the slope.

Once across the creek, it's a quick downhill hike back to the Beverly Creek Trail junction, barely 0.4 mile from the trailhead.

Afternoon thunderstorms roll in frequently during high summer, posing a hazard to hikers on the high ridges. If a storm develops, hurry down off the ridges, and find a safe spot to sit and wait out the storm. Flash floods may occur in creek bottoms during downpours, so avoid them when heavy rain threatens.

Options

As with other hikes in this area, there are many options to consider. Several additional loop hikes can be made, including loops down Fourth Creek and back up Hardscrabble Creek, or down Hardscrabble Peak and up Cascade Creek, or around Navaho Peak via Falls and Cascade Creeks. It all depends on how much time you have and how much energy. You could spend a day here, or three, or five. An advantage to hiking here is that these trails are usually far less crowded than other nearby trails, such as Ingalls Lake and Beverly-Turnpike. A disadvantage is that the trails are not as well maintained as others in the wilderness. But they definitely offer a sense of adventure and discovery. Just look at a trail map of the area, pick a loop, and go for it.

Several popular scrambles can be done from this loop, including 7,036-foot Earl Peak and 7,223-foot Navaho Peak, both of which are fairly straightforward ridge scrambles via climbers' trails or easy ridges directly from the trail. As always, these scrambles are recommended only for experienced scramblers and off-trail travelers. The views are great but not so much better than you will already see from the various high points along the trail. Day hikers on this loop may opt to skip the summits to save time and energy, although of the two, Earl Peak is the shortest climb.

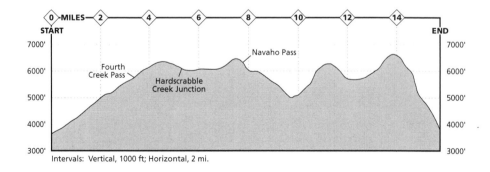

Intervals: Vertical, 1000 ft; Horizontal, 2 mi.

Key Points

0.0   Beverly Creek trailhead.

0.4   Bean Creek Trail junction; stay left.

2.8   Fourth Creek Trail junction; turn right.

3.2   Fourth Creek Pass and junction with County Line Trail 1226.1; turn right.

5.4   Hardscrabble Creek Trail junction; stay right.

7.9   Navaho Pass; descend right (south).

9.6   Standup Creek Trail junction; turn right (west).

12.3   Bean Creek Trail junction; turn right.

15.3   Beverly Creek Trail junction; turn left.

15.7   Beverly Creek trailhead.

18 Ingalls Creek

A long backpack up Ingalls Creek to Stuart Pass.

Start: Ingalls Creek trailhead.
Distance: 31 miles out and back.
Difficulty: Easy to moderate the first 12 miles; strenuous the last 3.5 miles to Stuart Pass.
Best season: Late spring for first few miles, summer and fall for upper trail.
Traffic: Foot and stock use; moderate use. No dogs.
Total climbing: About 4,500 feet.
High point: About 6,400 feet.

Fees and permits: A Northwest Forest Pass is required.
Maps: USGS Blewett, Enchantment Lakes, Mount Stuart; Green Trails No. 210 (Liberty), 209 (Mount Stuart).
Trail contacts: Wenatchee National Forest, Leavenworth Ranger District, 600 Sherbourne, Leavenworth, WA 98826; (509) 548-6977; www.fs.fed.us/r6/wenatchee.

Finding the trailhead: Ingalls Creek Trail 1215 begins just off of the Blewett Pass Highway (U.S. Highway 97) between Cle Elum and Leavenworth. Drive US 97 to the Ingalls Creek Road (Forest Road 7310) turnoff, which is 7.1 miles south from the "Big Y" junction of US 2 and US 97 and 14.2 miles north from Blewitt Pass, at milepost 178. Follow FR 7310 about 1.2 miles to the Ingalls Creek trailhead.

The Hike

Ingalls Creek Trail is one of the longest and loneliest trails in the Alpine Lakes Wilderness. Few hikers complete the entire trail. Early season hikers go 5 or 6 miles before they are turned back by snow. Late season hikers usually bypass the first dozen miles of the trail, favoring a shortcut into the upper canyon via Beverly-Turnpike or Ingalls Way Trails, which allow quicker access to the "best" part of the hike. But the lower portion of the trail, though lacking in sublime views, has its own rewards. Wildflowers are everywhere along the trail in early season; fall colors are spectacular. Throw in a few waterfalls and some impressive mountain views, and you have a hike that deserves your attention.

Get your permit at the trailhead register, and start hiking. The trail begins along Ingalls Creek's north bank and stays there, always close above the creek, leading gradually upward through deep fir, hemlock, and cedar forest for the first 3 miles or so, with only occasional window views of the canyon slopes and ridge points. At 3.6 miles the trail crosses the wilderness boundary just before crossing a stream, then meanders through a basin, crossing open slopes below talus slides that offer glimpses of McClellan Peak and the Three Brothers. After a short climb out of the basin,

Mount Stuart and Stuart Pass

Ingalls Creek

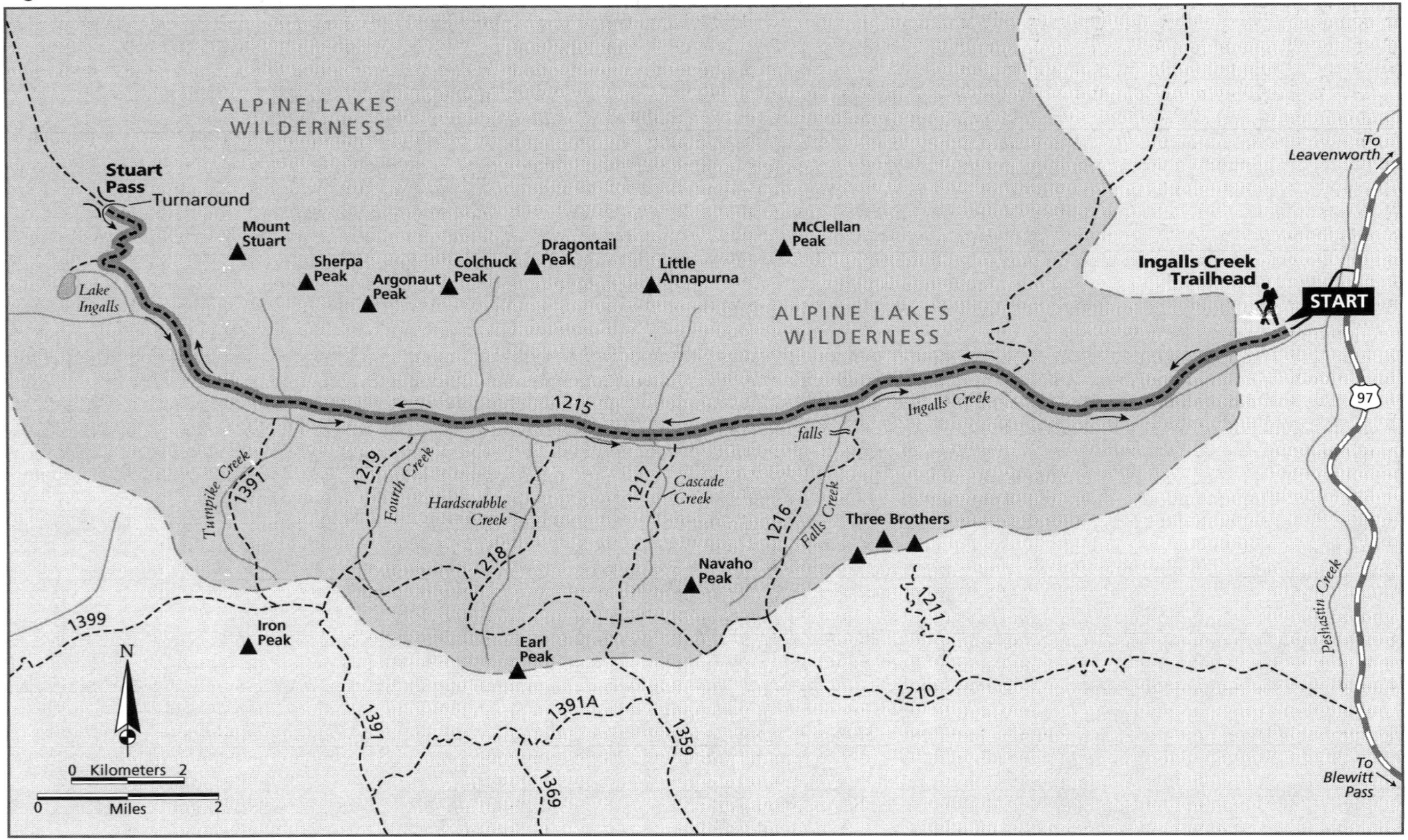

To Leavenworth

To Blewitt Pass

Peshastin Creek

97

START

Ingalls Creek Trailhead

ALPINE LAKES WILDERNESS

Ingalls Creek

ALPINE LAKES WILDERNESS

McClellan Peak

Little Annapurna

Three Brothers

1211

1210

falls

Falls Creek

1216

Navaho Peak

Dragontail Peak

Cascade Creek

1217

1359

1215

Colchuck Peak

Earl Peak

1391A

1369

Argonaut Peak

Hardscrabble Creek

1218

Sherpa Peak

Fourth Creek

1219

1391

Mount Stuart

Turnpike Creek

1397

Iron Peak

Stuart Pass

Turnaround

Lake Ingalls

1399

N

0 Kilometers 2

0 Miles 2

including a rare switchback, the trail levels out again and contours along above the creek as before, in and out of woods. At 5.7 miles is Falls Creek Trail junction, the usual turnaround point for day hikers, especially early season hikers who can expect to be slowed down looking at the abundant wildflowers, including the to-be-expected lupine, penstemon, bead lily, and trillium, as well as varieties of orchids and other flowers. In early season, avalanche-piled snow may linger in the gully crossings in the last couple of miles to the Falls Creek Trail junction. Those not prepared for snow crossings should turn back. In the first 5.7 miles the trail has gained only about 1,500 feet, making for a reasonably easy 11.4-mile round trip. Falls Creek Trail 1216 leads 3.8 miles up to Negro Pass to join Negro Creek Trail 1211. There is a campsite near the trail junction for those passing through.

Beyond the Falls Creek Trail junction, the trail continues as before, contouring close above the creek on the north side, through thinning fir, hemlock, and pine forest, passing occasional talus slopes and brushy gullies. Views expand as you climb higher, including glimpses of the granite walls and peaks of the Stuart Range. In another 2.4 miles is the Cascade Creek Trail junction. Cascade Creek Trail 1217 leads 3.6 miles up to Navaho Pass to join Stafford Creek Trail 1359. As always, there is a campsite near the trail junction.

The next several miles is more of the same, mostly flat, easy hiking along the creek, through increasingly subalpine forest and occasional grassy meadows as the trail climbs gradually from trail junction to trail junction. In 1.2 miles is the Hardscrabble Creek Trail junction. The unmaintained Hardscrabble Creek Trail 1218 leads 3.5 miles up to join County Line Trail 1226.1. In another 1.6 miles up Ingalls Creek is a junction with Fourth Creek Trail 1219, a 3.9-mile climb up and over a pass to join Beverly-Turnpike Trail. And 1.4 miles farther up the trail is Beverly-Turnpike Trail 1391, one of the "shortcut" trails leading to upper Ingalls Creek in 6.2 miles, about half as far as the 12-mile hike up from Ingalls Creek for those who just can't wait to hit the high country. There are campsites at each trail junction and in between. A campsite just beyond the Beverly-Turnpike junction is popular with climbers heading up Mount Stuart, whose looming presence increases with every step up the trail.

From Hardscrabble Creek on up, the trail begins to climb away from the creek. By the time you reach the Beverly-Turnpike junction, the creek is nearly 0.5 mile distant and 200 vertical feet below. The next 0.5 mile is fairly level, as the trail follows the 4,800-foot contour to within a short distance of the creek before climbing once again away from the creek for about a mile, gaining 600 feet, the steepest section of the trail so far. The Longs Pass Trail junction is passed in a mile from the Beverly-Turnpike junction; this is a way trail that leads steeply up to 6,200-foot Longs Pass, a path best left to mountain climbers. All along this section of trail the views expand. Mount Stuart lords over the trail, while Ingalls Peak and the tawny ridges of the Wenatchee Mountains unfold across the canyon. The trail crosses several talus slides, some with gigantic boulders dislodged from the granite walls of Mount Stuart. Until late summer, there may be snow crossings here and there; the hard-packed avalanche snow from Mount Stuart takes a long time to melt off, especially after winters with heavy snowpack.

The trail continues climbing steadily in the final 2 miles to Stuart Pass, elevation 6,400 feet, the high point of the trail. Just below the pass, the trail switches back once; a side trail leads off to the left 0.4 mile to Ingalls Lake. Camping is not allowed at the lake. The main trail continues up another 0.3 mile to the pass and supreme views of Mount Stuart, Ingalls Peak, and down the Ingalls and Jack Creek canyons. The upper part of the hike is spectacular in fall, when the larches turn yellow and the maples, mountain-ash, and other foliage turn all shades of yellow, orange, and red.

Options

Those not content with merely hiking the 16 miles to Stuart Pass and back, and who can arrange transportation, can continue another 12 miles down Jack Creek Trail to make a one-way hike of 28 miles, finishing at Icicle Creek. There are a number of one-way hike options, including exiting via Ingalls Lake or Beverly-Turnpike Trail. Of course, the hike can be done in reverse direction, approaching via one of the higher trails and descending Ingalls Creek 16 miles from Stuart Pass.

Side trails are abundant on this hike, but they are often ignored and thus offer even more solitude than the Ingalls Lake Trail itself. Falls Creek, Cascade Creek, Hardscrabble Creek, and Fourth Creek Trails are not the best maintained and are not often traveled. A variety of loops can be concocted by linking these creek trails via County Line Trail. Beverly-Turnpike Trail is used by climbers aiming for the summit of Mount Stuart, as well as by hikers seeking to avoid the lower 12 miles of the Ingalls Creek Trail. It can also be part of a loop including Fourth Creek Trail or Hardscrabble Creek Trail. There are sections of trail here that are faint to nonexistent, best left to experienced hikers with plenty of off-trail experience. It would be easy to lose the trail and end up lost, especially without a map and compass.

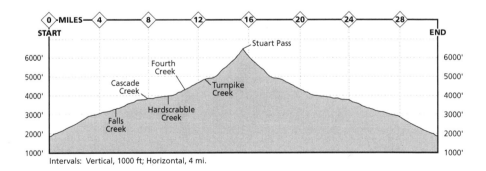

Key Points

0.0   Ingalls Creek trailhead.

3.6   Alpine Lakes Wilderness boundary.

5.7   Falls Creek Trail junction; stay right.

7.5   Cascade Creek Trail junction; stay right.

9.0   Hardscrabble Creek Trail junction; stay right.

10.5   Fourth Creek Trail junction; stay right.

12.0   Beverly-Turnpike Trail junction; stay right.

13.0   Longs Pass Trail junction.; stay right.

15.2   Side trail to Ingalls Lake; stay right.

15.5   Stuart Pass.

31.0   Back to Ingalls Creek trailhead.

19 Enchantment Lakes

The quintessential Alpine Lakes Wilderness hike to the fabled Enchantment Lakes.

Start: Snow Creek trailhead.
Distance: 25 miles out and back or 20 miles one way.
Difficulty: Strenuous.
Best season: Late summer through fall.
Traffic: Foot traffic only; moderate to heavy use in season. No dogs.
Total climbing: About 6,500 feet from the Snow Creek trailhead.
High point: About 7,840 feet.

Fees and permits: A Northwest Forest Pass is required. This is one trailhead where you can count on getting ticketed if you don't display a pass.
Maps: USGS Blewett, Enchantment Lakes, Mount Stuart; Green Trails No. 210 (Liberty), 209 (Mount Stuart).
Trail contacts: Wenatchee National Forest, Leavenworth Ranger District, 600 Sherbourne, Leavenworth, WA 98826; (509) 548-6977; www.fs.fed.us/r6/wenatchee.

Finding the trailhead: Enchantment Lakes Trail 1553.1 begins from Snow Lakes and is approached via Snow Creek Trail 1553. Approach from Leavenworth via Icicle Road (Forest Road 7600). Take U.S. Highway 2 to Icicle Junction at the west end of Leavenworth. Follow Icicle Road 4.1 miles to the Snow Creek Trail parking lot. The parking lot is big, but it gets crowded on summer and fall weekends, when everybody seems to be hiking Snow Creek Trail to the Enchantments. Theft is common at this trailhead, so park and lock your car, leaving no valuables behind.

The Hike

No hike in the Alpine Lakes Wilderness compares with a walk through the Enchantment Lakes. Not even close. It is the hike against which all other hikes are compared, and they all woefully fail to measure up. This high plateau sparkles with dozens of pristine lakes, from tiny ponds to deep pools, set in finely polished granite basins adorned with golden larch trees, guarded by rows of angular granite peaks. Every superlative one could heap upon the Enchantments would not begin to describe just how absolutely lovely and sublime—how enchanting—these lakes are. I will not attempt to do justice to the Enchantments; you will have to experience them for yourself. That may not be easy. Because of their remoteness, the Enchantment Lakes are not a day hike for any but the most fit and determined hikers. And because a permit is required to camp at or anywhere near the Enchantment Lakes, and only so many permits are available, only a lucky few are able to visit the Enchantments each season. You increase your chances by coming during the week before or after peak season, although the best time to visit is early fall, just before the season's first snowfall, when the larches turn from delicate green to blazing gold.

Lake Viviane, Enchantments ▶

Enchantment Lakes

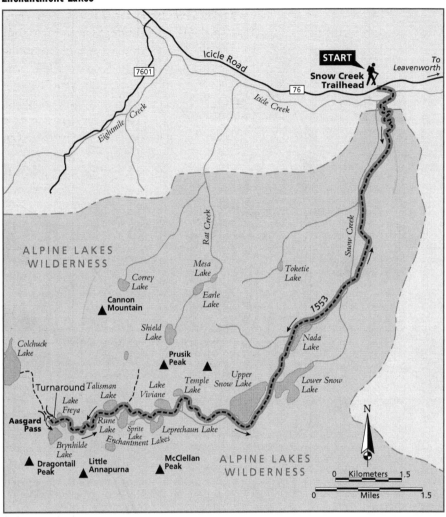

Begin via the 6.7-mile hike up Snow Creek Trail to Snow Lakes. From the kiosk at the south end of the parking lot, descend briefly to Icicle Creek, cross via an over-sized footbridge, then meander up a dusty road grade to an aqueduct channel, cross, and start climbing a series of hot, dusty switchbacks. The 1994 firestorm left these initial slopes exposed to the sun, so begin your hike early in the day to beat the heat, and bring plenty of water. The fire left behind charred trees and other hazards, so stay on the trail in this area. Eventually the switchbacks abate and the trail levels out, contouring rocky, occasionally brushy slopes just across the canyon from Snow Creek Wall.

The trail continues up the canyon, leaving the burn area and entering shady fir and pine forest. It ascends gradually up the canyon for a distance, switchbacks, levels out briefly, switchbacks again, before finally contouring the dusty canyon slope. About 4 miles up the trail, cross Snow Creek via a good bridge and parallel Nada Creek for a short mile, with a final few switchbacks to overcome before easing through grassy marshes to Nada Lake, elevation 4,800 feet. Nada Lake is a long, narrow lake lined by talus and timber, set in a narrow, granite-walled canyon. There are several campsites at Nada Lake, near the outlet stream and halfway up the lakeshore. Although most backpackers are in a hurry and continue on to Snow Lakes to get a head start to the Enchantment Lakes, Nada Lake is a usually quiet lake worthy of an overnight stay.

From the outlet stream, the trail rounds the western lakeshore, then crosses Nada Creek on footlogs before starting the climb to Snow Lakes, up an exposed talus slope. After several rocky switchbacks, the trail levels off and traverses subalpine forest over a rise and down to Snow Lakes, elevation 5,417 feet. The lakes are separated by a masonry dam, which keeps the upper lake from flooding the lower lake. The upper lake is drawn down during the summer to ensure a steady water supply for the fish hatchery miles downstream. By late summer, the upper lake may be several dozen feet low; in drought years, it is a blight on the otherwise pristine wilderness landscape.

There are numerous campsites at Snow Lakes, the traditional base camp for exploration of the Enchantment Lakes. Those making a day trip up to the lakes and back to camp will find the best base camp at the upper end of the upper lake, close to the inlet stream. Cross the dam separating the two lakes, and hike 1.3 miles along the upper lake's eastern shoreline to a footlog crossing the inlet stream. Once across the stream, the trail starts climbing and doesn't let up until the first lake is reached. The trail leads up through dusty forest at first, close to cascading Snow Creek, but soon angles away from the creek and ascends granite slabs and gullies. There are rebar footholds cemented in at the steepest spots; these are helpful when the slabs are wet and slippery. You may need to use your hands in a couple of spots, mostly for balance, but the rest of the climb up this slope, though steep, isn't too difficult during dry conditions. Scramblers might consider this Class 2 in a couple of spots but not harder unless you stray off route. Near the top, follow cairns up glacier-polished slabs, across ledges, and over a ridge. Here is the first lake, Lake Viviane, set in a granite-walled bowl below Prusik Peak. Some hikers push all the way to Lake Viviane in a day from the trailhead, a prodigious undertaking of over 9 miles with 5,500 feet of elevation gain.

The trail continues from Lake Viviane, crossing the outlet steam via an old log footbridge and skirting around and briefly up steep slabs and rocky steps, then down into a basin and an inlet of Leprechaun Lake. Follow the cairns up and over a rocky shelf and down to Leprechaun Lake proper. Climb up through lovely meadows and across white granite slabs, following Snow Creek upstream into a middle basin, lovely parkland with quiet ponds below granite domes. Cross the creek and hike up a long, polished slab, following cairns up along the creek as it splashes down a narrow gully, to little Sprite Lake, a scenic spot with a sublime view across the middle basin to Prusik Peak. Just up and around the corner from Sprite Lake is Rune Lake, which is one of the prettiest lakes anywhere, set in a narrow meadow basin that is enflamed with golden larch trees in early fall, with craggy Little Annapurna in the background. Wander up the lakeshore to a lovely meadow and a trail junction. This trail leads 0.5 mile or so up to 7,480-foot Prusik Pass, a grand viewpoint.

(A note here about nomenclature. The USGS maps don't show Rune, Talisman, Freya, or Brynhilde Lakes, but rather Perfection, Inspiration, Tranquil, and Isolation Lakes. The lakes were named by early visitors to the area to follow a mythological theme, but "official" names were later bestowed by unimaginative cartographers, and they stuck. Hikers and guidebook authors have disregarded these names and continue to refer to the lakes by their original names.)

Continuing on the main trail from Rune Lake, climb up a meadowy slope, past granite cliffs and golden larches to Talisman Lake, a near-twin of Lake Viviane, set in a cliff-lined bowl below craggy Enchantment Peak. Cross the outlet stream, and contour around the lakeshore to a rocky gully that leads to the upper Enchantments. This is a potentially hazardous gully in early season, when it is a steep snow slope. An ice ax and crampons may be useful here; beware of undermined snow as the gully melts out. Once past the gully, the trail meanders along a larch-filled meadow bench to a rocky point overlooking sparkling Crystal Lake, with views of McClellan Peak and its craggy ridges, Little Annapurna, and down into Ingalls Creek canyon and across to Navaho Peak.

Keep hiking up the basin, following cairns along trickling Snow Creek and past several small ponds and a unique waterfall pouring in a sheet down a polished granite slab. The trail climbs a bit more, across the high alpine basin, passing a few more desolate lakes below the blindingly white glaciers and ridges of Dragontail Peak. The lakes in this highest basin are snowbound most of the year and only melt out in late summer, if at all. Freya Lake is the final lake passed on the trail, a sparkling sheet of water draped over a bare granite bed; Brynhilde Lake is the big lake just south, nestled at the foot of Dragontail Peak's craggy eastern summit. Continue up the trail a short distance farther, to its high point at Aasgard Pass, elevation 7,840 feet, for a dizzying view down to Colchuck Lake and across the Wenatchee Mountains.

Because of the overwhelming popularity of this area, permits are required for overnight camping in the Enchantments and at Snow Lakes. Permits are available by mail while supplies last, and a few are given out each morning at the Leavenworth Ranger Station; they go fast, so get yours early, or try your luck in the daily lottery. Refer to the Enchantment Lakes Wilderness Permit section in Appendix A, or call the Leavenworth Ranger Station for permit information.

To alleviate sanitation problems, there are several privies in the Enchantments. A word of caution: They all have unobstructed views of the surrounding terrain, and vice versa. If you are hiking in the vicinity, as a courtesy you should perhaps yodel or make some noise to warn of your approach.

Options

A shorter but more rugged approach to the Enchantments is via Colchuck Lake and Aasgard Pass. Although one guidebook dismisses this approach as "tasteless" and "silly" if not downright deadly, it is as popular if not more popular than the Snow Lakes approach. Because it is only about 6 miles one way to the pass, gaining "only" 4,300 feet of elevation, the Aasgard Pass approach allows determined hikers to make a day hike to the upper Enchantments, or a one-way hike across the Enchantments (affectionately dubbed the "Death March") for those who can arrange transportation. However, this is a very strenuous option, with some serious off-trail travel over loose rock and snow, and it is not recommended for any but the most experienced and conditioned off-trail travelers. An ice ax is recommended for the climb to and descent from Aasgard Pass if there is any snow; crampons may be useful. Although climbers routinely use the Aasgard Pass approach, hikers should not try it until the path is snow free. A slip on snow or rock here could be and has been fatal. It is generally easier going up than down, so if you are making a traverse of the Enchantments, the recommended and popular direction is to approach via Aasgard Pass and descend via Snow Creek Trail.

There is a lot to explore in the Enchantments, too much to list here. Most of the lakes not reached by the trail are accessible via off-trail routes. Some are easy walks; others require good scrambling and route-finding skills. The ridge above Sprite and Rune Lakes makes for a scenic traverse, over granite domes, with incredible views of the entire Enchantment Lakes area. Gnome Tarn, a tiny pond set on this ridge, is a most sublime spot, with up-close views of Prusik Peak. Get out your map and see where you might wander.

Scrambling and technical climbing is a popular activity in the Enchantments. A popular side trip is an ascent of Little Annapurna, the prominent 8,000-foot peak rising gradually to the south, which offers easy, enjoyable scrambling up rock and snow slopes to its broad summit, with inspiring views overlooking the Enchantment Lakes and down into Ingalls Creek and beyond. This rocky scramble takes about two hours round trip from the "trail" and has no technical difficulty under ordinary con-

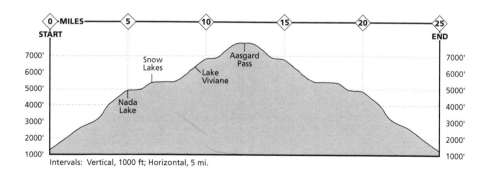

Intervals: Vertical, 1000 ft; Horizontal, 5 mi.

ditions, just some loose, sandy rock and moderately steep snow. There are also scrambling routes to the summit of Dragontail Peak and Enchantment Peaks. You will no doubt see climbers on top of Prusik Peak; one of the classic alpine rock climbs in the Cascade Range follows the west ridge. This is a technical climb, for experienced climbers only. Again, an ice ax and crampons are recommended if your route involves snow travel, and travel carefully over rock, especially talus and loose rock. Also beware of afternoon thunderstorms, which are common in this area. Climbing and scrambling should not be attempted except by those with proven skills and proper equipment.

Key Points

0.0 Snow Creek trailhead.

5.0 Nada Lake.

6.7 Snow Lakes.

8.0 Snow Lake inlet stream crossing.

9.3 Lake Viviane.

9.7 Leprechaun Lake.

10.0 Middle basin.

10.2 Sprite Lake.

10.6 Prusik Pass junction at Rune Lake.

10.9 Talisman Lake.

11.3 Crystal Lake viewpoint.

11.6 Upper basin.

12.2 Lake Freya.

12.5 Aasgard Pass.

25.0 Back to Snow Creek trailhead.

20 Windy Pass

Climb along Eightmile Creek and up through subalpine meadows to Lake Caroline and Windy Pass.

Start: Eightmile Creek trailhead.
Distance: 13.8 miles out and back to Windy Pass.
Difficulty: Easy to Eightmile Lake; strenuous to Lake Caroline and beyond.
Best season: Summer through fall.
Traffic: Foot and stock traffic; moderate to heavy use. No dogs.
Total climbing: About 3,900 feet.

High point: About 7,220 feet.
Fees and permits: A Northwest Forest Pass is required.
Maps: USGS Cashmere Mountain; Green Trails No. 209S (The Enchantments).
Trail contacts: Wenatchee National Forest, Leavenworth Ranger District, 600 Sherbourne, Leavenworth, WA 98826; (509) 548-6977; www.fs.fed.us/r6/wenatchee.

Finding the trailhead: Eightmile Creek and Lake Caroline Trails begin from the Eightmile Creek trailhead in Icicle Canyon. Take U.S. Highway 2 to Icicle Junction at the west end of Leavenworth. Turn onto Icicle Road, and follow 8.3 miles to Bridge Creek Campground. Turn left on Forest Road 7601, and follow 3 miles to the Eightmile Creek trailhead.

The Hike

The hike to Lake Caroline and Windy Pass is an Alpine Lakes Wilderness favorite, especially among those who enjoy hiking through high subalpine meadows and don't mind sweating a little to get there. This hike packs a lot into 7 miles, reaching two lakes in the first 3 miles, climbing through fire-scarred forest slopes and flower-strewn meadows, meandering through high lakes, and climbing wide-open meadows and basins to a high pass and sublime views.

Get your permit and begin hiking up the trail, which climbs up a grassy ridge above Eightmile Creek about 0.5 mile to a junction with an old logging road, follows the logging road briefly to a stream crossing, then departs the road and soon crosses the Alpine Lakes Wilderness boundary. The trail winds up the valley, amid fire-ravaged snags and dense underbrush, coming near the creek here, climbing away there, until finally leveling out and descending slightly to Little Eightmile Lake, 2.6 miles, elevation 4,404 feet. There are campsites here, but most hikers continue on to Eightmile Lake or Lake Caroline. The trail junction is just ahead. Continue on up the canyon another 0.5 mile to Eightmile Lake, elevation 4,641 feet, a big lake tucked into a craggy basin. A majority of hikers on this trail are bound for Eightmile Lake, which makes a nice 6-mile round-trip hike for families or day hikers who want to beat the traffic back across the mountains. However, enough

overnight hikers visit to fill up the available campsites on summer weekends, so come early or on a weekday if you are planning to camp at Eightmile Lake.

Lake Caroline Trail 1554 climbs from the junction in a series of switchbacks leading up the fire-razed slopes, then contouring up canyon into a basin, then switches back again up the ridge and climbs even more steeply. If you get a late start, you'll be suffering on this part of the trail; with all the trees burned, there is no shade. Just over a mile from the lake, the trail reaches a rocky viewpoint, from where you get a good view of Eightmile Lake and, just now peeking over the intervening ridge, the peaks of the Stuart Range. Continue up amid rust-colored talus, then across a flat, boggy basin, from where the trail leaves the ghost forest behind and enters meadows, steep at first but soon tapering back. Wildflowers are here and everywhere in season, all the way to the divide above Lake Caroline—aster, lupine, paintbrush, skyrocket—framed by subalpine firs and sienna cliffs. You stand a good chance of seeing deer here, maybe a bear, or a red-tailed hawk swooping overhead scouting the meadows for chipmunks, ground squirrels, and deer mice. The trail passes a campsite (and a horse camp) midway up the meadows, then switches back twice to reach the divide. Pause for effect, taking in the views of the Stuart Range and Enchantment peaks—steep rock walls, craggy ridge lines, glaciers, and all—then drop over the divide and switchback abruptly down to Lake Caroline, 4.8 miles, elevation 6,190 feet, a lovely, quiet lake ringed by subalpine firs and silver snags. There are several good campsites near the outlet stream and beyond, as well as a pit toilet. (Day-use area only for stock; tie line just before outlet stream.)

The trail loops around the east shore of the lake, then climbs over a rocky ridge, with views of craggy Cashmere Mountain, then drops into subalpine parkland, soon crossing a stream and contouring above the shore of Little Caroline Lake, 5.4 miles, 6,300 feet elevation, a small, shallow lake surrounded by meadows. There are a few more campsites here, including a horse camp just before the lake.

Continuing up the trail to Windy Pass is obligatory if you've come this far. The trail switches back through the meadows and traverses a rocky slope, then turns a ridge and contours above a lovely meadow basin at the foot of Cashmere Mountain. Near the basin head the trail crosses a small stream, last water until it runs dry in late summer, then climbs into a higher basin and switches back lazily through grassy alpine meadows, through dwarf firs, pines, and a few larches, to Windy Pass, elevation 7,220 feet. Take a moment to catch your breath, not only because of the altitude, but because of the views of mountains near and far, valleys, lakes, and countless high ridges. Mount Stuart and the other peaks of the Stuart Range dominate to the south, Mount Daniel and the crest peaks to the west, Sloan and other Monte Cristo peaks to the northwest, and Cashmere Mountain close to the north. For better

◀ *Ridge hiking above Windy Pass*

Windy Pass

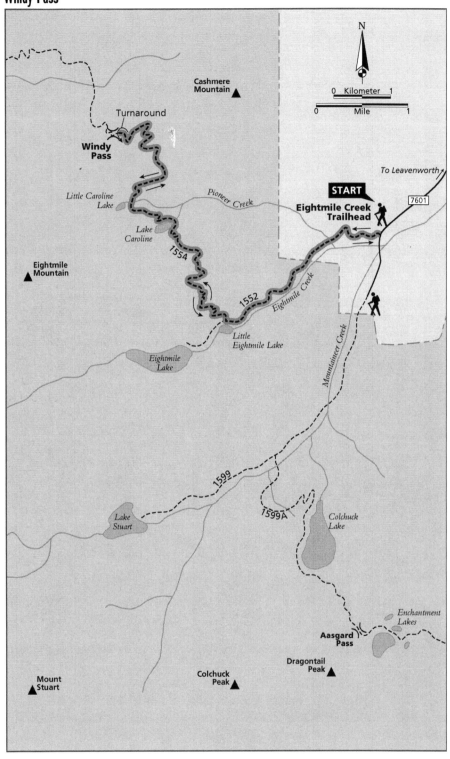

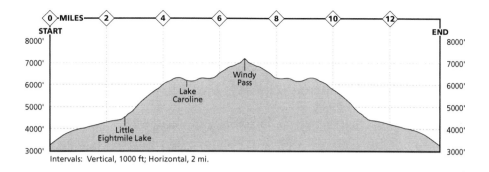

Intervals: Vertical, 1000 ft; Horizontal, 2 mi.

views, hike up the 7,380-foot-high point just south of the pass, or up the ridge toward Cashmere Mountain, but only as far as the going is easy.

Dogs are not allowed on this hike. Because of the popularity of this area, a permit is required for overnight camping at the lakes and elsewhere along this trail. Get your permit from the U.S. Forest Service Leavenworth office. A self-issued permit from the trailhead register is all that is required for day hiking here and elsewhere in the Alpine Lakes Wilderness.

Options

The trail continues down the other side of Windy Pass another 8.6 miles, descending to Trout Creek and out to Icicle Road near Scatter Creek Campground, with a short side trip to Trout Lake. This makes for an excellent 16-mile one-way day or overnight hike if you can arrange transportation.

Experienced scramblers and climbers can make the ascent of 8,501-foot Cashmere Mountain. There is a reasonable route up the west ridge, although it is quite exposed and not at all recommended for hikers lacking mountaineering experience. Refer to *Climbing Washington's Mountains* (Falcon, 2001) for details.

Key Points

0.0 Eightmile Creek trailhead.

2.6 Little Eightmile Lake; a 0.5-mile side trail leads to Eightmile Lake. Turn right to Lake Caroline.

4.0 Meadow camp.

4.8 Lake Caroline.

5.4 Little Caroline Lake.

6.9 Windy Pass.

13.8 Back to Eightmile Creek trailhead.

21 Trout Lake

A day hike or backpack to an alpine lake tucked between Jack Ridge and Eightmile Mountain.

Start: Jack-Trout trailhead.
Distance: 12.4 miles out and back to Trout Lake, or a 13.7-mile loop via Jack Ridge.
Difficulty: Strenuous.
Best season: Summer through fall.
Traffic: Foot and stock traffic only; light use.
Total climbing: About 2,100 feet gain to Trout Creek; 3,000 feet gain and loss on loop.
High point: About 4,800 feet.

Fees and permits: A Northwest Forest Pass is required.
Maps: USGS Jack Ridge; Green Trails No. 177 (Chiwaukum Mtns.)
Trail contacts: Wenatchee National Forest, Leavenworth Ranger District, 600 Sherbourne, Leavenworth, WA 98826; (509) 548-6977; www.fs.fed.us/r6/wenatchee.

Finding the trailhead: Trout Lake Trail 1555 begins from near the end of Icicle Road (Forest Road 7600) west of Leavenworth. Take U.S. Highway 2 to the western end of Leavenworth. Turn off on Icicle Road, and follow over 17 miles to Rock Island Campground. Continue on FR 7600 just across the bridge over Icicle Creek, then turn left in 0.1 mile to the Jack-Trout trailhead turnoff, on the left, then follow that spur road 0.3 mile to the trailhead.

The Hike

Trout Lake is a small lake tucked in a basin above Jack Creek, below Windy Pass, reached via a 6.2-mile trail starting at Icicle Creek. This trail is more popular with fishermen and horsemen than hikers. That said, if you are looking for a quiet lake hike that isn't crowded, Trout Lake may be a good one. The trail was rerouted a few years back and now begins from the Jack-Trout trailhead.

Get your permit at the trailhead and start hiking. Stay left at the first junction shortly up the trail, and drop briefly to cross Jack Creek, cross the very sturdy footbridge, then climb the opposite stream bank and ascend forested slopes another 0.7 mile to the Trout Creek Trail junction. Switch back sharply to the left, and climb a series of long, lazy, dusty switchbacks, gaining only 500 feet in the next mile, then contour around the foot of Jack Ridge into Trout Creek canyon. The trail ascends the canyon, contouring several hundred feet above Trout Creek amid pines and silver firs, gaining scarcely 500 feet in the next 2.5 miles.

At 5.7 miles, the trail reaches a junction with Lake Caroline Trail 1554, which leads 3 miles and 2,600 feet up to 7,220-foot Windy Pass, a worthwhile but lonesome side trip. Trout Lake is just 0.5 mile beyond this junction. There are several campsites at the lake, including a horse camp. Camping within 200 feet of the lake is prohibited, and, as at other alpine lakes, campfires are not allowed.

Trout Lake

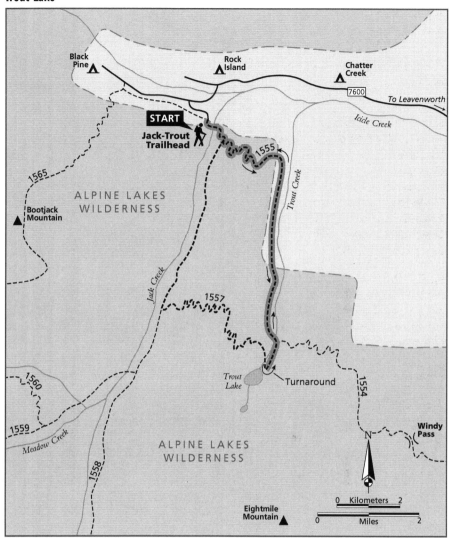

Options

This hike can be done in a convenient 13.7-mile loop over Jack Ridge and down to Jack Creek and out. This loop is best done by approaching via Trout Creek Trail, then hiking Jack Ridge Trail 1557 up to the 5,700-foot ridge crest, then steeply down 3 miles of unrelenting switchbacks, losing some 2,000 feet of elevation to Jack Creek. Don't do it the other way unless you enjoy climbing hot, steep switchbacks. This loop adds only 1 mile to the total distance of the hike, allowing a variation from the usual there-and-back hiking routine.

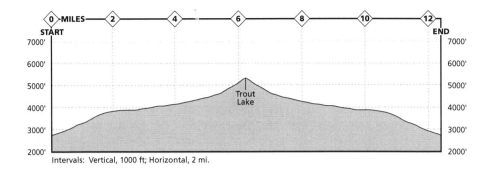

Intervals: Vertical, 1000 ft; Horizontal, 2 mi.

Key Points

0.0 Jack-Trout trailhead.

0.3 The trail crosses Jack Creek and enters the Alpine Lakes Wilderness.

1.0 Trout Lake Trail junction; turn left.

5.7 Lake Caroline Trail junction; stay right.

6.2 Trout Lake.

12.4 Back to Jack-Trout trailhead.

22 Jack Creek

A long backpack up lonesome Jack Creek to Stuart Pass, with side trail options.

Start: Jack-Trout trailhead.
Distance: 24 miles out and back to Stuart Pass.
Difficulty: Moderate.
Best season: Early summer through fall.
Traffic: Foot and stock traffic only; light hiker use.
Total climbing: About 3,700 feet.
High point: About 6,400 feet.

Fees and permits: A Northwest Forest Pass is required.
Maps: USGS Jack Ridge, Mount Stuart; Green Trails No. 177 (Chiwaukum Mtns.) and 209 (Mount Stuart).
Trail contacts: Wenatchee National Forest, Leavenworth Ranger District, 600 Sherbourne, Leavenworth, WA 98826; (509) 548-6977; www.fs.fed.us/r6/wenatchee.

Finding the trailhead: Jack Creek Trail 1558 begins from the Jack-Trout trailhead just off Icicle Road (Forest Road 7600) west of Leavenworth. Take U.S. Highway 2 to the western end of Leavenworth. Turn off on Icicle Road (FR 7600), and follow over 17 miles to Rock Island Campground. Continue on FR 7600 just across the bridge over Icicle Creek, then turn left in 0.1 mile to the Jack-Trout trailhead turnoff, on the left, then follow that spur road 0.3 mile to the trailhead.

The Hike

Jack Creek Trail follows a tributary of Icicle Creek some 12 miles to Stuart Pass, a high pass dividing Jack and Ingalls Creek drainages. It is a long creek hike, with very little elevation gain except in the first and last miles. If you like long, easy hikes without much excitement but some solitude and get along well with horses, you will enjoy this hike. If you prefer lakes or mountain views, you may wish to try a different hike.

Get your permit at the trailhead, and start hiking up the trail. At the first fork, just 100 yards up the trail, stay left and drop down briefly to cross Jack Creek. Cross the very sturdy footbridge, then climb the opposite stream bank and climb through open pine and fir forest to the Trout Lake Trail junction at 1 mile. Continue upstream, contouring along the east bank of Jack Creek, gaining elevation steadily but not always perceptibly. In early season, bright yellow balsamroot (a sunflower lookalike) blooms profusely along the first part of the trail, along with lupine, which seems to grow everywhere in the Alpine Lakes Wilderness. Mature pines tower above the trail in places. At 3.2 miles is the Jack Ridge Trail junction, from where a steep, punishing 3.5-mile side trip can be made up and over Jack Ridge to Trout Lake. For day hikers, this is a good option that makes for a 12.7-mile loop back to the trailhead via Trout Lake Trail.

Jack Creek

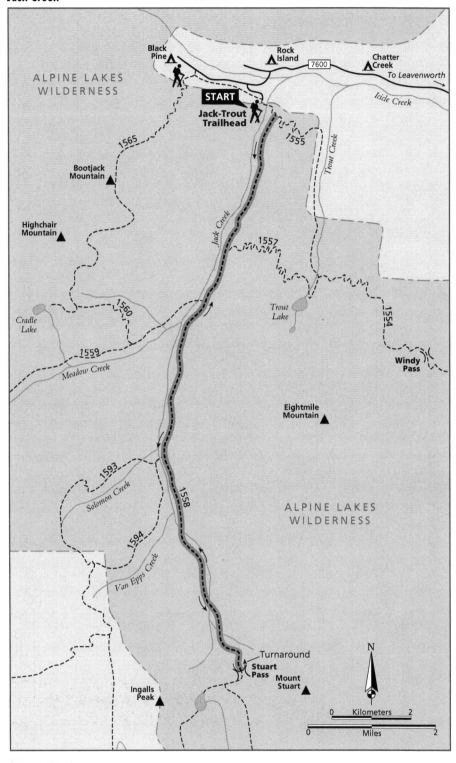

Black Pine
Rock Island
Chatter Creek
7600
To Leavenworth

ALPINE LAKES
WILDERNESS

Icicle Creek

START
**Jack-Trout
Trailhead**

1565

1555

Trout Creek

Bootjack
Mountain

Highchair
Mountain

Jack Creek

1557

1560

*Cradle
Lake*

*Trout
Lake*

1554

1559

Meadow Creek

Windy
Pass

Eightmile
Mountain

1593

Solomon Creek

1558

ALPINE LAKES
WILDERNESS

1594

Van Epps Creek

Turnaround

Stuart
Pass

Mount
Stuart

Ingalls
Peak

N

Kilometers
0   2

Miles
0   2

Hikers intent on continuing will proceed along Jack Creek Trail, still gaining little elevation, to the Meadow Creek Trail junction, 4.6 miles, elevation 3,800 feet. This is the turning off point for those hiking to Cradle Lake or making a loop up Meadow Creek and down French Creek Trail or back to Icicle Road via Blackjack Ridge. Cradle Lake is a good destination for backpackers on an overnight trip, providing a 21-mile round trip or loop back via Blackjack Ridge.

Past the Meadow Creek junction, Jack Creek Trail continues upstream, contouring along the east bank of Jack Creek, gaining elevation so slowly you hardly notice except that the trees are getting smaller and trending toward silver fir and hemlock. At 8.1 miles is the Van Epps Creek Trail junction, elevation 4,200 feet. Van Epps Creek Trail 1594 leads 3.5 miles up to and over Van Epps Pass, passing an old mining camp along the way. A side loop up to Van Epps Pass and down Solomon Creek Trail 1593 is an option here, although Solomon Creek Trail is not well maintained and is difficult to follow in places.

The final 4 miles of the trail climbs more steeply, gaining 2,200 feet, mostly in the final mile to 6,400-foot Stuart Pass. Ascend subalpine meadows, past diminutive silver and subalpine firs and mountain hemlocks, traversing below talus slopes from Jack Ridge and Mount Stuart, with views of Ingalls Peak and Mount Stuart looming close overhead as you approach the pass. From Stuart Pass are expansive views down the Ingalls Creek canyon and across to the Teanaway peaks, as well as back down Jack Creek and out over the Wenatchee Mountains.

Options

Just 0.5 mile down from the pass, via a way trail leading southward from a switchback, is Lake Ingalls, one of the gems of the Alpine Lakes Wilderness. Camping is not allowed at the lake, but you can camp just outside the lake basin. No campfires; no dogs.

Assuming you can arrange transportation, Jack Creek Trail is best done as a 16-mile one-way hike starting at Icicle Creek and hiking up over Stuart Pass and out via Ingalls Way Trail. This makes for a long day hike, but it is reasonably done as a two- or three-day backpack. There are camps at most of the trail junctions along Jack Creek Trail.

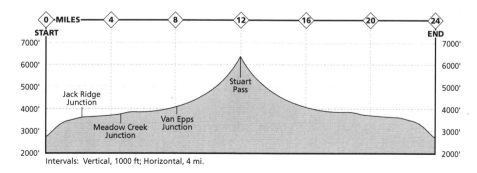

Intervals: Vertical, 1000 ft; Horizontal, 4 mi.

More challenging yet is a link-up of the 16-mile Ingalls Creek Trail with Jack Creek Trail. This 28-mile hike can be done in two, three, or four days, depending on your fitness and resolve, whether you have side trips in mind, and, of course, your transportation arrangements.

Key Points

0.0   Jack-Trout trailhead.

0.3   Jack Creek crossing and Alpine Lakes Wilderness boundary.

1.0   Lower Trout Lake Trail junction; stay right.

3.2   Jack Ridge Trail junction; stay right.

4.6   Meadow Creek Trail junction; stay straight.

7.4   Solomon Creek Trail junction; stay straight.

8.1   Van Epps Creek Trail junction; stay straight.

12.0   Stuart Pass.

24.0   Back to Jack-Trout trailhead.

23 Cradle Lake

A high alpine lake nestled in a basin above Meadow Creek.

Start: Jack-Trout trailhead.
Distance: 7.6 miles out and back from the Jack Creek Trail junction; 16.8 miles out and back from the trailhead.
Difficulty: Strenuous.
Best season: Summer through fall.
Traffic: Foot and stock traffic; light use.
Total climbing: About 3,400 feet.
High point: About 6,200 feet.

Fees and permits: A Northwest Forest Pass is required.
Maps: USGS Jack Ridge; Green Trails No. 177 (Chiwaukum Mtns.).
Trail contacts: Wenatchee National Forest, Leavenworth Ranger District, 600 Sherbourne, Leavenworth, WA 98826; (509) 548-6977; www.fs.fed.us/r6/wenatchee.

Finding the trailhead: This hike begins via Jack Creek Trail west of Leavenworth. Take U.S. Highway 2 to the western end of Leavenworth. Turn off on Icicle Road (Forest Road 7600), and follow over 17 miles to Rock Island Campground. Continue on FR 7600 just across the bridge over Icicle Creek, then turn left in 0.1 mile to the Jack-Trout trailhead turnoff, on the left, then follow that spur road 0.3 mile to the trailhead.

The Hike

Cradle Lake is a small lake perched in a high meadow basin about 1 mile south of Highchair Mountain on Blackjack Ridge. This approach to Cradle Lake is long, about 9.7 miles total via Jack Creek and Meadow Creek trails, and is more popular with horseback riders than hikers.

Get your permit at the trailhead, and start hiking up the trail. At the first fork, just 100 yards up the trail, stay left. Stay right going upstream at the junction with Trout Lake Trail. At the Jack Ridge Trail junction, stay right, continuing upstream to the Meadow Creek Trail junction at 4.6 miles. Leave Jack Creek Trail, and hike west up Meadow Creek Trail 1559, crossing Pablo Creek 0.8 mile along and reaching the Snowall Creek Trail 1560 junction at 1.3 miles. Follow Snowall Creek Trail up a long series of switchbacks, gaining about 1,100 feet in just over 1 mile. The switchback slope is south facing, making for hot, sweaty going on a sunny summer day. Hit the trail early or late in the day to beat the heat. The switchbacks end at a ridge crest not far above Pablo Creek, from where the trail ascends westward up the ridge to a junction with Blackjack Ridge Trail, 3.2 miles from the Jack Creek junction. From here, continue west to a creek and up alongside the creek another 0.6 mile to Cradle Lake, elevation 6,170 feet, a quiet lake set in a talus and meadow basin below a shoulder of Highchair Mountain. There are a few campsites near the lake. As elsewhere in the Alpine Lakes Wilderness, campfires are not allowed above 5,000 feet or within 0.5 mile of the lake.

Cradle Lake

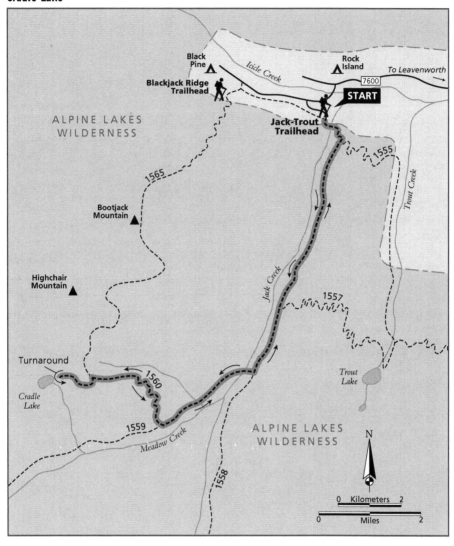

Wander up to the 6,400-foot divide 0.5 mile west of the lake, or scramble up the 6,623-foot peak just south of the gap for views.

Options

Cradle Lake may be reached via Blackjack Ridge Trail. This path-less-traveled has better views and provides an opportunity to scramble up Bootjack and Highchair Mountains, which are fairly simple climbs by scrambling standards and provide outstanding views of Mount Stuart and the surrounding peaks and valleys.

For those who prefer something more than a there-and-back hike to Cradle

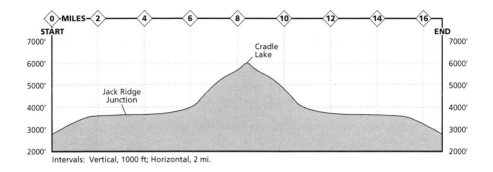

Intervals: Vertical, 1000 ft; Horizontal, 2 mi.

Lake, there are several longer loop options. You can hike in via Jack Creek and out via Blackjack Ridge; this 18-mile loop requires just over 1 mile of hiking on the Blackpine Creek Campground road, but if you stash a mountain bike at either trailhead, you can bike back to your car and save some time. A longer loop continues past Cradle Lake and over a 6,400-foot divide, then down Snowall Creek Trail 1560 about 7 miles to French Creek. From there, hike up French Creek Trail 1595 about 8 miles to the French-Meadow Creek divide, elevation 5,300 feet, then descend 5 miles to Jack Creek Trail and another 4.6 miles out for a 34-mile loop. This loop can also be done starting via French Creek Trail.

Key Points

0.0 Jack-Trout trailhead.

0.3 Jack Creek crossing and Alpine Lakes Wilderness boundary.

1.0 Lower Trout Lake Trail junction; stay right.

3.2 Jack Ridge Trail junction; stay right.

4.6 Meadow Creek Trail junction; turn right (west).

5.9 Cradle Lake Trail junction; turn right.

7.8 Blackjack Ridge Trail junction; stay left.

8.4 Cradle Lake.

16.8 Back to Jack-Trout trailhead.

24 Blackjack Ridge

A high ridge hike leading to Cradle Lake.

Start: Blackjack Ridge trailhead.
Distance: 7.2 miles out and back to Bootjack Mountain meadows; 17 miles out and back to Cradle Lake.
Difficulty: Very strenuous.
Best season: Midsummer through fall.
Traffic: Foot and stock traffic only; light hiker use.
Total climbing: About 3,900 feet.

High point: About 6,700 feet.
Fees and permits: A Northwest Forest Pass is required.
Maps: USGS Jack Ridge; Green Trails No. 177 (Chiwaukum Mtns.).
Trail contacts: Wenatchee National Forest, Leavenworth Ranger District, 600 Sherbourne, Leavenworth, WA 98826; (509) 548-6977; www.fs.fed.us/r6/wenatchee.

Finding the trailhead: Blackjack Ridge Trail 1565 begins near Blackpine Campground at the end of Icicle Road. Take U.S. Highway 2 to Icicle Junction at the west end of Leavenworth. Follow Icicle Road (Forest Road 7600) over 17 miles to Rock Island Campground, then continue across the Icicle Creek bridge another 1.3 miles to the Blackjack Ridge trailhead, on the left just before Blackpine Creek Campground.

The Hike

Blackjack Ridge is the high divide separating Jack and Black Pine Creeks, culminating in 7,016-foot Highchair Mountain. Blackjack Ridge is traversed by a rugged 8-mile trail that climbs nearly 4,000 feet out of Icicle Canyon and maintains an elevation of over 6,000 feet for several miles, providing wide-open views up Jack Creek, across to Jack Ridge, Cashmere Mountain, Mount Stuart, and other surrounding peaks. The trail leads to a junction with Snowall–Cradle Lake Trail, from where Cradle Lake is only 0.5 mile away. This hike can be done as part of a loop including Cradle Lake and Jack Creek. The trail is not popular because it is steep, strenuous, and dry, and literally disappears in several places in the upper meadow basins. It is not recommended for any but the most experienced wilderness hikers.

Fill out your permit and start up the trail, which leads through dusty pine forest briefly before starting to climb a long series of lazy switchbacks, first up a steepening forest slope, then up a ridge above an unnamed creek, with expanding views across Icicle Canyon and up to Icicle Ridge. The switchbacks do not relent for over 2 miles, and even after the final switchback the trail continues climbing steeply, just without the luxury of switchbacks. From the final switchback, the trail ascends about

View across French, Snowall, and Jack Creeks to Jack Mountain

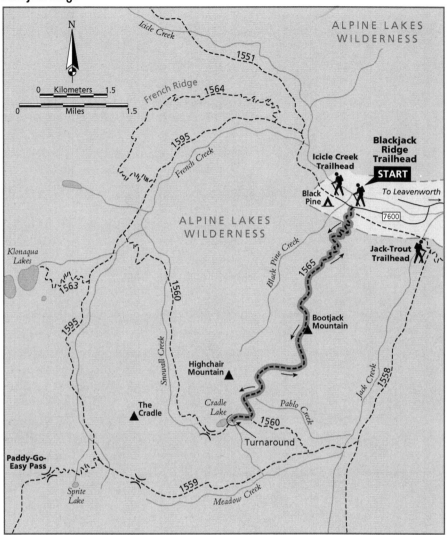

0.5 mile to a ridge point at 6,060 feet, the first good viewpoint of the hike. From here you see a panorama of high peaks and ridges, including Mount Stuart to the south, Cashmere Mountain to the east, Icicle Ridge to the north, and the Wenatchee Mountains to the west, with volcanoes poking up in the distance. The hike this far is 2.8 miles, with over 3,000 feet of elevation gain. Some hikers call it a day and head back, but the hard work is done, and there are meadows and peaks not far along.

From the ridge point, the trail continues southward 0.3 mile up the ridge to another high point (about 6,300 feet elevation), then drops down into a meadow basin on the east side of Bootjack Mountain. This is a lovely basin, with grassy meadows and hardy wildflowers, talus slides and subalpine firs. In early season, while snow lingers in the basin, there is water; by late summer, the trail may be completely dry until Pablo Creek, another 2 miles along. Most parties call this far enough, and cap off the hike with a scramble up 6,789-foot Bootjack Mountain. The usual route is up the northern ridge, nothing an experienced alpine scrambler should not be able to manage.

The trail becomes increasingly faint beyond the meadows, contouring around Bootjack Mountain's east ridge and several intervening ridges, descending here, ascending there across subalpine meadow slopes, talus slides, and rocky ridges toward 7,016-foot Highchair Mountain. The trail traverses the basin just below Highchair Mountain, then climbs up over a ridge and descends into Pablo Creek Basin, a meadow basin. In each meadow basin, the trail vanishes. Use your instincts and follow the path of least resistance to the other side of the basin, and hopefully pick up the trail there. The trail climbs a final 0.7 mile out of Pablo Creek Basin and over a ridge to join Snowall Creek Trail 1560 just 0.5 mile east of Cradle Lake. Most hikers spend a night at Cradle Lake before continuing on down Snowall or Meadow Creeks, or returning the way they came.

Options

As mentioned above, Bootjack Mountain is a fairly direct scramble up the north ridge. Highchair Mountain is also a relatively easy climb from the trail, usually approached from the saddle on the northeast side. It is easy by climbing standards, but it and Bootjack Mountain, like other mountains, are best summited by those with alpine scrambling experience.

Bootjack Ridge Trail can be linked with Jack Creek Trail for a 20-mile loop, or 18.3 miles if you stash a mountain bike at the trailhead and ride the last 2 miles of road. Likewise, from Cradle Lake you can hike up and over the divide and down Snowall Creek and loop out via French Creek Trail for a 22-mile loop, including a short stretch of road hiking in between trailheads.

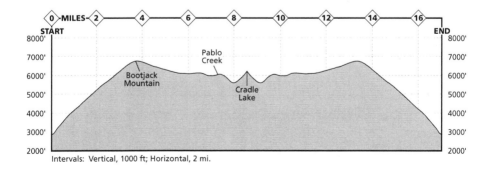

Intervals: Vertical, 1000 ft; Horizontal, 2 mi.

Key Points

0.0 Blackjack Ridge trailhead.

2.8 First ridge point.

3.6 Bootjack Mountain.

6.4 Highchair Mountain Basin.

7.3 Pablo Creek Basin.

8.0 Junction with Snowall Creek Trail; turn right (west).

8.5 Cradle Lake.

17.0 Back to Blackjack Ridge trailhead.

25 Icicle Creek

A backpack up Icicle Creek to Lake Josephine, with many options.

Start: Icicle Creek trailhead.
Distance: About 11 miles one way to Josephine Lake.
Difficulty: Moderate.
Best season: Early summer through fall.
Traffic: Foot and stock traffic; moderate use.
Total climbing: About 1,800 feet.
High point: About 4,700 feet.

Fees and permits: A Northwest Forest Pass is required.
Maps: USGS Chiwaukum Mountains, Stevens Pass; Green Trails 177 (Chiwaukum Mtns.), 176 (Stevens Pass).
Trail contacts: Wenatchee National Forest, Leavenworth Ranger District, 600 Sherbourne, Leavenworth, WA 98826; (509) 548-6977; www.fs.fed.us/r6/wenatchee.

Finding the trailhead: Icicle Creek Trail 1551 begins from the end of Icicle Road (Forest Road 7600) just beyond Blackpine Campground. From Leavenworth, follow Icicle Road just over 19 miles to road's end and the Icicle Creek trailhead.

The Hike

Icicle Creek is the major drainage of the northeastern portion of the Alpine Lakes Wilderness. The creek flows through one of the deepest canyons in the Cascade Range, more than a mile deep as measured from the top of Icicle Ridge to the depths of Icicle Creek. A popular hiking trail follows the creek some 11 miles to its source at Josephine Lake. The hike is not popular in its own right so much as it is heavily used to access the many trails leading to sparkling lakes and scenic ridges in this corner of the wilderness. Hikers, horsemen, and fishermen swarm up the trail all summer. Don't expect solitude here, unless you find it at a remote lake or high ridge away from the canyon floor.

From the trailhead, cross Blackpine Creek and continue along the trail through dusty, open pine forest. In 0.3 mile is the wilderness boundary; the trail continues as before, crossing streams and traversing dusty forest. In 1.5 miles, just across the footbridge crossing French Creek, is the junction with French Creek Trail. The trail this far is a popular late spring hike, at least among those who can't wait another month for the snow to melt out and the entire trail to be passable. Bright yellow and orange balsamroot flowers bloom profusely along the trail in early season, adding color to the otherwise drab forest. There is a campsite at this junction and one or two more at every other trail junction along the way.

A short distance farther up the trail is the junction with French Ridge Trail. Beyond this junction, the trail climbs away from the creek, then descends back to the creek bottom, where the creek has meandered away to the other side of the

Icicle Creek

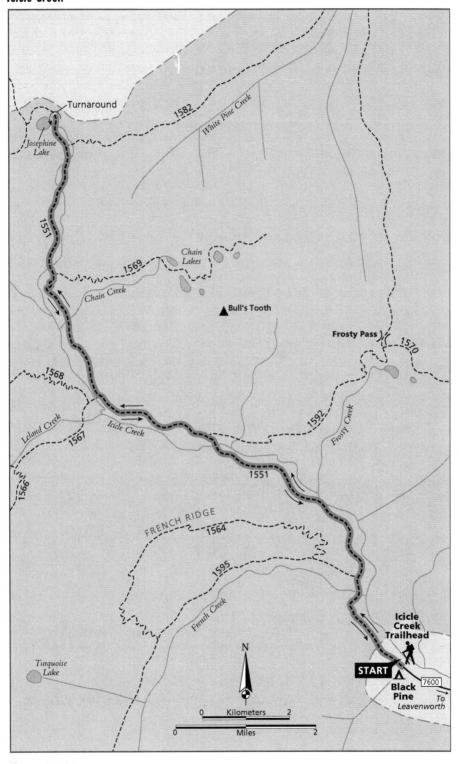

canyon. Continue through quiet forest to the junction with an abandoned segment of Frosty Pass Trail. The bridge washed out, and the trail was relocated a couple of miles upstream. Not far beyond the junction, the creek reappears and is followed closely for another mile. The trail passes a junction with the old, abandoned Dough-god Creek Trail, which still shows up on some maps as leading up to Doelle and Chain Lakes. A hiker I talked to said he had tried to follow it down from the lakes once; he told a tale of wading through miles of brush. Enough said. Pass it by and continue up the trail another 0.6 mile to a footbridge over Icicle Creek. There are several campsites near the crossing, popular with hikers and horsemen. The trail his far is about 5 miles, making for a good day hike of about 10 miles round trip.

Just across the creek is the junction with the new Frosty Pass Trail. Continue on, passing a grassy marsh, then through open fir and pine forest and across bushy avalanche swaths nearly 2 miles to the junction with Leland Creek Trail. Beyond, the trail keeps contouring along the creek bottom for another 1.5 uneventful miles, then suddenly starts climbing away from the creek in a short burst of switchbacks, gaining a quick 400 feet in 0.6 mile to the junction with Chain Lakes Trail. The trail crosses Icicle Creek once more, then again, and again in the next 1.8 miles as it climbs the steeper, narrower canyon, then meets the junction with Whitepine Creek Trail. The montane forest trends to subalpine as you climb higher, with meadows opening to reveal views of the surrounding ridges. In a final 0.5 mile, the trail ascends to the head of a basin, climbs a few switchbacks, then crosses a meadow swale and drops slightly to the shore of Josephine Lake.

Options

In another short mile above Josephine Lake, the trail officially ends at the Pacific Crest Trail junction. One-way hikers may continue about 4 miles north from here to Stevens Pass for a 16-mile trip. Some hikers prefer to hike the trail in the reverse direction, which is nearly all downhill except for the initial 1,100-foot climb up the ski slopes and a brief climb to the Josephine Lake junction. If you can arrange transportation, this is the easiest way to hike Icicle Creek Trail.

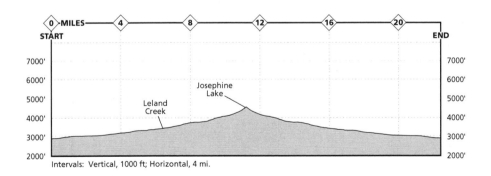

Intervals: Vertical, 1000 ft; Horizontal, 4 mi.

Icicle Creek Trail is not usually hiked in its entirety, but as a trail to approach other trails. The several trails passed along the hike lead to high ridges and lakes, which are described in separate chapters.

Key Points

0.0	Icicle Creek trailhead.
0.3	Alpine Lakes Wilderness boundary.
1.5	French Creek Trail junction; stay right on creek trail.
2.2	French Ridge Trail junction; stay right.
2.8	Old Frosty Pass Trail junction.
4.3	Old Doughgod Creek Trail.
4.9	Icicle Creek crossing and new Frosty Pass Trail junction; stay left.
6.7	Leland Creek Trail junction; stay right.
8.9	Chain Lakes Trail junction; stay left.
10.7	Whitepine Creek Trail junction; stay left.
11.2	Josephine Lake.
22.4	Back to Icicle Creek trailhead.

26 French Creek

A long hike up French Creek, with a side trip to Klonaqua Lakes.

Start: Icicle Creek trailhead.
Distance: 18 miles out and back to Klonaqua Lakes; 23 miles out and back to Paddy-Go-Easy Pass.
Difficulty: Moderate.
Best season: Midsummer through fall.
Traffic: Foot and stock traffic only; light to moderate.
Total climbing: About 3,200 feet.

High point: About 6,100 feet.
Fees and permits: A Northwest Forest Pass is required.
Maps: USGS Chiwaukum Mtns., Stevens Pass, The Cradle; Green Trails No. 177 (Chiwaukum Mtns.), 176 (Stevens Pass).
Trail contacts: Wenatchee National Forest, Leavenworth Ranger District, 600 Sherbourne, Leavenworth, WA 98826; (509) 548-6977; www.fs.fed.us/r6/wenatchee.

Finding the trailhead: French Creek Trail 1595 begins from the end of Icicle Road (Forest Road 7600) just beyond Blackpine Campground. From Leavenworth, follow Icicle Road just over 19 miles to road's end and the Icicle Creek trailhead.

The Hike

French Creek is one of the major tributaries of Icicle Creek. It is a long creek and a long, lonesome hike. There are no pretty lakes or mountaintop views on the majority of this hike, just quiet forest hiking for miles on end. A majority of visitors to French Creek come on horseback. As a consequence, some sections of the trail are muddy and rough, and the trail is not especially popular with hikers.

From the trailhead, hike up Icicle Creek Trail 1.5 miles to the French Creek Trail junction. Take the left fork and hike up French Creek canyon, contouring above the creek, climbing a bit here and dropping a bit there, crossing an occasional stream or dry streambed. The going is mostly flat but has some of the up-and-down typical of eastern Cascades stream hiking. After about 3.5 miles is the upper junction with French Ridge Trail. This steep trail climbs up to a fishermen's trail leading to Turquoise Lake, one of the most remote lakes in this area.

The trail continues up French Creek another mile to a junction with Snowall Creek Trail 1560, which leads about 7 miles up and over a high divide to Cradle Lake, another hike more popular with horseback riders than hikers. In another mile, the trail crosses Klonaqua Creek. At last report there is no footlog or bridge, and no plans to install one, so ford the creek. Like other creek crossings, it is best to wait until later in the season, after the snowmelt has subsided, when the creek is more easily forded. You'll get your feet wet on this crossing, but by August that should be all that gets wet unless you slip. Just past the creek, at 7.1 miles, is Klonaqua Lakes Trail 1563, a side trip to two big lakes with several campsites. For many hikers on

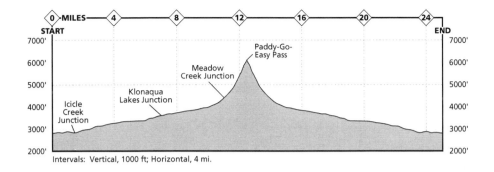

Intervals: Vertical, 1000 ft; Horizontal, 4 mi.

French Creek Trail, Klonaqua Lakes is the destination. This trail is steep and well worn by hikers and fishermen, climbing rocks and roots up through boulderfields and meadows some 2.2 miles to the lower of the two lakes. A fishermen's path leads to the upper lake. There are many campsites; campfires are not permitted. Although over 9 miles distant from the nearest trailhead, these lakes are hardly lonesome, although the fact that the path is hiker-only helps keep the traffic down. The lakes are lovely, surrounded by subalpine meadows and forest below snowy granite peaks and ridges. This 18.6-mile round trip is best done in three days, allowing a full day to relax and explore at the lakes.

For those continuing upstream from the Klonaqua Lakes junction, French Creek Trail meanders through a broad meadow basin, then climbs up the basin headwall alongside the creek, eventually crossing the creek and climbing the opposite bank to its junction with Meadow Creek Trail (Forest Trail 1559), 11.4 miles from the trailhead. Here the trail climbs 1,200 feet in 1.4 miles, past Sprite Lake, to Paddy-Go-Easy Pass. One-way hikers will continue 3 miles down from the pass to the trailhead at Tucquala Meadows, if they have transportation waiting.

Options

Side trips are abundant on French Creek Trail. French Ridge Trail is an excellent high ridge loop hike of 14.5 miles. Snowall Creek Trail climbs 7 lonesome miles to Cradle Lake, from where you can loop back to the trailhead via Blackjack Ridge Trail for a 22-mile loop, or down to Meadow Creek Trail and over the divide to French Creek Trail for a 33-mile semi-loop hike, or out via Jack Creek.

French Creek Trail can be hiked one way from Black Pine to Salmon la Sac. This 16-mile hike is a good long day hike, but it is better enjoyed over two or three days, with an overnight stop at Klonaqua Lakes. The difficulty of arranging transportation at both ends of the trail deters most would-be one-way hikers, who opt for the more convenient there-and-back or loop hikes.

◀ *French Creek Canyon and Mount Stuart*

French Creek

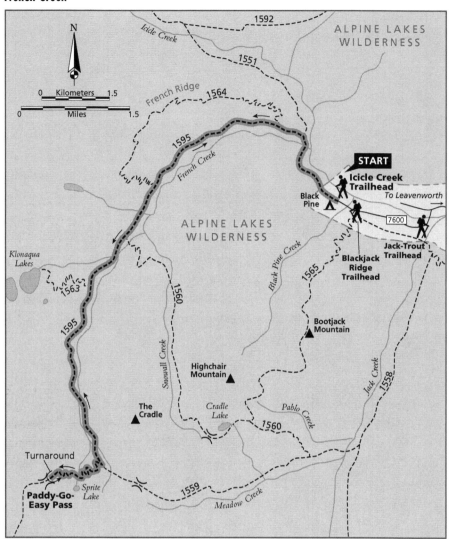

Key Points

0.0 Icicle Creek trailhead.

1.5 French Creek Trail junction; turn left.

4.9 French Ridge Trail junction; stay left.

5.9 Snowall Creek Trail junction; stay right.

7.1 Klonaqua Lakes Trail junction; stay left.

11.4 Meadow Creek Trail junction; stay right.

12.4 Sprite Lake.

12.5 Paddy-Go-Easy Pass.

25.0 Back to Icicle Creek trailhead.

27 French Ridge Loop

A loop hike over French Ridge and along French Creek, with views and wildflowers aplenty.

Start: Icicle Creek trailhead.
Distance: 13.6-mile loop.
Difficulty: Strenuous.
Best season: Midsummer through fall.
Traffic: Foot and stock traffic only; light to moderate use.
Total climbing: About 3,000 feet.
High point: About 5,840 feet.

Fees and permits: A Northwest Forest Pass is required.
Maps: USGS Chiwaukum Mtns., Stevens Pass, The Cradle; Green Trails No. 177 (Chiwaukum Mtns.), 176 (Stevens Pass).
Trail contacts: Wenatchee National Forest, Leavenworth Ranger District, 600 Sherbourne, Leavenworth, WA 98826; (509) 548-6977; www.fs.fed.us/r6/wenatchee.

Finding the trailhead: French Ridge Trail 1564 begins from the end of Icicle Creek Road (Forest Road 7600) just beyond Blackpine Campground. From Leavenworth, follow Icicle Road just over 19 miles to road's end and the Icicle Creek trailhead.

The Hike

French Ridge is the high ridge dividing the French Creek and Icicle Creek drainages. French Ridge Trail provides a convenient but strenuous loop hike to a former lookout site, featuring wide views of the Wenatchee Mountain and Stuart Range peaks. The hike is steep, strenuous, and dry by summer and not especially popular. If you are looking for a good view hike away from the crowds, this might be a good one. Just be sure to go light, and pack an extra water bottle.

The hike begins via Icicle Creek Trail 1.5 miles to the French Creek Trail junction. The loop portion of the hike begins here. You can do the loop in either direction, but if you're averse to long, steep, switchbacking trails, stay right on Icicle Creek Trail another 0.6 mile to the French Ridge Trail junction.

From the junction, French Ridge Trail climbs out of the canyon bottom, gradually at first but soon switching back in earnest to gain the ridge crest, then climbing steadily along the crest. This section of the trail can be miserably hot and sweaty on a summer day, making it wise to get an early start, especially if you are lugging overnight gear along. The views increase as the trees thin out and open up in subalpine parkland liberally sprinkled with wildflowers, including lupine, aster, penstemon, and skyrocket. After a few miles of climbing up the ridge, the trail contours southeast of the crest and climbs a bit more to an old lookout site atop the ridge, elevation 5,840 feet, a supreme viewpoint. A day hike to the lookout site is a 12-mile round trip, well worth the sweat and strain, but the loop hike is only a couple of miles longer and equally worthwhile.

French Ridge Loop

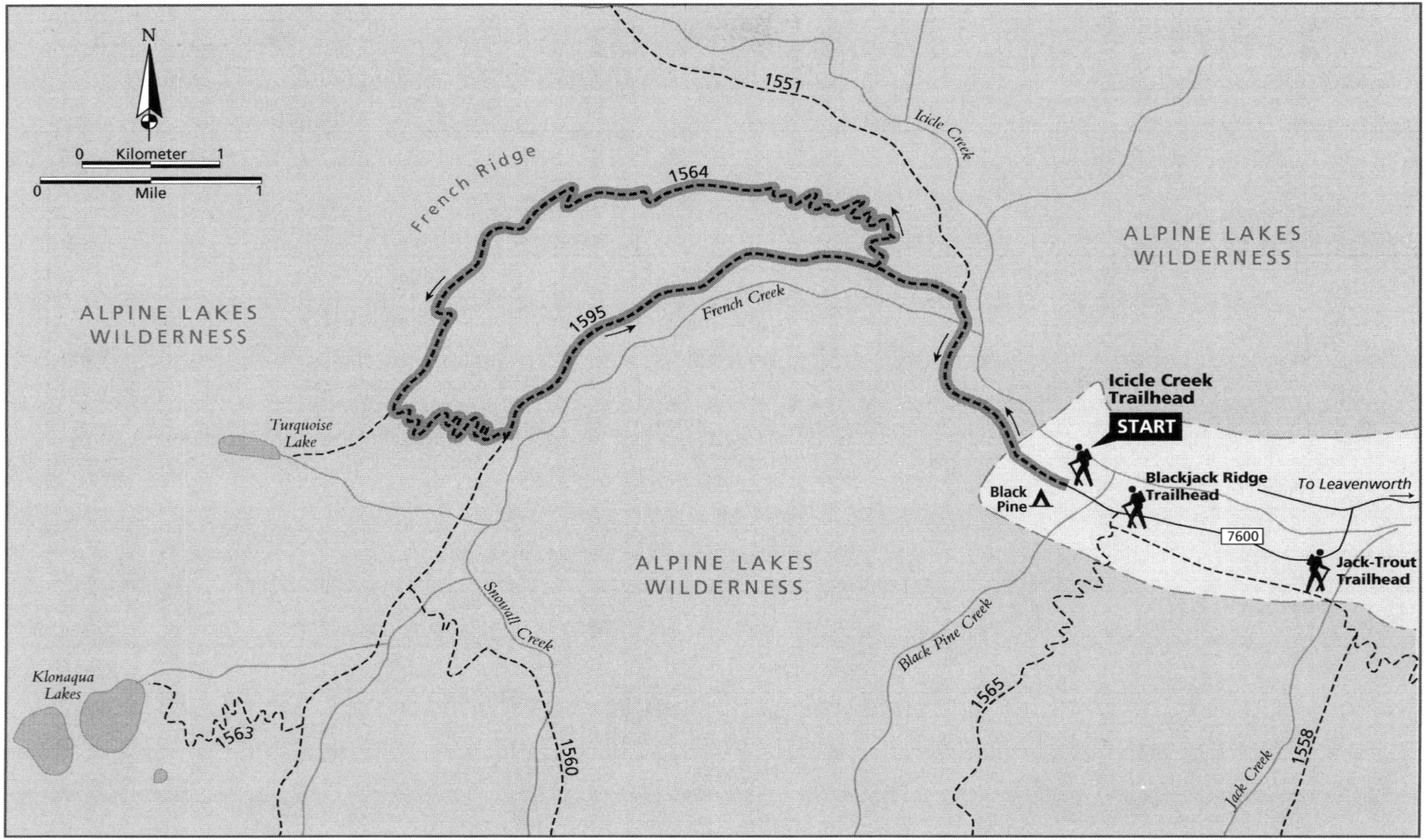

N

Kilometer
0   1

Mile
0   1

ALPINE LAKES
WILDERNESS

ALPINE LAKES
WILDERNESS

ALPINE LAKES
WILDERNESS

Icicle Creek
Trailhead

START

Blackjack Ridge
Trailhead

Jack-Trout
Trailhead

To Leavenworth

Blackjack Ridge

Black
Pine

Icicle Creek

Black Pine Creek

Jack Creek

1558

1565

7600

1551

1564

1595

French Creek

French Ridge

Snowall Creek

1560

Turquoise
Lake

1563

Klonaqua
Lakes

It's pretty much all downhill from the lookout site. The trail drops to a saddle, where abandoned Cuitin Creek Trail leads down the north side of the ridge. Stay on the ridge trail, and continue along the crest. The trail contours east of the ridge crest a bit farther and passes a side trail leading afar to Turquoise Lake. This trail doesn't show on maps and is only mentioned in one hiking guide, which describes it as hard to follow, up and down. It's an abandoned trail, now traveled only by fishermen and wayward hikers. Those doing the loop hike will bypass this path and start down now on their way back to French Creek, gradually at first, but then down relentless switchbacks for the final mile to rejoin French Creek Trail some 3.5 miles up from the Icicle Creek Trail junction. Hike down French Creek Trail back to Icicle Creek, then a final 1.5 miles back to the Icicle Creek trailhead.

Options

Again, this hike can be done in reverse direction if you prefer, but be forewarned. The climb up from French Creek gains over 2,000 feet in under 2 miles and faces east, making for a hot, sweaty, strenuous climb except in the very early morning and very late afternoon most summer days.

Several of the high points of French Ridge may be reached via straightforward ridge scrambles. The going is open and easy but rocky in places, and is recommended only for those with off-trail hiking and alpine scrambling experience.

Key Points

0.0   Icicle Creek trailhead.
1.5   French Creek Trail junction; turn left (south).
2.1   French Ridge Trail junction; turn right.
6.0   French Ridge lookout.
6.2   Cuitin Creek Trail junction (abandoned).
7.5   Turquoise Lake side trail junction.
8.6   French Creek Trail junction; turn left.
12.1 Icicle Creek Trail junction; turn right.
13.6 Back to Icicle Creek trailhead.

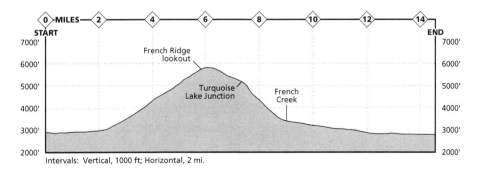

28 Leland Creek to Lake Leland

A long hike up Leland Creek to Lake Leland.

Start: Icicle Creek trailhead.
Distance: 24 miles out and back to Lake Leland.
Difficulty: Moderate.
Best season: Midsummer through fall.
Traffic: Foot traffic only; light use.
Total climbing: About 1,700 feet.
High point: About 4,500 feet.

Fees and permits: A Northwest Forest Pass is required.
Maps: USGS Stevens Pass; Green Trails No. 176 (Stevens Pass).
Trail contacts: Wenatchee National Forest, Leavenworth Ranger District, 600 Sherbourne, Leavenworth, WA 98826; (509) 548-6977; www.fs.fed.us/r6/wenatchee.

Finding the trailhead: Leland Creek Trail 1566 begins about 6.6 miles up Icicle Creek Trail from the Icicle Creek trailhead just beyond Blackpine Campground. From Leavenworth, follow Icicle Road (Forest Road 7600) just over 19 miles to road's end and the Icicle Creek trailhead.

The Hike

Leland Creek is another major tributary of Icicle Creek. From the Icicle Creek junction, a lonesome trail leads over 5 miles up the creek to Lake Leland. A difficult creek crossing right at the start deters all the but the most determined hikers and fishermen and limits the season to late summer and fall. Farther on, windfalls block the path. If this trail had reliable creek crossings and was maintained more regularly, it would be more popular. But then, if this hike became popular, where would anyone go to get away from the crowds?

Hike up Icicle Creek Trail some 6.6 miles to the Leland Creek Trail junction, staying right at the French Creek Trail junction and left at the Frosty Pass Trail junction. This far, the trail has gained only about 450 feet of total elevation. There are camps at the Icicle Creek crossing at about 5 miles and at the Leland Creek junction. From the junction, follow Leland Creek Trail across Icicle Creek via a good footbridge. Just across the creek is another trail junction, this one for Lake Lorraine Trail. Stay left on the main trail, dropping down to cross Leland Creek. This is the tough one; there is no bridge, so either find a log crossing up or down stream or ford. Don't try in early season; during high water this is a risky crossing. Once across, continue through flat, cool forest briefly, then climb a bit to yet another junction, this one with abandoned Cuitin Creek Trail, a faint path on the left. Proceed another 1.2 flat, easy miles along the edge of a broad basin to the Prospect Creek Trail junction, the final trail junction on the hike. This trail leads some 3.5 miles up to Square Lake.

Continue from the junction along Leland Creek. After a couple of switchbacks leading up and away from the creek, the trail levels out and traverses the wooded slope, crossing a few side streams. Except for the switchbacks, the first 2 miles past the Prospect Creek Trail junction are relatively flat and easy, gaining only 400 feet

Leland Creek to Lake Leland

Map showing trail from Icicle Creek Trailhead to Lake Leland within the Alpine Lakes Wilderness. Labeled features include Icicle Creek Trailhead (START), Black Pine, Frosty Pass, Frosty Creek, Bull's Tooth, Icicle Creek, French Ridge, French Creek, Trapper Creek, Lake Lorraine, Thunder Mountain, Square Lake, Lake Wolverine, Prospect Creek, Mac Peak, Leland Creek, Lake Leland, Turnaround, Trico Mountain, Klonaqua Lakes. Trail numbers: 1570, 1592, 1551, 1595, 1564, 1568, 1567, 1566. Road 7600 to Leavenworth. Scale in Kilometers and Miles.

of elevation, but the trail begins climbing more noticeably farther on, gaining 400 feet in the next 0.5 mile as the valley narrows and steepens, although the going isn't too strenuous, at least not for long. The final mile to the lake eases off some, still gaining gradually but not like before. The creek is close, chattering and splashing down the steep, narrow canyon. Soon you arrive at Lake Leland, elevation 4,461 feet, a small lake set in a wooded basin below the craggy slopes of Trico Mountain. There are a few campsites at the lake; you may have them all to yourself. Campfires are not allowed at or within 0.5 mile of the lake.

Options

Off-trail explorations at Lake Leland include cross-country hiking to a broad, lake-dotted basin southwest of the lake. Ambitious off-trail hikers and scramblers with good route-finding skills can find their way to the Granite Potholes and up Trico Mountain, or across the Wenatchee Mountains to Robin and Tuck Lakes, then back across the divide and down to Klonaqua Lakes. These high routes are not recommended for any but experienced off-trail hikers and alpine scramblers.

Side trips to Square Lake and Lake Lorraine are more popular than Lake Leland and are discussed in their own chapters.

Key Points

0.0 Icicle Creek trailhead.
0.3 Alpine Lakes Wilderness boundary.
1.5 French Creek Trail junction; stay right on the creek trail.
2.8 Old Frosty Pass Trail junction.
4.3 Doughgod Creek Trail.
4.9 Icicle Creek crossing and new Frosty Pass Trail junction; stay left.
6.6 Leland Creek Trail junction; turn left (southwest).
6.7 Lake Lorraine Trail junction; stay left.
7.2 Cuitin Creek Trail junction (abandoned).
8.5 Prospect Creek Trail junction; stay left.
12.0 Lake Leland.
24.0 Back to Icicle Creek trailhead.

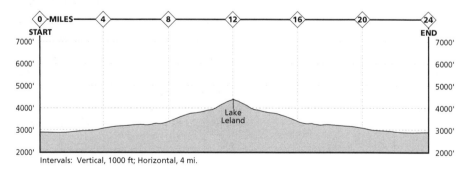

Intervals: Vertical, 1000 ft; Horizontal, 4 mi.

29 Square Lake

Backpack to Square Lake, a lovely alpine lake near the crest of the Wenatchee Mountains.

Start: Icicle Creek trailhead.
Distance: 3.5 miles one way from Leland Creek Trail junction, 23.8 miles round trip from Icicle Creek trailhead.
Difficulty: Moderately strenuous, difficult.
Best season: Midsummer to fall.
Traffic: Foot and stock traffic only; moderate use.
Total climbing: About 2,300 feet.

High point: About 5,100 feet.
Fees and permits: A Northwest Forest Pass is required.
Maps: USGS Stevens Pass; Green Trails No. 176 (Stevens Pass).
Trail contacts: Wenatchee National Forest, Leavenworth Ranger District, 600 Sherbourne, Leavenworth, WA 98826; (509) 548-6977; www.fs.fed.us/r6/wenatchee.

Finding the trailhead: Square Lake Trail 1567 begins about 2 miles up Leland Creek Trail, which is approached via Icicle Creek Trail from the Icicle Creek trailhead just beyond Blackpine Campground. From Leavenworth, follow Icicle Road (Forest Road 7600) just over 19 miles to road's end and the Icicle Creek trailhead.

The Hike

Square Lake is a large lake set in a deep, rocky basin against the east slope of the Wenatchee Mountains divide, just southeast of Thunder Mountain, less than 1 mile as the eagle flies from Surprise Gap. It is reached via a 3.5-mile spur trail from Leland Creek Trail. The trail is rugged and not well maintained, but that's just fine with the handful of hikers who visit; it keeps the casual hikers away.

Follow Icicle Creek Trail some 6.6 miles to the Leland Creek Trail junction. From the junction, follow Leland Creek Trail about 1.9 miles, contouring along the edge of the broad creek basin, to the Square Lake Trail junction. There is a difficult stream crossing just 0.2 mile past the Icicle Creek footbridge; if you can't find a good log to cross on, ford the creek carefully or turn back.

From the Square Lake Trail junction, the trail crosses Leland Creek (another ford or log crossing) and climbs the opposite slope briefly, then crosses Prospect Creek about 0.6 mile farther and 500 feet higher (yet another ford), then contours along the creek another mile or so before climbing a series of switchbacks, contouring again briefly, then climbing steeply a final 0.4 mile to Lake Wolverine, elevation 5,041 feet, set in a craggy basin. One might find a spot near Lake Wolverine to bivouac, but the camps are at the big lake just up the trail. From Lake Wolverine, the trail traverses subalpine meadow slopes as it descends gradually a quick 0.5 mile to

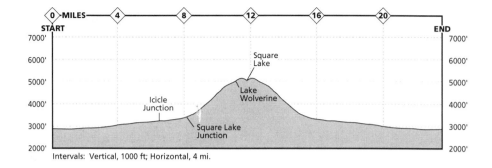

Intervals: Vertical, 1000 ft; Horizontal, 4 mi.

trail's end at the outlet of Square Lake, elevation 4,989 feet. Square Lake is set in a wide talus basin below soaring granite spires and ridges; 6,556-foot Thunder Mountain, one of several 6,000-foot peaks, rises to the northwest. Like Snow Lakes, Square Lake has a masonry dam spanning the outlet stream, put in before the area was designated wilderness. There are a few campsites at Square Lake. As always, campfires are not permitted at or within 0.5 mile of the lakes.

Options

Off-trail adventurers will find plenty to do at Square Lake. Milk Lake and a smaller "square" lake are hidden above the southeast shore of Square Lake. Adventuresome scramblers can find a route up to Mac Peak to the south or Thunder Mountain and Lakes to the north.

Key Points

0.0   Icicle Creek trailhead.

0.3   Alpine Lakes Wilderness boundary.

1.5   French Creek Trail junction; stay right on the creek trail.

2.8   Old Frosty Pass Trail junction.

4.3   Doughgod Creek Trail.

4.9   Icicle Creek crossing and new Frosty Pass Trail junction; stay left.

6.6   Leland Creek Trail junction; turn left (southwest).

6.7   Lake Lorraine Trail junction; stay left.

8.5   Square Lake Trail junction; turn right (west).

11.3 Lake Wolverine.

11.9 Square Lake.

23.8 Back to Icicle Creek trailhead.

Square Lake

30 Lake Lorraine

Backpack over a high ridge and down to Lake Lorraine, a remote lake nestled in a high basin.

Start: Icicle Creek trailhead.
Distance: 7 miles out and back from Leland Creek Trail junction, 20 miles out and back from Icicle Creek trailhead.
Difficulty: Strenuous.
Best season: Midsummer to fall.
Traffic: Foot and stock traffic only; light use.
Total climbing: About 2,600 feet gain, 400 feet loss one way.

High point: About 5,600 feet.
Fees and permits: A Northwest Forest Pass is required.
Maps: USGS Stevens Pass; Green Trails No. 176 (Stevens Pass).
Trail contacts: Wenatchee National Forest, Leavenworth Ranger District, 600 Sherbourne, Leavenworth, WA 98826; (509) 548-6977; www.fs.fed.us/r6/wenatchee.

Finding the trailhead: Lake Lorraine Trail 1568 begins from a junction on Leland Creek Trail, about 6.6 miles up from the Icicle Creek trailhead just beyond Blackpine Campground. From Leavenworth, follow Icicle Road (Forest Road 7600) just over 19 miles to road's end and the Icicle Creek trailhead.

The Hike

Lake Lorraine is a small lake set in a deep basin above Trapper Creek. It is reached via a 3.5-mile spur trail from Leland Creek Trail. Given that Lake Lorraine is a strenuous 20-mile round trip from Icicle Creek trailhead, it is not usually overcrowded. The trail climbs up and over a ridge, past a former lookout site, with wildflowers and views. If you're looking to get away from the crowds and don't mind pounding out some miles, this is a good hike.

Hike 6.6 miles up Icicle Creek Trail to the Leland Creek Trail junction, then follow Leland Creek Trail a quick 0.1 mile to the Lake Lorraine Trail junction. In the first 6.7 miles from the trailhead, the trail has gained only about 450 feet of total elevation, but that's about to change, and how. From the junction, the trail crosses the creek bottom, gaining elevation gradually at first, then more steeply as it climbs the forested ridge slopes just below an old lookout site just below Lake Lorraine Point. A short side trail leads to the lookout site and the best views on the hike. In 1.9 miles from the valley bottom, the trail has gained about 2,100 feet, hot and sweaty going on a summer day, with only a few switchbacks. Get here early, before the sun hits the slope, or wait for late afternoon shade. If you're doing this as a weekend backpack, consider camping at the trail junction on the first night, then climbing to the ridgetop early the next morning.

Lake Lorraine

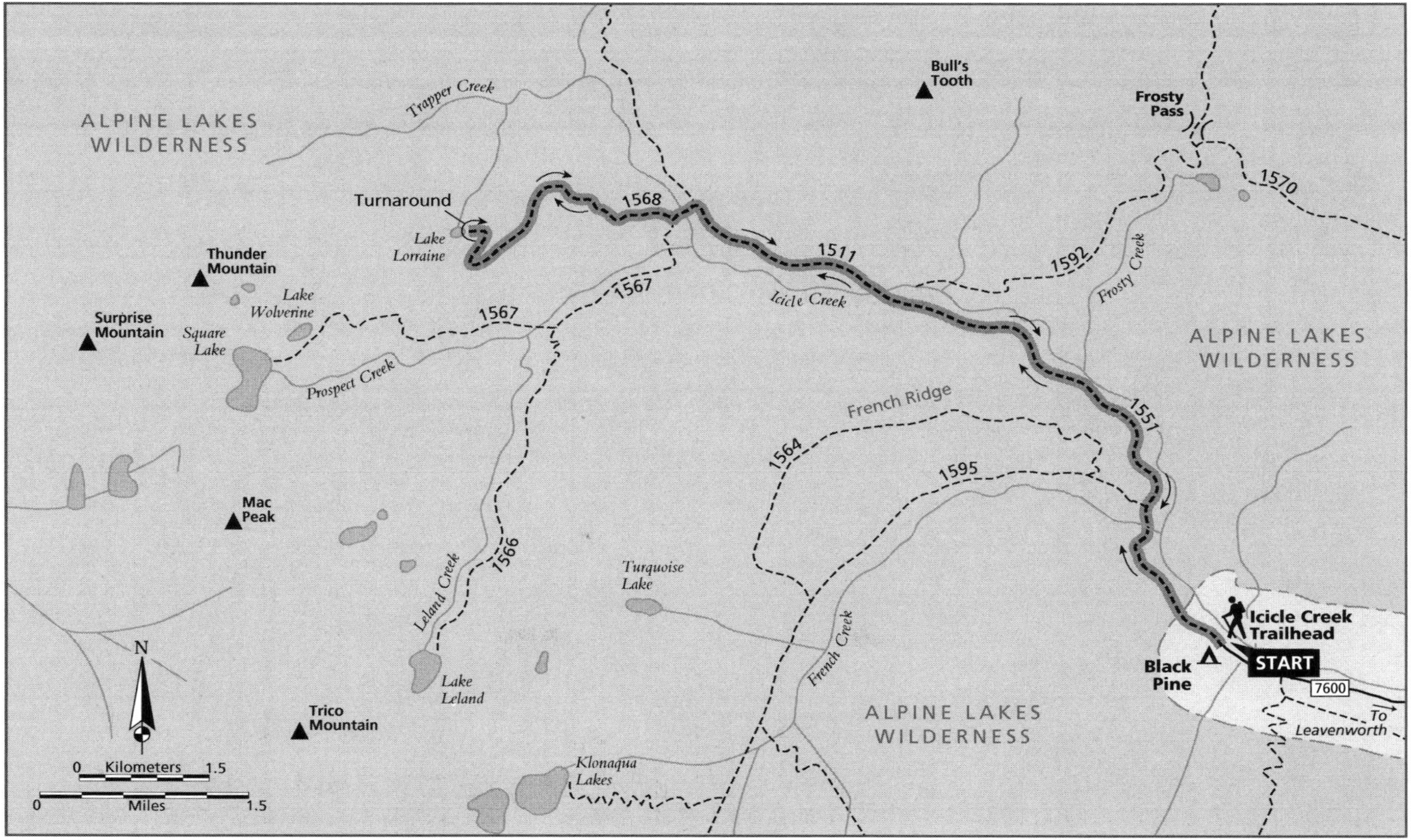

ALPINE LAKES WILDERNESS

ALPINE LAKES WILDERNESS

ALPINE LAKES WILDERNESS

ALPINE LAKES WILDERNESS

Icicle Creek Trailhead

START

To Leavenworth

7600

Black Pine

Frosty Pass

1570

1592

Frosty Creek

1551

Bull's Tooth

1511

Icicle Creek

French Ridge

1595

French Creek

1564

1568

1567

Turnaround

Lake Lorraine

Trapper Creek

Thunder Mountain

Lake Wolverine

1567

Surprise Mountain

Square Lake

Prospect Creek

Turquoise Lake

Klonaqua Lakes

Leland Creek

1566

Lake Leland

Mac Peak

Trico Mountain

N

Kilometers   0   1.5

Miles   0   1.5

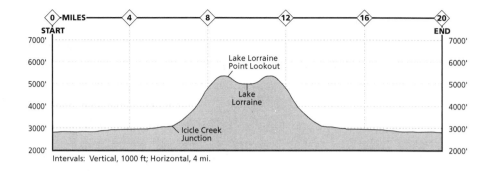

Intervals: Vertical, 1000 ft; Horizontal, 4 mi.

Once the climbing is done, the trail contours grassy flower meadows to a saddle, then another saddle, then climbs briefly up the ridge before dropping over the other side and descending a quick 600 feet in 0.5 mile to Lake Lorraine, elevation 5,056 feet. There are few campsites at the lake, but since so few people hike this trail, you shouldn't have any trouble finding a place to pitch your tent. Camping on the ridgetop is another option, although there is no water. Campfires are not permitted at or within 0.5 mile of the lake, or above 5,000 feet.

Options

Lake Lorraine Point, elevation 5,500 feet, is an easy hike from the trail and offers panoramic views, although the views aren't better than those found at other points along the ridge. For the best views, scramble up the little 5,889-foot peak just west of the trail's high point.

Key Points

0.0 Icicle Creek trailhead.

0.3 Alpine Lakes Wilderness boundary.

1.5 French Creek Trail junction; stay right on the creek trail.

2.8 Old Frosty Pass Trail junction.

4.3 Doughgod Creek Trail.

4.9 Icicle Creek crossing and new Frosty Pass Trail junction; stay left.

6.6 Leland Creek Trail junction; turn left (southwest).

6.7 Lake Lorraine Trail junction; turn right (west).

8.6 Lake Lorraine Point lookout site.

9.5 Divide above Lake Lorraine.

10.0 Lake Lorraine.

20.0 Back to Icicle Creek trailhead.

31 Chain Lakes

A backpack to remote Chain and Doelle Lakes.

Start: Pacific Crest Trail trailhead at Stevens Pass (south).
Distance: 21.2 miles out and back from Stevens Pass to Doelle Lakes; 22 miles via Icicle Creek.
Difficulty: Mostly moderate, but strenuous climb to lakes.
Best season: Midsummer to fall.
Traffic: Foot and stock traffic only; light use.
Total climbing: About 2,800 feet gain, 900 feet loss via Stevens Pass; 2,900 feet gain via Icicle Creek.

High point: About 5,700 feet.
Fees and permits: A Northwest Forest Pass is required.
Maps: USGS Stevens Pass, Chiwaukum Mtns.; Green Trails No. 176 (Stevens Pass), 177 (Chiwaukum Mtns.).
Trail contacts: Wenatchee National Forest, Leavenworth Ranger District, 600 Sherbourne, Leavenworth, WA 98826; (509) 548-6977; www.fs.fed.us/r6/wenatchee.

Finding the trailhead: Chain Lakes Trail 1569 begins from Icicle Creek Trail. As described in this guide, the hike begins from Stevens Pass, the shortest approach option. Take U.S. Highway 2 to the pass, and turn into the south parking lot. The Pacific Crest Trail trailhead is found just up a service road; follow the signs. This hike may also be approached from the Icicle Creek trailhead just beyond Blackpine Campground. From Leavenworth, follow Icicle Road (Forest Road 7600) just over 19 miles to road's end and the Icicle Creek trailhead.

The Hike

Chain Lakes are a string of small lakes set high in an enclosed basin high above Icicle Creek. The lakes are fairly remote; the shortest path to the lakes is over 9 miles long. These lovely lakes are among the most lonesome in the Alpine Lakes Wilderness. Although they are as beautiful as the Enchantment Lakes, precious few hikers visit, allowing a greater sense of solitude for those who do.

The hike described begins via the Pacific Crest Trail (PCT) from Stevens Pass, the shortest approach. From the summit, follow the PCT about 4 miles to the junction above Josepine Lake. Follow Icicle Creek Trail down a short, steep mile to Josephine Lake, the source of Icicle Creek, at 4,681 feet. Continue down Icicle Creek Trail, switching back a few times. In about 0.5 mile from the lake is the junction with Whitepine Creek Trail. Continue past the junction another 2.1 miles to the Chain Lakes Trail junction.

From the junction, hike eastward up the canyon slope, climbing a series of tight switchbacks that gain 1,000 feet in the first mile, where the trail levels off some and contours above Chain Creek, gaining only 600 feet in the next mile, with increasing

Chain Lakes

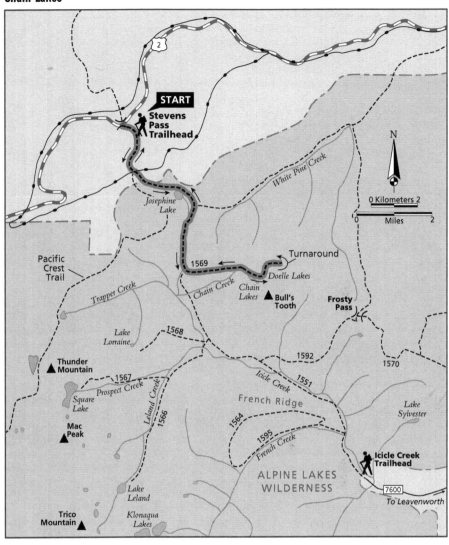

views down to the upper Icicle Creek canyon. The trail soon reaches Chain Creek and, not far beyond, the lowest of the three Chain Lakes set in a granite basin below craggy Bull's Tooth, a granite tower on the 6,840-foot ridge above the lakes, the highest summit in the area. There are campsites near the lakes; campfires are not allowed.

Don't stop at Chain Lakes, but continue another mile to Doelle Lakes, a pair of larger lakes set in an even lovelier granite basin across a 6,200-foot pass, if you need to get away from the "crowds" at Chain Lakes.

◀ *Bull's Tooth above Wildhorse Creek*

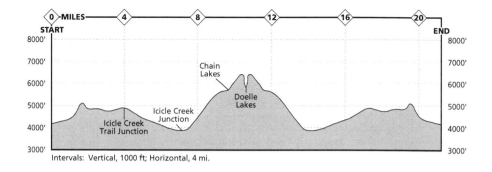

Intervals: Vertical, 1000 ft; Horizontal, 4 mi.

Options

An approach via Icicle Creek Trail is longer, taking 9 miles to reach the Chain Lakes Trail junction, 9 miles of mostly flat, boring creek hiking, gaining just over 100 feet of elevation per mile. Those driving from the east may prefer this option, which doesn't take much longer than the Stevens Pass approach and has fewer ups and downs, especially on the hike out. For details on this approach variation, refer to the description given for Icicle Creek Trail. A better option is to start at Stevens Pass, hike down and then up to Chain Lakes, then out via Icicle Creek Trail. This requires arranged transportation but allows for the maximum amount of downhill hiking.

Old maps show a trail leading down Doughgod Creek from Doelle Lakes. This long-abandoned trail is very brushy and hard to follow, and it is downright nonexistent in places, a surprise for some who come thinking they can make an easy loop back to Icicle Creek Trail. Don't try it. There is also a cross-country route following the high ridge from Doelle Lakes to Frosty Pass. Both of these options are for the most experienced off-trail travelers only.

Hikers can scramble up to various points on the ridge above the lakes; experienced scramblers can find a route to the highest point of Bull's Tooth ridge, elevation 6,840 feet. The actual "tooth" is a sharp rock spire slightly west of the highest point; for climbers only.

Key Points

0.0 Pacific Crest Trail trailhead at Stevens Pass.

4.0 Icicle Creek Trail junction; turn left.

4.6 Josephine Lake.

5.2 Whitepine Creek Trail junction; stay right.

7.3 Chain Lakes Trail junction; turn left.

9.3 Lower Chain Lake.

9.6 Middle Chain Lake.

10.6 Doelle Lakes.

21.2 Back to Stevens Pass.

32 Frosty Pass

Hike up Frosty Creek to Frosty Pass and Lakes Margaret and Mary.

Start: Icicle Creek trailhead.
Distance: 21.6 miles out and back to Frosty Pass.
Difficulty: Strenuous.
Best season: Midsummer to fall.
Traffic: Foot and stock traffic only; moderate use.
Total climbing: About 3,000 feet

High point: About 5,780 feet.
Fees and permits: A Northwest Forest Pass is required.
Maps: USGS Chiwaukum Mtns.; Green Trails No. 177 (Chiwaukum Mtns.).
Trail contacts: Wenatchee National Forest, Leavenworth Ranger District, 600 Sherbourne, Leavenworth, WA 98826; (509) 548-6977; www.fs.fed.us/r6/wenatchee.

Finding the trailhead: Frosty Pass Trail 1592 begins about 5 miles up Icicle Creek Trail from the Icicle Creek trailhead just beyond Blackpine Campground. From Leavenworth, follow Icicle Road (Forest Road 7600) just over 19 miles to road's end and the Icicle Creek trailhead.

The Hike

Frosty Pass is a high pass at the upper end of Icicle Ridge, dividing Frosty and Wildhorse Creek drainages. This is a popular backpacking hike through some of the most scenic country in the Alpine Lakes Wilderness, but it's a long weekend outing since the first lake is 10 miles up the trail, with about 3,000 feet of elevation gain, a bit stiff for one day with a heavy backpack. The hike is best done as a three- or four-day backpack, allowing time to rest, relax, and explore. Old maps and guidebooks show the trail being only about 2.8 miles up from the trailhead, but a bridge washed out and the Forest Service relocated the trail, adding some 3 miles to the one-way distance.

Follow Icicle Creek Trail 4.9 miles, staying right on the creek at the French Creek Trail junction to where it crosses Icicle Creek via a footbridge. Just across the creek is the new Frosty Creek Trail junction. There are camps here, on both sides of the creek. In the first 4.9 miles from the trailhead, the trail has gained only a few hundred feet of elevation. From the junction, take the right fork and follow Frosty Creek Trail downstream along Icicle Creek to Doughgod Creek. The old Doughgod Creek Trail, long abandoned since its bridge washed out, leads faintly off up the creek into a brushy hell traveled only by a few anguished souls. Keep to the main path, which begins climbing away from the creek through dry pine and fir forest, and in another mile joins the old Frosty Creek Trail. The trail contours into a broad basin, coming closer and closer to Frosty Creek as you climb higher.

Frosty Pass

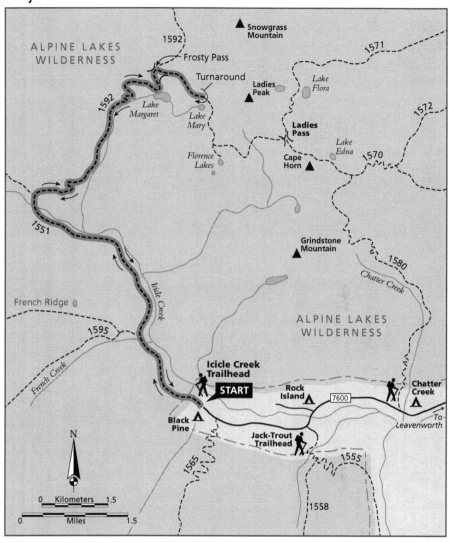

This portion of the trail isn't as steep as other hikes leading up to Icicle Ridge, but it faces south and can be hot and sweaty going on a sunny summer afternoon, especially with a fully laden backpack. At 8.2 miles, the trail enters a meadow basin with a popular campsite. The trail has gained about 2,000 feet from Icicle Creek so far, and it isn't over. It climbs a bit more, switching back twice and contouring to the head of the basin, where it levels out and a side trail leads to the shore of Lake Margaret, at 5,220 feet, a lovely lake set in woodsy meadows, very popular with backpackers. There are several campsites near the lake; campfires are not allowed here or anywhere in the vicinity.

◀ *Lower Grace Lake near Frosty Pass*

The trail continues 0.5 mile and another 500-plus feet up to Frosty Pass, elevation 5,780 feet, a broad, grassy saddle dividing Frosty Creek and Wildhorse Creek drainages, where three trails converge. Take your time here, soaking in the wide-open views.

To reach Lake Mary, another pretty lake and a very popular place to camp, take the Icicle Ridge Trail eastward a short mile, climbing up the broad, rocky meadow ridge briefly before traversing open subalpine meadows above Lake Margaret, crossing a stream, and finding the short side trail leading down to Lake Mary, elevation 6,100 feet, smaller than her sister, Florence, but equally lovely.

Options

A shorter approach to Frosty Pass is via Wildhorse Creek, which saves over a mile of hiking each way in addition to less driving time for those approaching over Stevens Pass.

An excellent loop hike option is to continue past Lake Mary to Chatter Creek Trail and out, providing a 20-plus-mile loop. This requires arranging transportation or stashing a mountain bike at the Chatter Creek Guard Station, or hiking 2 miles up the road. A better option is to hike this loop in reverse direction, up Chatter Creek and down Frosty Creek, leaving a bike at the upper trailhead so you can coast the 2 miles down the road to the car. Although over 20 miles long, this allows trail runners and other "death march" enthusiasts to do the loop as a day hike.

The 6,489-foot peak just west of Frosty Pass is an easy ridge hike and provides excellent views. Snowgrass Mountain, elevation 7,993 feet, the second-highest peak of the Chiwaukum Mountains, is a 1.5-mile ridge hike the other way, first east and then north up the grassy ridge from Frosty Pass. It, too, is easy by climbing standards, and although scrambling is best left to those with experience, determined hikers often manage this summit without incident. For more information about this and other scrambles in this area, refer to *Climbing Washington's Mountains* (Falcon, 2001).

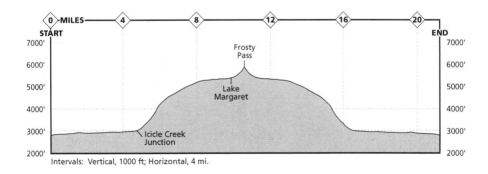

Key Points

0.0   Icicle Creek trailhead.

0.3   Alpine Lakes Wilderness boundary.

1.5   French Creek Trail junction; stay right on the creek trail.

2.8   Old Frosty Pass Trail junction.

4.3   Doughgod Creek Trail.

4.9   Icicle Creek crossing and new Frosty Pass Trail junction; turn right (east).

5.7   Frosty Creek crossing.

10.3   Lake Margaret.

10.8   Frosty Pass.

21.6   Back to Icicle Creek trailhead.

33 Icicle Ridge

A long backpack along the crest of Icicle Ridge.

Start: Icicle Ridge trailhead.
Distance: 26 miles one way from Leavenworth to Frosty Pass; 37.3 miles one way to Whitepine Creek trailhead via Wildhorse Creek Trail.
Difficulty: Strenuous.
Best season: Late spring for first few miles; midsummer to fall for upper ridge.
Traffic: Foot and stock traffic only; moderate use.
Total climbing: About 5,600 feet.

High point: About 7,100 feet.
Fees and permits: A Northwest Forest Pass is required.
Maps: USGS Leavenworth, Cashmere Mountain, Big Jim Mountain, Chiwaukum Mountains; Green Trails No. 178 (Leavenworth), 177 (Chiwaukum Mtns.).
Trail contacts: Wenatchee National Forest, Leavenworth Ranger District, 600 Sherbourne, Leavenworth, WA 98826; (509) 548-6977; www.fs.fed.us/r6/wenatchee.

Finding the trailhead: Icicle Ridge Trail 1570 begins from Icicle Road just south of Leavenworth. Take U.S. Highway 2 to Leavenworth. Take Icicle Road from the west end of town, and follow 1.4 miles on what looks like a private road leading up to several houses. A small brown sign points to the Icicle Ridge trailhead. Turn right, then left, and drive about 50 yards or so to the trailhead.

The Hike

Icicle Ridge is one of the longest, highest hikes in the Alpine Lakes Wilderness. The ridge forms the divide between Tumwater and Icicle Canyons, two of the deepest gorges in the Cascade Range. The relief is incredible; the trail begins from only about 1,600 feet elevation on the outskirts of the town of Leavenworth, then climbs up to and traverses along and beside a 7,000-foot-high ridge for over 20 miles. It goes without saying that the views from the ridge are far and wide. Although steep in places, especially in the first several miles, the majority of the trail is relatively gentle ridge hiking with the usual ups and downs one might expect, sometimes steep. Wildflowers bloom in abundance in the spring and early summer on the lower ridge and stay late higher up. Because of its length, this hike is more popular with horse packers than backpackers. Few hike the entire trail in one push; most hike segments of the trail as part of other hikes.

Get your permit at the trailhead register, and start hiking. From the trailhead, the trail climbs through open pine forest that was burned over a decade ago, leaving grassy meadows in place of brush. Pine needles litter the trail; in early season, yellow balsamroot flowers brighten the path. In 2 miles, after a healthy 1,600-foot gain, the trail reaches a saddle on the ridge, from where a quick trip along the ridge leads

Icicle Ridge

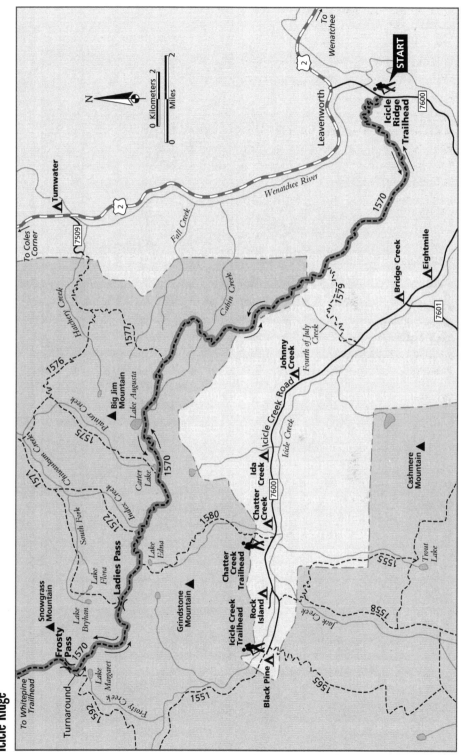

to a rocky viewpoint overlooking the town of Leavenworth and the highway snaking up Tumwater Canyon. There's a campsite here, offering a unique perspective of the sights and sounds of Leavenworth at night, but no water.

Continuing upward, the trail contours along the eastern side of the crest, switching back occasionally as it climbs through open pine and fir forest. In another 1.5 miles, sometimes on the ridge crest with views down into Tumwater Canyon, is the steepest part of the trail, climbing a series of tight switchbacks and gaining a quick 600 feet. The trail levels out just as suddenly, meandering through open forest and meadows along the gentle ridge crest to a 5,580-foot-high point at 4.8 miles, a good place for a rest stop, with views down into Icicle Canyon and beyond to the Stuart Range.

The trail continues along the gradual ridge crest for just over a mile, then contours across the head of the Power Creek basin on the Tumwater Canyon side, with views down into the canyon, then climbs back up to the ridge and keeps traversing. This section of the trail was burned over recently when lightning struck the ridge crest, igniting a series of forest fires. Although the burn area is not especially pretty now or fun to hike through, in the coming years the heights of Icicle Ridge will be covered with grassy meadows and wildflowers, so don't give up on this hike just yet.

After dropping briefly to a saddle above Bridge Creek, the trail climbs up and over a 6,905-foot-high point and at the 9-mile mark meets Fourth of July Creek Trail. A short distance beyond is the old lookout site, a supreme viewpoint at 7,029 feet. Conventional wisdom says this is the turnaround point for day hikers, making for a prodigious 18-mile round trip with 5,500 feet of elevation gain and loss. An alternative is to descend Fourth of July Creek Trail (when reopened) some 5 sooty miles to Icicle Road, and either mountain bike or drive back to the trailhead, depending on your transportation arrangements. This option is only 14 miles, much more reasonable as a day hike, but check with the Forest Service to make sure the trail has been restored following the forest fires; otherwise, it is too dangerous to hike.

Beyond the lookout point, Icicle Ridge Trail continues along or near the ridge crest, always with good views either north or south, especially of the Stuart Range peaks. Near the 11-mile mark is a 6,885-foot viewpoint. Beyond this, the trail descends, first gradually through open, fire-scarred woods and meadows, then more steeply down into meadowy Cabin Creek basin. By late summer, after snow has melted away, Cabin Creek is the first reliable water source crossed on the trail. There are campsites here, conveniently, as this is the halfway point of the hike. If there are horse parties on the trail, you will likely find them encamped at Cabin Creek watering the horses.

The trail climbs even more steeply out of Cabin Creek basin, gaining nearly 1,200 feet elevation in a mile, to gain a spur ridge of Big Jim Mountain. After a mile of hiking along this crest, the trail meets Hatchery Creek Trail. From the junction, the trail descends a bit back into upper Cabin Creek basin, then contours through subalpine meadows, crossing the creek, then climbing briefly to its source, Lake Augusta, elevation 6,850 feet, 17 miles along the trail. In 0.5 mile above the lake, the trail crosses a barren, rocky saddle, then descends steeply into upper Painter Creek basin 1 mile to the Painter Creek Trail junction and tiny Carter Lake. There are campsites at both Lake Augusta and Carter Lake; campfires are not allowed here or anywhere else for the remainder of the hike.

Beyond Carter Lake the trail climbs over another saddle, then descends 1,600 feet in 1.6 miles to the Index Creek Trail junction in upper Index Creek basin. It then climbs just as steeply up the opposite slope, gaining a whopping 1,400 feet in the next 1.2 miles to the junction with Chatter Creek Trail. From here the trail traverses easy high meadow slopes just over 0.5 mile to little Lake Edna at the head of Index Creek. There are usually hikers hereabouts, as Lake Edna is only about 5 miles up from the road via Chatter Creek Trail. Camping is not permitted in the Lake Edna basin, so keep moving through. Above Lake Edna the trail reaches its zenith as it crosses over a ridge just below 7,316-foot Cape Horn, a rocky high point that lures many a hiker away from the trail for spectacular views. Just beyond is Ladies Pass and the Chiwaukum Creek Trail junction. Just 1.4 miles down Chiwaukum Creek Trail are Lakes Brigham and Flora, two of the "Mormon Ladies Lakes," although the 1,000 feet of elevation loss on the way down and corresponding gain on the way back up to the pass makes this side trip not very popular with hikers doing the complete ridge traverse.

Continuing on from Ladies Pass, the trail contours across the head of Spanish Camp Creek Basin and across a saddle, then drops to a spur trail leading to upper Florence Lake. After crossing over another little saddle, the trail drops down into Frosty Creek basin above Lake Mary, also reached via a short side trail through the grassy meadows. After crossing a branch of Frosty Creek, the trail continues contouring, losing elevation slowly for another 0.7 mile to trail's end at Frosty Pass.

From here, there's another several miles and hours of hiking out via Frosty Creek Trail or Wild Horse Creek Trail. After tacking on the extra 9 or 11 miles of hiking out, this becomes a 35- or 37-mile hike. Definitely allow four or five days unless you are an absolute animal.

As the recent forest fires attest, summer thunderstorms are a hazard to hikers on Icicle Ridge. Lightning strikes the high ridges in this region with some frequency,

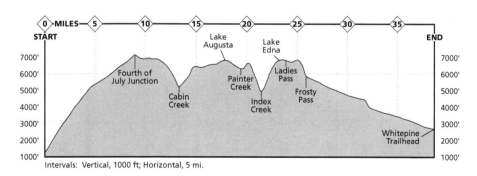

Intervals: Vertical, 1000 ft; Horizontal, 5 mi.

and if a thunderstorm approaches, you should descend from the ridge crest quickly and wait in a safe place until the storm has passed.

Options

Icicle Ridge Trail can be hiked in segments via spur trails, including Forth of July Trail (14 miles to Fourth of July trailhead, check with Forest Service for trail status), Hatchery Creek Trail (23 miles to Hatchery Creek trailhead), Chatter Creek Trail (28.1 miles to Chatter Creek trailhead), Frosty Trail and Icicle Creek Trail (35 miles to Icicle Creek trailhead). It can also be hiked in reverse direction from Whitepine Creek trailhead or Icicle Creek trailhead. From Frosty Pass the way is mostly downhill.

The first several miles of the trail are often hiked in late spring, and the lower ridge is a popular snowshoe hike in winter and spring.

Key Points

0.0   Icicle Ridge trailhead.

2.0   A saddle below Leavenworth viewpoint.

9.0   Fourth of July Creek Trail junction; stay on ridge trail at this and all junctions.

9.1   The old lookout site atop Icicle Ridge.

16.5   Hatchery Creek Trail junction; stay left.

18.0   Lake Augusta.

19.5   Painter Creek Trail junction; stay left.

21.3   Index Creek Trail junction; stay left.

22.5   Chatter Creek Trail junction; stay right.

23.1   Lake Edna.

23.6   Ladies Pass; stay left.

26.0   Frosty Pass; turn right (north) onto Wildhorse Creek Trail.

32.2   Whitepine Creek Trail junction; turn right (northeast).

34.3   Whitepine Creek trailhead.

34 Hatchery Creek Trail to Lake Augusta

A day hike or backpack to a high meadow basin and Lake Augusta.

Start: Hatchery Creek trailhead.
Distance: 16.2 miles out and back to Lake Augusta.
Difficulty: Strenuous.
Best season: Midsummer through fall.
Traffic: Foot and stock traffic; mostly light.
Total climbing: About 5,400 feet.
High point: About 7,280 feet.

Fees and permits: A Northwest Forest Pass is required.
Maps: USGS Big Jim Mountain; Green Trails No. 177 (Chiwaukum Mtns.).
Trail contacts: Wenatchee National Forest, Leavenworth Ranger District, 600 Sherbourne, Leavenworth, WA 98826; (509) 548-6977; www.fs.fed.us/r6/wenatchee.

Finding the trailhead: Hatchery Creek Trail 1577 begins from U.S. Highway 2 near Tumwater Campground. Take US 2 to the campground entrance, 8.7 miles from Leavenworth and 5.8 miles from Coles Corner. Find Hatchery Creek Road (Forest Road 7905), which is 0.1 mile south of the campground, on the north side of the bridge. Follow Hatchery Creek Road about 2.5 miles to the trailhead. Stay on the main road, passing spur roads on the right.

The Hike

Hatchery Creek Trail is a steep, dry trail climbing to a high ridge, where high meadow wandering awaits. Although this trail offers one of the shortest approaches to the high subalpine meadows of Icicle Ridge, including wildflowers and views, it is not a popular hike, often overlooked by day hikers with their sights set on alpine lakes. Determined day hikers often make the 16-mile out and back to Lake Augusta, one of the highest lakes in the area, but it is usually the domain of backpackers willing to hump a ruck up a hot, dusty trail.

From the trailhead, the trail begins climbing and doesn't stop for 3 miles. Switchbacks up an old logging road lead through old clearcuts, then a trail proper continues up steep wooded ridges, through pine and fir and grassy meadows, with views down Tumwater Canyon. At 3 miles, the trail finally stops climbing and reaches a junction with Badlands Trail 1576. Continue left, climbing through open forest and meadows, then drop into upper Fall Creek Basin and contour across the basin, crossing Fall Creek, then climbing to a ridge crest and joining Icicle Ridge Trail at 6.5 miles. The traverse across Fall Creek Basin is through lovely subalpine meadows liberally splashed with wildflowers. Most day hikers turn around here, satisfied with the wildflowers and the views, but determined day hikers and the majority of backpackers continue another 1.6 miles to Lake Augusta.

From the junction, follow Icicle Ridge Trail westward. The trail descends briefly in a couple of switchbacks into upper Cabin Creek Basin, then traverses the

Hatchery Creek Trail to Lake Augusta

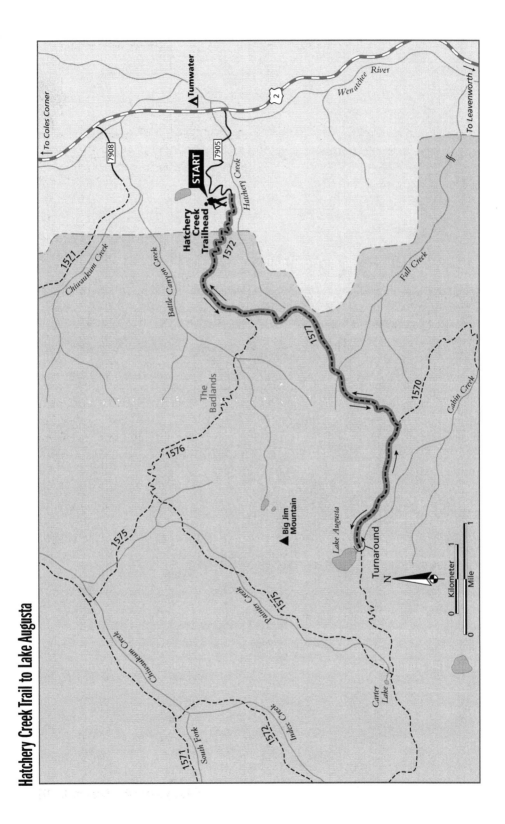

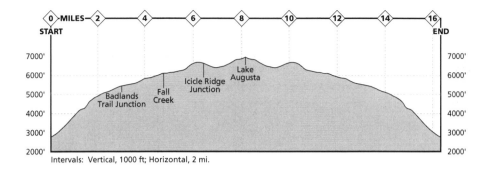

Intervals: Vertical, 1000 ft; Horizontal, 2 mi.

meadow basin to its head and climbs up a rocky, wooded slope to Lake Augusta, elevation 6,854 feet, a teardrop-shaped lake nestled in a barren subalpine meadow basin. The meadows here have been abused; please don't camp anywhere near the lake, and use existing campsites. As at other high lakes, no campfires are allowed.

Hikers who have come this far should continue a short 0.5 mile up to the 7,300-foot saddle west of the lake for views. Scramble up the ridge north or south from the saddle as far as you feel secure for even better views.

Options

A 20-plus-mile loop hike can be done by continuing over the saddle and down to Painter Creek, then hiking 3.1 miles down Painter Creek Trail 1575, then 5 miles up Badlands Trail 1576 to rejoin Hatchery Creek Trail at the first junction. The Painter Creek segment of the loop is the most difficult, following a brushy trail that fords the creek several times; it is not recommended for any but the most determined and experienced hikers who really want to get away from it all.

Experienced off-trail travelers can scramble up from Lake Augusta to the summit of Big Jim Mountain, elevation 7,763 feet. This scramble is relatively easy by climbing standards, but it is not recommended for hikers lacking scrambling and snow climbing experience. Refer to *Climbing Washington's Mountains* (Falcon, 2001) for route details.

Key Points

0.0   Hatchery Creek trailhead.

3.0   Badlands Trail junction; stay left.

6.5   Icicle Ridge Trail junction; turn right.

8.1   Lake Augusta.

16.2   Back to Hatchery Creek trailhead.

35 South Fork Chiwaukum Creek to Lake Flora

A backpack up South Fork Chiwaukum Creek to Lake Flora and Icicle Ridge.

Start: Chiwaukum Creek trailhead.
Distance: 27 miles out and back to Ladies Pass.
Difficulty: Moderate to Lake Flora, strenuous to Ladies Pass.
Best season: Late spring for lower Chiwaukum Creek trail; summer through fall to Timothy Meadow and beyond.
Traffic: Foot and stock traffic; moderate to heavy use.
Total climbing: About 5,000 feet.

High point: About 6,780 feet.
Fees and permits: A Northwest Forest Pass is required.
Maps: USGS Big Jim Mountain, Chiwaukum Mountains; Green Trails No. 177 (Chiwaukum Mtns.).
Trail contacts: Wenatchee National Forest, Leavenworth Ranger District, 600 Sherbourne, Leavenworth, WA 98826; (509) 548-6977; www.fs.fed.us/r6/wenatchee.

Finding the trailhead: Chiwaukum Creek Trail 1571 begins just off U.S. Highway 2 between Coles Corner and Leavenworth. Drive US 2 to Chiwaukum Creek Road (Forest Road 7908), 5 miles south from Coles Corner and 0.8 mile north of Tumwater Campground. Follow FR 7908 a short 0.3 mile to the Chiwaukum Creek Trail trailhead loop.

The Hike

Chiwaukum Creek, one of the major drainages of the Alpine Lakes Wilderness, has a reputation of being a long, lonely hike, and the reputation is partly right. This portion of the trail is over 13 miles long and leads to high meadows and lakes that are more readily reached via shorter trails coming up from Icicle Creek, making this a more lonesome hike than others in the area. The lakes, Flora and Brigham, popularly known as the "Mormon Ladies Lakes," are set in a high basin at the head of South Fork Chiwaukum Creek. The upper meadows and lakes don't melt out until midsummer, which is well enough since the fall colors are one of the main attractions. Those who come to see the wildflowers are usually content to turn around in the first 5 miles, or at Timothy Meadow.

Chiwaukum Creek Trail begins at a gate blocking access to a private road that once upon a time could be driven about a mile farther up the canyon. Get your permit at the trailhead register, then hike up the road grade 1 mile to a gate, where signs point rightward to Chiwaukum Creek Trail. Continue up the canyon, staying on the north side of the creek another 4.4 up-and-down miles to a fork. The trail is relatively flat and easy going, gaining elevation gradually all the way but never too steeply. The trail ascends through fir and hemlock forest, passing frequent stands of mature pine. In early season, wildflowers bloom alongside the road and trail, including balsamroot, Tweedy's lewisia, and the usual lupine, Indian paintbrush, bead lily,

South Fork Chiwaukum Creek to Lake Flora

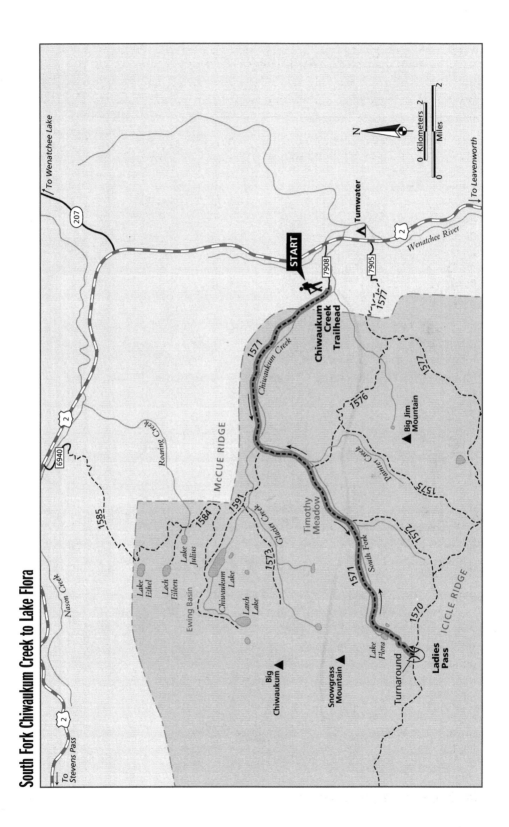

trillium, and bunchberry. The trail is well trodden by horse traffic, which is abundant. The loose, dusty soil can be irritating to walk on after a while. For the most part, the trail stays well above the creek. The trail drops down to a campsite next to the creek in a couple of miles, then reaches the creek again at a bouldery spot a bit farther on. Just past the 5-mile mark, the trail forks. The horse ford is down to the left; the footlog crossing is off to the right. The footlog crossing is recommended for two-footed travelers. Once across the convenient cedar footlogs, the trail meanders to the junction of the South and North Fork Chiwaukum Creek trails. There is a trail camp near the junction and at every trail junction along the way. Many hikers turn back here, especially late spring and early summer hikers who come merely to stretch their legs and see some wildflowers.

North Fork Chiwaukum Creek Trail 1591 continues upstream from the junction to Chiwaukum and Larch Lakes, but if you're headed to Timothy Meadow and Lake Flora, stay left and continue up the South Fork Chiwaukum Creek. The trail climbs gradually up the narrow canyon, through dusty pine and fir forest, well trodden by horses. In 1.6 miles is the junction with Painter Creek Trail 1575, a loop option described below; as always, there is a campsite at the junction. Continue up the South Fork Trail, which curves gradually eastward and climbs a rocky step past a waterfall. In just 1 mile beyond the Painter Creek junction you reach Timothy Meadow, a lovely, broad meadow framed by an aspen grove. In early season, the meadows here burst with wildflowers; in late summer and fall, autumn leaves turn every shade of yellow, red, and orange. Some make a day trip to Timothy Meadow; most backpackers spend a night at Timothy Meadow, then hike out, making for a 15.4-mile out and back. If done as a three-day backpack, Timothy Meadow is a convenient base camp for explorations up to Lake Flora and Icicle Ridge. Don't be surprised to find a pack train camped out near the meadows; this is one of the most popular horse trails in the area.

The trail continues up the canyon, through meadows and open forest. In 0.8 mile beyond Timothy Meadow is the Index Creek Trail junction, yet another loop option described below. Stay right and continue another 3.3 miles up the South Fork to Lake Flora, a small lake set at the head of South Fork Chiwaukum Creek Basin. The trail climbs a bit more steadily now, through subalpine forest and meadows, with wildflowers including lupine, aster, skyrocket, and paintbrush. Side trails lead off to the lakes, Flora to the east, Brigham to the west. There are campsites at each lake, often taken on summer and fall weekends. Having hiked nearly 12 miles to get here, you might wonder at all the people. They mostly come in via Chatter Creek Trail from Icicle Creek Canyon, a scant 8 miles distant.

From Lake Flora, the trail leads a final strenuous 1.8 miles up to 6,780-foot Ladies Pass, the high point of the trail. Here the trail joins Icicle Ridge Trail, from where you can roam in either direction.

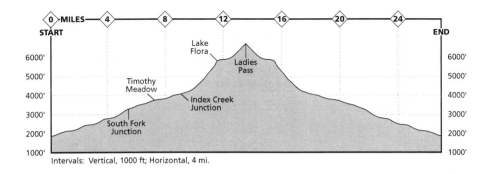

Intervals: Vertical, 1000 ft; Horizontal, 4 mi.

Options

Many hikers backpack in to Timothy Meadow or the Index Creek Trail junction, establish camp, then spend the second day hiking up to Lake Flora and Icicle Ridge. A convenient loop can be made from Ladies Pass by hiking 2.5 miles down Icicle Ridge Trail, then 2.8 miles down Index Creek Trail back to the junction. If you camped at Timothy Meadow, this is a good 11.3-mile day trip, providing a scenic highlight to the trip, although Index Creek is not often maintained and has a reputation for being brushy.

A great one-way hike with arranged transportation is to hike up Chiwaukum Creek Trail all the way to Ladies Pass, then traverse Icicle Ridge and follow Chatter Creek Trail or Frosty Creek Trail down to Icicle Creek, for a reasonable two- to four-day backpack of 20 to 25 miles.

Key Points

0.0 Chiwaukum Creek trailhead.

1.0 Trail forks off from access road.

5.4 South Fork Trail junction; turn left (south).

6.8 Painter Creek Trail junction; stay right.

7.6 Timothy Meadow.

8.4 Lower Index Creek Trail junction; stay right.

11.6 Lake Flora.

13.5 Ladies Pass.

27.0 Back to Chiwaukum Creek trailhead.

36 North Fork Chiwaukum Creek to Larch Lake

A backpack up North Fork Chiwaukum Creek to Chiwaukum and Larch Lakes.

Start: Chiwaukum Creek trailhead.
Distance: 23.2 miles out and back to Larch Lake.
Difficulty: Strenuous.
Best season: Late spring for lower Chiwaukum Creek trail; midsummer through fall to Larch Lake.
Traffic: Foot and stock traffic for first 7 miles, foot traffic only beyond Glacier Creek; moderate use.
Total climbing: About 4,300 feet.

High point: About 6,100 feet.
Fees and permits: A Northwest Forest Pass is required.
Maps: USGS Big Jim Mountain, Chiwaukum Mountains; Green Trails No. 177 (Chiwaukum Mtns.).
Trail contacts: Wenatchee National Forest, Leavenworth Ranger District, 600 Sherbourne, Leavenworth, WA 98826; (509) 548-6977; www.fs.fed.us/r6/wenatchee.

Finding the trailhead: Chiwaukum Creek Trail 1571 begins just off U.S. Highway 2 between Coles Corner and Leavenworth. Drive US 2 to Chiwaukum Creek Road (Forest Road 7908), 5 miles south from Coles Corner and 0.8 mile north of Tumwater Campground. Follow FR 7908 a short 0.3 mile to the Chiwaukum Creek Trail trailhead loop.

The Hike

Chiwaukum Creek Trail follows the first 5 miles of the main trail, then forks off up North Fork Chiwaukum Creek another 6-plus miles to high lakes including Chiwaukum and Larch Lakes. Although this trail provides the shortest public access to these lakes, it is not the recommended approach to the them. Although a bit longer and with more elevation gain, the hike in via Lake Ethel and McCue Ridge is more scenic. There is also a private shortcut to the lakes that cuts the hiking distance in half, making the upper lakes much less private than they ought to be.

Hike the first 5.4 miles of Chiwaukum Creek Trail, staying right at the gate to the private access road 1 mile from the trailhead. Once across the cedar footlogs, the trail meanders to the junction of the South and North Fork Chiwaukum Creek trails. Take a right and follow North Fork Chiwaukum Lake Trail 1591 upstream from the junction, through quiet woods and some brushy areas. About a mile from the junction, the trail climbs up over an old glacier moraine, where you get the first good views on the hike, including a look up Glacier Creek canyon to the snow-capped peak of Big Chiwaukum, the highest summit in the Chiwaukum Mountains and the source of the rocky debris underfoot. The trail continues along the southern edge of the canyon floor, through fir and hemlock forest, to the Glacier Creek

Fisherman at Larch Lake

Trail junction. Glacier Creek Trail 1573 leads about 2 miles into Glacier Creek Basin, a broad glacial valley just below the snowy Chiwaukum Mountains.

From Glacier Creek Trail junction, the trail climbs through forest to a footlog crossing of Chiwaukum Creek. Water up here; the next mile is brutal. Once across the logs, the trail starts climbing up a rocky slope and doesn't let up for over a mile. This section of trail is very steep, gaining some 1,200 feet in a mile, up a brushy scree slope. Although there are switchbacks, the trail grade is one of the steepest in the Alpine Lakes Wilderness, making for hot and miserable hiking on a sunny summer day. The trail bed is sandy and gravelly in places, and the slope is very steep and rocky, so take care with each step. After climbing several hundred feet, the trail traverses beneath cliffs, then climbs a bit more before finally leveling out and dropping into the Chiwaukum Lake basin. Contour above the lakeshore for 0.3 mile to the McCue Ridge Trail junction. There is a campsite here, close to the lakeshore.

From Chiwaukum Lake, the trail continues up into Ewing Basin, passing through wide, grassy meadows, then climbing briefly through woods before entering the basin proper. Ewing Basin is a broad subalpine meadow basin draped with rust-tinted talus. As the snow melts out of the basin by midsummer most years, wild-flowers bloom profusely, especially lupine and aster. In late summer and fall, the basin slopes are enflamed with all shades of yellow, red, and orange as the leaves turn their autumn colors.

The trail climbs up the basin, through grassy meadows, then ascends a series of switchbacks up a wooded ridge before leveling out in a broad lupine-filled meadow framed by larch trees. Larches, larches everywhere as you traverse the meadows up and over a final rise and behold Larch Lake, elevation 6,078 feet. The trail disappears in the meadows just above the lake; hike across the meadows, spreading out to do less damage. Fishermen's trails lead along the lakeshore in either direction. There are many lovely tarns among the rocky meadows north of the lake. No camping is permitted within 200 feet of the lakeshore; there are camps on the fringes of the meadows, but you may have to hunt around for a while to find a good one. Please don't camp on the meadows, and don't clear ground for new camps either. It's best if you camp at Chiwaukum Lake and make a day trip up to Larch Lake instead. No campfires, of course.

Options

Cup Lake, a little lake hidden in a cirque 500 feet above Larch Lake, can be reached via a short talus scramble from the southwest edge of Larch Lake. The going is a bit rugged, but hikers and fishermen regularly make the trip. Experienced scramblers and off-trail hikers sometimes climb up to one of the ridges above the lakes. Dead-horse Pass is one such destination, providing views down into Glacier Creek Basin and up to the Chiwaukum Mountains.

North Fork Chiwaukum Creek to Larch Lake

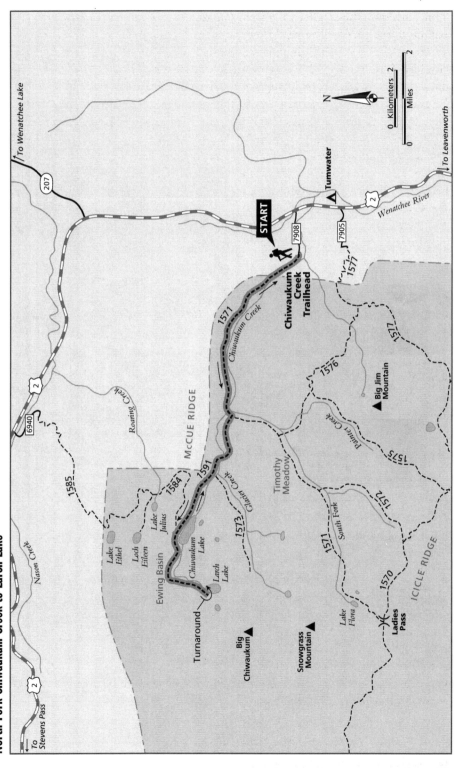

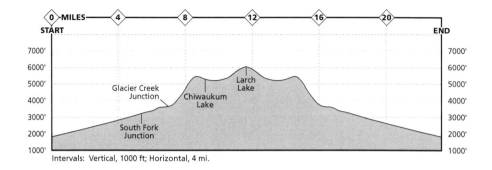

Intervals: Vertical, 1000 ft; Horizontal, 4 mi.

From the fork at 7 miles, Glacier Creek Trail 1573 leads 1.7 miles up into Glacier Creek Basin. This is a lovely meadow basin below the rugged, snow-clad peaks of the Chiwaukum Range. Although the trail officially ends at 1.7 miles, way trails continue up into the basin and onto the snowfields.

McCue Ridge Trail 1574 leads up from Chiwaukum Lake to a high ridge with expansive views. One can follow this trail 3.5 miles to the Lake Julius spur trail, then out to Lake Ethel. Approaching Larch Lake via Lake Ethel Trail is a more scenic option than Chiwaukum Creek Trail for those who don't mind hiking a couple of extra miles or enduring the "crowds" coming in from the High Camp.

For those who don't want to lug a heavy backpack all that way up to Larch Lake, a shortcut is available via the Scottish Lakes High Camp, a private lodging facility located just outside the Alpine Lakes Wilderness. Via a private trailhead, Larch Lake is only 5.5 miles one way, with very little elevation gain, making the lake very accessible as a day hike.

Key Points

0.0 Chiwaukum Creek trailhead.

1.0 Trail forks off from access road.

5.4 South Fork Trail junction; stay right (west).

7.0 Glacier Creek Trail junction; stay right.

9.4 McCue Ridge Trail junction; stay left.

10.4 Ewing Basin.

11.6 Larch Lake.

23.2 Back to Chiwaukum Creek trailhead.

37 Lake Ethel to Larch Lake

A more scenic path to Larch Lake via Lake Ethel and the Scottish Lakes.

Start: Lake Ethel trailhead.
Distance: 23.4 miles out and back to Larch Lake.
Difficulty: Strenuous.
Best season: Summer through fall.
Traffic: Foot traffic only; light to moderate use.
Total climbing: About 4,200 feet.
High point: About 6,100 feet.

Fees and permits: A Northwest Forest Pass is required.
Maps: USGS Chiwaukum Mountains, Mount Howard, Lake Wenatchee; Green Trails No. 177 (Chiwaukum Mtns.).
Trail contacts: Wenatchee National Forest, Lake Wenatchee Ranger District, 22976 State Highway 207, Leavenworth, WA 98826; (509) 763-3211; www.fs.fed.us/r6/wenatchee.

Finding the trailhead: Larch Lake may also be reached via Lake Ethel Trail 1585, which begins just off U.S. Highway 2 between Stevens Pass and Coles Corner. Take US 2 to Gill Creek Road, Forest Road 6940, about 15.2 miles east of Stevens Pass and 5.3 miles west of Coles Corner, on the south side of the highway. If approaching from Stevens Pass, the turnoff is just 1.2 miles past the White Pine turnoff; it is easily passed if you aren't paying attention. Follow FR 6940 across the railroad tracks to the power lines. The road forks; stay left and follow the main road as it skirts around and under the power lines, then curves up to the Lake Ethel trailhead in 0.8 mile. The road is a little rough in places but not too bad. Low-clearance passenger cars might bottom out here and there, but most manage to reach the trailhead just fine.

The Hike

The traditional path to Larch Lake is via Chiwaukum Creek, but a slightly longer alternative is available to those who prefer to get the climbing over with first, then meander through high lake country and across subalpine ridges, via Lake Ethel Trail and the Scottish Lakes.

Assuming you managed the drive to the trailhead, get your permit at the trailhead register and start hiking. (If the road proves too rough, park lower down and hike up the road to the trailhead.) The trail begins in fir and pine forest, climbing gradually at first, but soon switching back steadily up a dry, grassy slope. At one point, the trail comes close to a noisy creek, then switches back a few times and contours the slope to the edge of Gill Creek. In clearings below mature pines you get views down Nason Creek Canyon and across to Nason Ridge. About 1.5 miles up the slope, the trail begins to level out as it rounds the crest of a sparsely wooded ridge, then breaks into the first of several clearcuts, with views to Mount Howard and the other high peaks of Nason Ridge.

Lake Ethel to Larch Lake

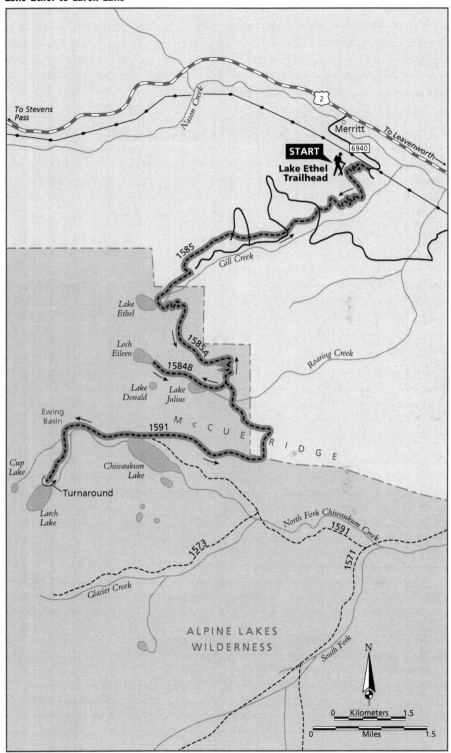

To Stevens Pass

Nason Creek

2

Merritt

6940

To Leavenworth

START

Lake Ethel Trailhead

1585

Gill Creek

Lake Ethel

Loch Eileen

1585A

1584B

Lake Donald

Lake Julius

Roaring Creek

Ewing Basin

1591

M c C U E   R I D G E

Cup Lake

Chiwaukum Lake

Turnaround

Larch Lake

North Fork Chiwaukum Creek

1591

1591

1571

1573

Glacier Creek

South Fork

ALPINE LAKES WILDERNESS

N

0   Kilometers   1.5

0   Miles   1.5

◀ *Ewing Basin, Larch Lake*

Shortly above the clearcut, the trail climbs up to the first of four logging road crossings. Once across the road, the trail leads up a wooded rib, which is soon paralleled by a cat track and logging debris. Not far above is the second logging road crossing, and soon above that is the third logging road crossing with a stone bench and fire pit. The trail continues up the ridge crest, a narrow island fir and pine forest between an ocean of clearcuts, and in 0.3 mile makes its fourth and final logging road crossing. Once past the logging roads and clearcuts, the trail leads up through silver fir and pine forest laced with lupine, still on the ridge, but not as steeply as before, then leaves the ridge and descends eastward, traversing steep, open slopes into a narrow meadow basin. After crossing a little creek, the trail climbs over a ridge and drops into a deeply wooded basin and curves leftward, seemingly the wrong direction, but soon doubles back up the basin, passing lovely meadows to the Alpine Lakes Wilderness boundary at a trail junction just a few hundred feet from Lake Ethel. Take a right at the junction, and hike to the lakeshore. There is a large campsite here, with others nearby.

From the Lake Ethel Trail junction, continue along Upper Roaring Creek Trail 1585A. You climb steeply up to and traverse an open ridge with great views, then drop down to a junction at a broad meadow, 2.5 miles from Lake Ethel. From here, it's 0.3 mile up Loch Eileen Trail 1585B to Lake Julius and another 0.8 mile to Loch Eileen, two of the "Scottish Lakes" (a third, Lake Donald, is hidden off-trail in a higher meadow basin). If you got an early start on the trail, it's a reasonable day's backpack to Loch Eileen, which makes a good base camp for a day jaunt to Larch Lake.

From the Loch Eileen Trail junction, the trail continues briefly through the meadow basin, then climbs up the opposite ridge and onto McCue Ridge. At first, you hike through thick pine forest flagged for cross-country skiers, but as you hike westward along the ridge, the trees diminish, and you traverse open, grassy meadows with great views of the surrounding mountains, valleys, and lakes. Eventually the trail descends to Chiwaukum Lake. From there, it's a short hike up Ewing Basin to Larch Lake.

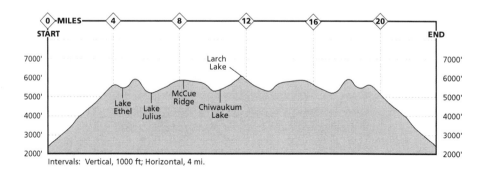

Intervals: Vertical, 1000 ft; Horizontal, 4 mi.

Options

Although the purist will prefer to hike in the long way, there is a shortcut to Lake Ethel and the Scottish Lakes via Scottish Lakes High Camp, a private lodge that has an access road to a trailhead just 1.3 miles from Lake Julius and 3.5 miles from Lake Ethel. Access via the High Camp is not only shorter but much more scenic, although it isn't free.

Key Points

0.0   Lake Ethel trailhead.

1.5   First logging road crossing.

2.5   Fourth logging road crossing.

4.0   Meadow basin.

4.5   Lake Ethel.

7.0   Loch Eileen Trail junction; stay left.

10.5 Chiwaukum Lake; turn right (west).

11.7 Larch Lake.

23.4 Back to Lake Ethel trailhead.

38 Whitepine-Frosty Loop

A long loop hike connecting Whitepine, Icicle, Frosty, and Wildhorse Creeks.

Start: Whitepine trailhead.
Distance: 25.3-mile loop.
Difficulty: Strenuous.
Best season: Summer through fall.
Traffic: Foot and stock traffic; light use.
Total climbing: About 4,500 feet gain and 4,500 feet loss.
High point: About 5,800 feet.
Fees and permits: A Northwest Forest Pass is required.

Maps: USGS Mount Howard, Chiwaukum Mountains, Stevens Pass; Green Trails No. 145 (Wenatchee Lake), 177 (Chiwaukum Mtns.), 176 (Stevens Pass).
Trail contacts: Wenatchee National Forest, Lake Wenatchee Ranger District, 22976 State Highway 207, Leavenworth, WA 98826; (509) 763-3211; www.fs.fed.us/r6/wenatchee.

Finding the trailhead: This loop hike is best started via Whitepine Creek Trail 1582, which begins just up the road from Whitepine Campground off U.S. Highway 2. Take US 2 to Whitepine Road, Forest Road 6950, about 14 miles east from Stevens Pass and 6.5 miles west of Coles Corner, on the south side of the highway. Follow Whitepine Road 3.1 miles to the Whitepine trailhead at road's end.

The Hike

The Whitepine-Frosty Loop is a 28-mile loop hike along some of the most remote, least traveled, and most scenic trail in the Alpine Lakes Wilderness. On portions of this hike, you are likely to see no one else all day, just wildflowers, mountains, and lakes.

The first segment of the hike follows Whitepine Creek Trail, one of the forgotten hikes of the Alpine Lakes Wilderness. The trail follows Whitepine Creek for nearly 8 miles, through pine and fir forest and a high meadow basin. It is a long, usually lonesome hike up a dusty, narrow creek canyon, without a lake or views to attract crowds. The trail has a reputation for being brushy and hard to follow, but the Forest Service recently brushed it out. The bridge is still out, though.

Get your permit at the trailhead register, and start hiking. The first 2.5 miles of the trail are straightforward, leading along the south bank of Whitepine Creek through silver fir and pine forest, well above the creek at first, with views up canyon to a craggy buttress of Arrowhead Mountain. There is a very brushy traverse across a broad stream gully about 1.2 miles up the trail; until the trail crews clear it out (if they bother), expect to bushwhack your way to the other side. Early morning dew on the assorted brush can soak you more thoroughly than a rainstorm. Watch your

Flowery meadow along Wildhorse Creek Trail ▶

footing on rocks hidden beneath the foliage; it is easy to slip or stumble. Once past the brush, the trail proceeds as before, climbing along the southern bank of the stream, soon dropping down to a rocky shelf directly above the stream, a good place to take a break. There is a campsite nearby, another at the junction. The trail continues along above the creek, barely gaining elevation in the final mile to the Wildhorse Creek Trail junction. So far the trail has gained only about 500 feet in 2.5 miles. Early season hikers usually turn around here and head back to the trailhead; the upper valley does not melt out until midsummer.

From the Wildhorse junction, the trail continues another 6 miles up Whitepine Creek. In just over 0.1 mile from the junction, Whitepine Creek is crossed just below the confluence of Wildhorse Creek; the bridge washed out some time ago, and there are no plans to replace it, so carefully ford the creek. Once across, the trail stays on that side and contours above Whitepine Creek through thinning pine and fir forest and below brushy talus slides, with views up the canyon of Jim Hill Mountain. The trail is not frequently brushed out, so be prepared for more wading. At about the 6-mile mark, the trail enters a broad meadow basin below the cliffs and talus slopes of Jim Hill Mountain. In early season there are wildflowers; in late season, autumn colors. There are a few campsites, rarely used.

At the head of the basin, the trail climbs away from Whitepine Creek to a 4,700-foot pass, gaining 400 feet in 0.8 mile, the steepest part of the hike so far. This section of the trail is not often traveled, even less often maintained; it was brushed out (more like logged out) not long ago, but it may again become brushy and hard to follow in places if not regularly maintained. From the pass, the trail drops a quick 0.4 mile to the Icicle Creek Trail junction. This is the end of Whitepine Creek Trail. Most hikers who come this far turn up Icicle Creek Trail to Lake Josephine, a mere 0.4 mile up the trail and a popular overnight stop.

From the junction, the loop continues down Icicle Creek Trail, descending a steep, narrow canyon 1.8 miles to the Chain Lakes Trail junction, then dropping a bit more to the canyon floor. Once the trail "levels out," it leads downstream in gentle ups and downs through open fir and pine forest and across brushy avalanche swaths for 1.8 miles to the Leland Creek Trail junction, then another 1.6 miles of the same continuing downstream to the Icicle Creek crossing and the Frosty Creek Trail junction. There are camps at this junction, and it's a popular location to camp, as it is 5 miles up from the Icicle Creek trailhead.

From the junction, follow Frosty Creek Trail downstream along Icicle Creek to Doughgod Creek, then begins climbing away from the creek through dry pine and fir forest, and in another mile joins the old Frosty Creek Trail. The trail continues up, contouring into a broad basin, coming closer and closer to Frosty Creek as you climb higher. This portion of the trail isn't as steep as other hikes leading up to Icicle Ridge, but it faces south and can be hot and sweaty going on a sunny summer afternoon, especially with a fully laden backpack. Higher up, the trail enters a meadow basin with a popular campsite. The trail has gained about 2,000 feet from

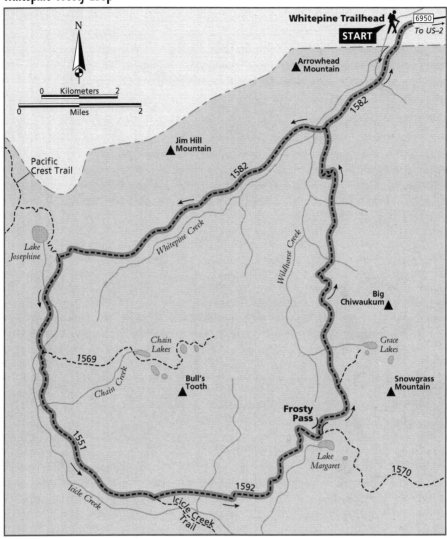

Icicle Creek so far, and it isn't over. It climbs a bit more, switching back twice and contouring to the head of the basin, where it levels out and a side trail leads to the shore of Lake Margaret, at 5,220 feet, a lovely lake set in woodsy meadows, very popular with backpackers. There are several campsites near the lake; campfires are not allowed here or anywhere in the vicinity. The trail continues another 0.4 mile and 400 feet up to Frosty Pass, elevation 5,780 feet, a broad, grassy saddle dividing Frosty Creek and Wildhorse Creek drainages, where three trails converge. Spectacular views can be found here of the Icicle Creek drainage, Stuart Range, and Wenatchee Mountains.

The final segment of the loop is a 6.5-mile downhill hike from Frosty Pass, following Wildhorse Creek Trail 1592. This is a scenic stretch of trail, traversing subalpine meadow slopes with wide-open views of the surrounding peaks. In about a mile down from Frosty Pass, a side trail leads up to Grace Lakes, a pair of lakes set in a basin between Snowgrass Mountain and Big Chiwaukum. A side trip to Grace Lakes beckons; the lakes are high and lonesome, the meadows bursting with wildflowers.

Past this junction, the trail passes several wide meadow basins liberally splashed with wildflowers by midsummer. Get off the trail and wade knee deep in aster, lupine, lousewort, and buzzing bees. Several creek crossings below 8,091-foot Big Chiwaukum allow thirsty hikers to water up for the remainder of the hike. The trail eventually descends into dusty pine forest and reaches the Whitepine Creek Trail, closing the loop. From here, it's a 2-mile downhill walk to the trailhead.

Options

This loop can be done in either direction. My preference is to always save the best for last; hence the counterclockwise direction described. Whitepine and Wildhorse Creek Trails can each be hiked as day hikes or easy overnight backpacking trips. Of the two, Wildhorse Creek is more popular with both hikers and horseback riders. All things considered, hiking Wildhorse Creek is the fastest route to Frosty Pass, especially for hikers driving over Stevens Pass from the Puget Sound region.

For those doing the loop, the 4.5-mile side trip to Chain and Doelle Lakes is worthwhile if you have an extra day or two to spend on the trail.

Key Points

0.0 Whitepine trailhead.

2.5 Wildhorse Creek Trail junction; stay right.

6.0 Whitepine Basin.

7.8 Whitepine-Icicle Divide.

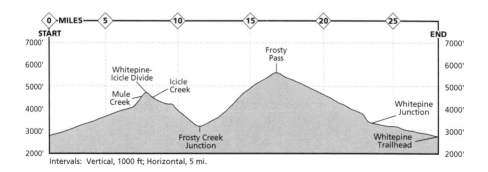

Intervals: Vertical, 1000 ft; Horizontal, 5 mi.

8.2 Icicle Creek Trail junction; turn left (south).

10.0 Leland Creek Trail junction; stay left.

11.6 Frosty Creek Trail junction; turn left.

16.0 Lake Margaret

16.7 Frosty Pass; turn left (north) onto Wildhorse Creek Trail.

23.2 Whitepine Creek Trail junction; turn right.

25.3 Back to Whitepine trailhead.

39 Nason Ridge

A high traverse along the crest of Nason Ridge.

Start: Snowy Creek trailhead.
Distance: 17.7 miles one way from Snowy Creek to Round Mountain.
Difficulty: Strenuous.
Best season: Midsummer to early fall.
Traffic: Moderate.
Total climbing: About 5,200 feet gain, 4,400 feet loss one way.
High point: 6,852 feet.

Fees and permits: A Northwest Forest Pass is required.
Maps: USGS The Labyrinth, Mount Howard, Lake Wenatchee; Green Trails No. 145 (Wenatchee Lake).
Trail contacts: Wenatchee National Forest, Lake Wenatchee Ranger District, 22976 State Highway 207, Leavenworth, WA 98826; (509) 763-3211; www.fs.fed.us/r6/wenatchee.

Finding the trailhead: Nason Ridge Trail 1583 traverses a high ridge rising just north of U.S. Highway 2 about 10 miles east of Stevens Pass. There are several places to begin this hike. The best, which is described here, is via Snowy Creek Trail 1531. To get there, drive US 2 to the Smith-Brook Road (Forest Road 6700) turnoff, about 4.2 miles east of Stevens Pass and 16.3 miles west of Coles Corner. Follow FR 6700, a typical winding, bumpy forest road, about 5 miles a fork; turn right and follow FR 6705 another 3.5 miles to the trailhead, on the south side of the road. Parking is limited.

This hike finishes at the Round Mountain Trailhead, which is reached via Butcher Creek Road (FR 6910). To get there, follow US 2 to the rest area east of Coles Corner. The road is 0.2 mile east of the rest area and leads about 4.5 uphill miles to the trailhead.

The Hike

Nason Ridge Trail is one of the best high ridge hikes of the eastern Cascades. The hike described is the popular way, approaching via a quiet, uncrowded meadow trail that climbs abruptly to the ridge crest, getting the elevation gain over with right away, then savoring the long, high traverse before descending gradually the last few miles out. Of course, the hike can be done in the opposite direction just as well, or in an abbreviated fashion by approaching from one of two more direct trails. However it is done, it is a memorable high traverse with great views, memorable wildflower displays, and solitude in places. Nason Ridge is not within the Alpine Lakes Wilderness, but it is as impressive and worthwhile as any hike across the way.

Beginning from the Snowy Creek trailhead, hike 2.4 miles along Snowy Creek to a lovely meadow nestled in a steep-walled basin below Rock Mountain. This meadow is a popular campsite. The meadow is shaded in the morning and evening,

Mount Howard and Nason Ridge from Wildhorse Creek Trail

and chilly winds blow through, so batten down your tent. Camp in the trees at the northern fringe of the meadow, away from the stream. Watch for deer in the early morning and late evening, pika shrieking in the talus, and, if you are lucky, goats on the craggy ridge above the meadow. If you are unlucky, you will have bears lurking about; be sure to hang your food, and cook well away from your camp. From the meadow, the trail climbs a quick 2,000 feet in just over 2 miles, wading waist-deep in wildflowers in midsummer, to the summit ridge of Rock Mountain, from where a short trail leads to the summit, site of a former fire lookout and, at 6,852 feet, the high point of the hike. The summit is a great place to set your pack down, sit back, and enjoy the panoramic view, including Glacier Peak to the north and Mount Stuart to the south, and the ridges radiating off in all directions. A hike up Rock Mountain from the Snowy Creek side is a good 11-mile day hike, one you might have to yourself.

Descending from the summit ridge, the rocky trail soon passes the Rock Mountain Trail junction and continues a short distance to Rock Lake, elevation 5,850 feet. If you're making a three-day trip of it, Rock Lake is a good place to make camp on the first night. Or continue another 1.3 miles to Crescent Lake, elevation 5,440 feet, which is a bit more private since fewer day hikers venture that far. Both lakes have a couple of decent campsites nearby, and there is plenty to explore. Rock Lake is fed by an old glacier remnant that sometimes shows crevasses near the abutting rocks, so be careful if hiking on the snowfield.

Continuing from Crescent Lake, the trail traverses the southern slopes of Nason Ridge, crossing Royal Creek in 1 mile and continuing to the Merritt Lake Trail junction. From here, Merritt Lake, elevation 5,003 feet, is another 0.4 mile along the trail. Merritt Lake is usually occupied by interlopers who came in the short way, just 3.5 miles from the road. From just beyond Merritt Lake, a 1.3-mile abandoned trail leads off to Lost Lake, elevation 4,930 feet. Lost Lake is hard to get to, down a faint trail of slippery rocks and roots, but if you want to get lost, it will get you away from the crowds. From Merritt Lake, the trail leads up to and along or near the Nason Ridge crest another 2.5 miles to the summit of Alpine Peak, elevation 6,237, which is occupied by a fire lookout. You stand your best chance of seeing mountain goats here, as well as the best views since Rock Mountain. The trail descends the other side of Alpine Peak, still on the craggy crest, to the Round Mountain Trail junction in 3 miles. The 5,700-foot summit of Round Mountain is not far off, although it's not really worth the effort unless you want to summit every peak along the ridge, a dubious achievement.

The final segment of the trail descends 6 uneventful miles to Nason Creek Campground, some by trail, much by road, where, hopefully, you have a car or ride waiting. The disadvantage to this finish, aside from the length and the sheer tedium of hiking along a road, is that the last 6 miles is open to motorbikes. Most hikers don't finish at the campground, but take the shorter option via Round Mountain

Nason Ridge

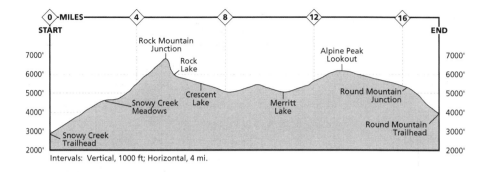

Intervals: Vertical, 1000 ft; Horizontal, 4 mi.

Trail 1529, a 1.6-mile spur trail leading to FR 6910. This shortens the one-way distance by 4.4 miles. Either way, you must have a ride waiting at the other end; if not, it's a long walk back to the car.

Summer afternoon thunderstorms are frequent on the eastern side of the Cascade crest. Be prepared to descend quickly from high ridges and peaks as soon as you see a storm coming.

Options

Nason Ridge can be hiked in either direction, or starting from any one of several trailheads. Starting via Rock Mountain Trail will shave off a few miles, but this is a much more strenuous hike and will not save you much in the way of wear and tear in the long run, plus you miss the meadows at Snowy Creek.

A climber's route from Crescent Lake leads up to 7,063-foot Mount Howard, the highest summit of Nason Ridge. It isn't a technical climb, but it isn't a hike either, and it should not be attempted by any but experienced alpine scramblers and climbers. Refer to *Climbing Washington's Mountains* (Falcon, 2001) for more information.

Key Points

0.0   Snowy Creek trailhead.

2.4   Snowy Creek meadows.

4.7   Junction with Rock Mountain summit trail.

5.2   Rock Mountain Trail junction; stay left.

5.6   Rock Lake.

6.9   Crescent Lake.

10.2   Merritt Lake Trail junction; stay left.

10.6   Merritt Lake.

13.2   Alpine Peak lookout.

16.2   Round Mountain Trail junction; turn right.

17.7   Round Mountain trailhead.

40 Deception Creek to Deception Lakes

A long, mostly lonesome hike up Deception Creek to Deception Lakes.

Start: Deception Creek trailhead.
Distance: 17 miles out and back to Deception Lakes.
Difficulty: Moderate.
Best season: Early summer through late fall.
Traffic: Foot traffic only; moderate to heavy use.
Total climbing: About 3,100 feet.
High point: About 5,100 feet.

Fees and permits: A Northwest Forest Pass is required.
Maps: USGS Scenic; Green Trails No. 176 (Stevens Pass).
Trail contacts: Mt. Baker-Snoqualmie National Forest, Skykomish Ranger District, 74920 NE Stevens Pass Highway, P.O. Box 305, Skykomish, WA 98288; (360) 677-2414; www.fs.fed.us/r6/mbs.

Finding the trailhead: Deception Creek Trail 1052 begins from U.S. Highway 2 between Skykomish and Stevens Pass. Drive US 2 to the Deception Falls picnic area, about 8 miles east of Skykomish and 8 miles west from Stevens Pass. Just 0.2 mile east of Deception Falls, turn south up Forest Road 6088, and follow it shortly to the Deception Creek trailhead at road's end.

The Hike

Deception Creek flows northward from Deception Pass, cascading some 10 miles down a quiet wilderness valley into the Tye River just west of Stevens Pass. Deception Creek is probably best known by one of its waterfalls, Deception Falls, which splashes down a rocky gorge directly beside U.S. Highway 2. The falls is one of the scenic highlights of this creek, but hikers who follow the trail up Deception Creek aren't the kind who come looking for pretty scenery. This is a quiet, moderately strenuous forest hike up a seldom-traveled trail, a hike for hiking's sake, not at all for casual hikers. The first 4.5 miles of Deception Creek Trail are among the least traveled in the Alpine Lakes Wilderness. This part of the trail has a reputation for isolation and difficulty, which is sometimes well founded.

From the trailhead, hike down into the woods, following the creek 0.4 mile to the first crossing via a footlog if one is there. This and other footlogs have washed out during flood years; they have been replaced, but there's no guarantee that they will survive future flooding. If there is no footlog, find a log up or downstream, or ford the creek carefully, at your peril. Once across, the trail climbs steadily away from the creek through old-growth fir and hemlock forest, then contours the steep canyon slope, gaining elevation gradually before rounding a subtle ridge and entering a creek basin. In 2 miles the trail crosses Sawyer Creek, climbs to a wooded ridge, then drops back to Deception Creek at the 2.7-mile mark and follows the creek's western bank another 2 miles to the Tonga Ridge Trail junction. This section of trail was recently

Deception Creek to Deception Lakes

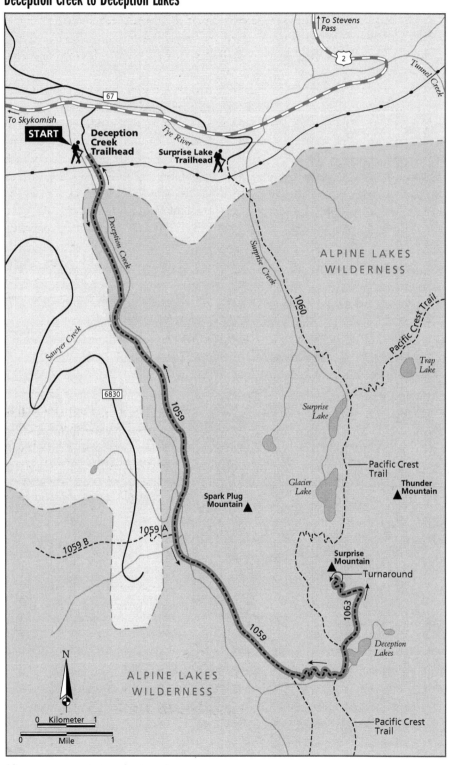

To Stevens Pass

2

Tunnel Creek

67

To Skykomish

START

Deception Creek Trailhead

Tye River

Surprise Lake Trailhead

Deception Creek

Surprise Creek

ALPINE LAKES WILDERNESS

1060

Pacific Crest Trail

Trap Lake

Sawyer Creek

6830

1059

Surprise Lake

Spark Plug Mountain ▲

Glacier Lake

Pacific Crest Trail

Thunder Mountain ▲

1059 A

1059 B

Surprise Mountain ▲

Turnaround

1063

1059

Deception Lakes

N

ALPINE LAKES WILDERNESS

Pacific Crest Trail

0   Kilometer   1

0   Mile   1

rerouted to avoid two perilous creek crossings. If you haven't seen a soul on the trail so far, savor the solitude you have enjoyed, because it may be over. Hikers in a hurry to hit the high country often use Tonga Ridge Trail 1059A as a shortcut, bypassing the first 4.7 miles of Deception Creek Trail.

From Tonga Ridge junction, cross Fisher Creek, and soon cross Deception Creek for the second time, this time via a sturdy footbridge. Continue along the eastern side of the creek for a short distance, crossing a side stream. Here the trail begins to climb away from the creek through silver fir and hemlock forest, and in over a mile of steady climbing it crosses another creek. Just beyond this creek crossing is the junction with Deception Lakes Trail 1059B. This trail leads 0.9 mile up to Deception Lakes, the usual destination for overnight hikers. This cluster of lakes is set in a subalpine meadow basin just west of the Cascade crest, a popular, often crowded, stop along the Pacific Crest Trail. From the lower trailhead to Deception Lakes is 8.5 miles one way; via the Tonga Ridge shortcut, the lakes are only about 8 miles round trip.

Those who hike the entire Deception Creek Trail, rare as they are, will continue from the Deception Lakes junction, contouring and descending gradually through the upper creek basin to cross the creek three more times before climbing through subalpine forest and meadows to 4,470-foot Deception Pass.

As on most hikes in the Alpine Lakes Wilderness, there are campsites near major trail junctions and creek crossings, and of course near the lakes.

Options

If you want to shortcut the first 4.5 miles of the trail, follow Tonga Ridge Road (FR 6830) 14-plus miles to its junction with Tonga Ridge Trail. From here, a short 0.7-mile hike down Trail 1059A leads to Deception Creek Trail, allowing you to bypass the lower trail, making a more feasible day hike to Deception Pass and Deception Lakes, or even Marmot Lake. A popular variation to the hike is to make a loop from Deception Pass to Deception Lakes via the Pacific Crest Trail, then down Deception Lakes Trail 1059B to Deception Creek Trail and out, or vice versa.

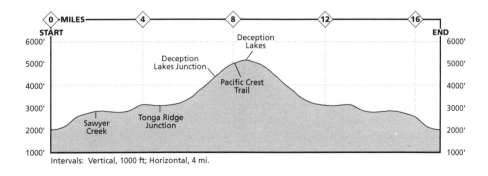

Intervals: Vertical, 1000 ft; Horizontal, 4 mi.

A mandatory side trip is to hike the 1.3-mile trail up Surprise Mountain. This 6,830-foot summit offers spectacular views of the surrounding wilderness, including an unobstructed view of glacier-clad Mount Daniel and other nearby peaks, lakes, and valleys.

Those making a multiday backpacking trip in this area can include Deception Pass, Tuck and Robin Lakes, and Marmot Lake as destinations, then hike out via the entire Deception Creek Trail. Another option is to hike out via Surprise Lake Trail 1060.

Key Points

0.0   Deception Creek trailhead.

0.4   First crossing of Deception Creek.

1.9   Trail crosses Sawyer Creek.

4.7   Tonga Ridge Trail junction at Fisher Creek.

4.9   Second crossing of Deception Creek.

7.2   Deception Lakes Trail junction; turn left (east).

8.1   Pacific Crest Trail junction; turn left (south).

8.5   Deception Lakes.

17.0   Back to Deception Creek trailhead.

41 Necklace Valley

A long river hike leads to these remote, beautiful alpine lakes.

Start: Necklace Valley trailhead.
Distance: 17.8 miles out and back to Opal Lake.
Difficulty: Easy for the first 5 miles; strenuous to Necklace Valley.
Best season: Spring through early winter for the first 5 miles; summer through fall to lakes.
Traffic: Foot traffic only; moderate use.
Total climbing: About 3,200 feet.
High point: About 4,800 feet.

Fees and permits: A Northwest Forest Pass is required.
Maps: USGS Skykomish, Big Snow Mountain, Mount Daniel; Green Trails No. 175 (Skykomish), 176 (Stevens Pass).
Trail contacts: Mt. Baker-Snoqualmie National Forest, Skykomish Ranger District, 74920 NE Stevens Pass Highway, P.O. Box 305, Skykomish, WA 98288; (360) 677-2414; www.fs.fed.us/r6/mbs.

Finding the trailhead: Necklace Valley Trail 1062 is approached via Foss River Road from Skykomish on U.S. Highway 2. Take US 2 to Foss River Road (Forest Road 68), about 2 miles east of Skykomish, just 0.6 mile east of the Skykomish ranger station. Follow Foss River Road 1.1 paved miles to a fork, where a sign points the way to various trailheads, including East Fork Foss River Trail. Take the right fork, continuing 3 gravel miles on FR 68 to the Necklace Valley trailhead parking lot.

The Hike

Necklace Valley is a narrow subalpine basin framed by granite cliffs and liberally endowed with a string of lakes set like jewels among pristine subalpine meadows. Hikers rave about this hike, as well they should, although it is the destination, not the hike itself, that most justifies the praise. The hike getting there is, indeed, no gem. It is a primitive trail, in places as steep and as badly eroded as any trail in the Alpine Lakes Wilderness. Trail repairs are under way, but slowly. No matter. The long, sometimes difficult trail deters many from visiting Necklace Valley, leaving some semblance of solitude for those willing to endure.

Necklace Valley Trail (or East Fork Foss River Trail) begins via an old railroad grade used in early 1900s mining operations. The going is flat and easy through quiet hemlock and fir forest. Moss carpets the forest floor, ferns shoot up everywhere, the river is a faint murmur in the distance. At 1 mile, the trail leaves the railroad grade and climbs briefly to cross Burn Creek via a wobbly old footbridge. At last visit, the bridge was supported by a stick; if it is not replaced soon, it will probably fall over. There is a campsite on either side of the creek. The trail continues another 0.5 mile on the railroad grade, then leaves it and climbs through hemlock and silver fir forest, past old cedar stumps and snags, nurse logs sprouting hemlocks and huckleberries. After a few gradual ups and downs, the trail drops to the marshy river bottom, then

Necklace Valley

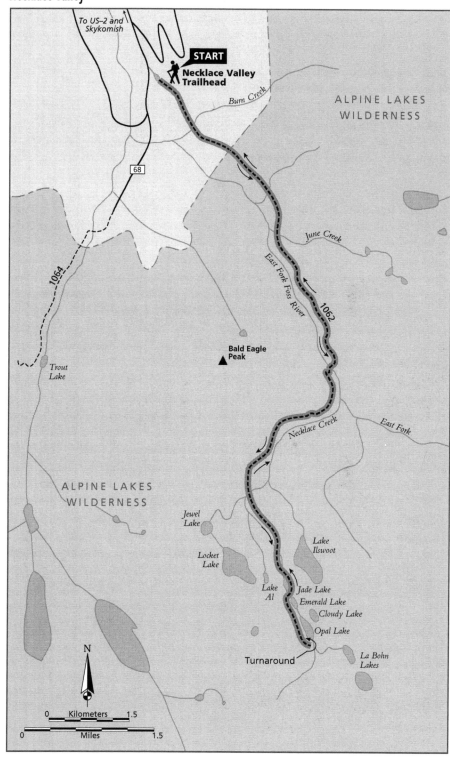

To US–2 and
Skykomish

START
**Necklace Valley
Trailhead**

Burn Creek

ALPINE LAKES
WILDERNESS

68

June Creek

1064

East Fork Foss River

1062

Trout
Lake

**Bald Eagle
Peak**

Necklace Creek

East Fork

ALPINE LAKES
WILDERNESS

Jewel
Lake

Lake
Ilswoot

Locket
Lake

Lake
Al

Jade Lake

Emerald Lake

Cloudy Lake

Opal Lake

La Bohn
Lakes

Turnaround

N

0   Kilometers   1.5

0   Miles   1.5

◀ *Jade Lake, Necklace Valley*

crosses a boggy area via an old, crooked puncheon pathway above devil's club and skunk cabbage. After climbing again through quiet silver fir and hemlock forest, the trail drops over a wooded ridge and descends close to the river, which drops noisily through granite boulders. Side trails lead to the river's edge. Farther on the way is more open but sometimes brushy, passing below an imposing 1,000-foot granite cliff. A short distance farther the trail passes a big campsite near the river, with century-old mining relics lying beside the trail. Soon beyond is the footbridge crossing East Fork Foss River, 4.9 miles, elevation 2,150 feet. The gentle grade and low elevation make the hike this far a popular and often recommended hike for early and late season. The trail gains only 550 feet of net elevation, although given the ups and downs along the way, actual elevation gain is somewhat more.

Once across the river, hike into woods on the other side until the trail turns abruptly and crosses an old footlog, then ascends talus to a mossy old trail section pressed back into service by a washout higher up. The trail has been rerouted here more than once; this reroute is presently marked by cairns. No doubt this section of the trail will be rerouted in the future; perhaps a new footbridge may be built. Once across the river and back on the trail, climb steeply up through talus and hemlock forest. This is slow, strenuous hiking, exposed to sun by midmorning. The trail angle eases off higher up, contouring above a stream, then curving southward and crossing an open talus slope at 6 miles, then traversing shady hemlock forest above the stream, much more pleasant going than that last steep section. Just past the 6-mile marker, the trail drops to the stream, then starts climbing again, now up roots and rocks. Seasonal streams flow down the trail; it's slippery when wet. In 0.4 mile of steepness, the trail crosses a footbridge over a noisy stream, then continues up as before, passing a memorable section that is steep, mucky, and badly eroded. After climbing to the head of a narrow rock canyon, you pass the 7-mile marker (seems farther), then climb through a quiet talus basin and scramble up a steep rocky gully, then climb a little more before dropping down to Jade Lake, elevation 4,600 feet, a pretty lake set in a narrow talus and cliff-lined basin, the portal to Necklace Valley. Officially, Jade Lake is 7.5 miles from the trailhead, but if you feel like you hiked farther, you're not the only one.

The hiking eases up once you reach Jade Lake. Skirt the lake's east shore and cross the inlet stream via a narrow footlog or boulders, then continue up through cliff-lined, talus-strewn heather meadows another 0.3 mile to the Necklace Shelter, a log shelter built in 1950. The shelter has served as a register of sorts for hikers, who have variously carved and written their names and stories on the beams and logs inside. Best entry: "7/19–22/73, rainy, women complained all 4 days." Just down from the shelter is Emerald Lake, a shallow, golden green lake. Not far beyond is Opal Lake, the gem of Necklace Valley, a narrow lake set below white granite cliffs. Side trails lead off to other lakes. Just before the shelter, a trail departs to Al Lake and Locket Lake, and farther to Jewel Lake. From the outlet stream of Emerald Lake, hike over a divide to Ilswoot Lake. Contour the east shore of Opal Lake to reach Cloudy

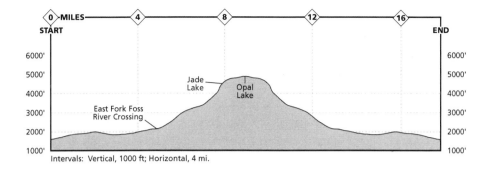

Intervals: Vertical, 1000 ft; Horizontal, 4 mi.

Lake. Hike up to a talus basin at the head of the valley, then look back for views of distant peaks. There's much to explore here, enough for at least a full day.

There are also several campsites here, but Necklace Valley gets crowded on sunny summer weekends. Use existing bare-ground campsites; don't create new ones. Also, don't come expecting the shelter to be available. If the trailside lakes are crowded, find a campsite near one of the other lakes. Campfires are not permitted in Necklace Valley.

Options

Experienced cross-country hikers can find the route up to La Bohn Lakes, a group of lakes set in a rocky basin about 1,000 feet higher than Necklace Valley. The route is quite steep and rocky, and not at all recommended. A less risky route to La Bohn Lakes leads over La Bohn Gap from Williams Lake via Dutch Miller Trail. Experienced climbers equipped for steep snow travel (ice ax, crampons) can ascend to the gap visible from Opal Lake and climb 6,585-foot La Bohn Peak. Mere hikers should be content with exploration of the lakes, and leave the snow and rock to the climbers.

Key Points

0.0 Necklace Valley trailhead.

1.1 Footbridge across Burn Creek.

1.6 Alpine Lakes Wilderness boundary.

4.9 East Fork Foss River crossing.

6.0 Talus traverse above creek.

6.9 Nestby Memorial footbridge.

8.0 Jade Lake.

8.5 Shelter cabin at Emerald Lake.

8.9 Opal Lake.

17.8 Back to Necklace Valley trailhead.

42 West Fork Foss River to Foss Lakes

A popular trail linking a group of alpine lakes above the West Fork Foss River.

Start: West Fork Foss River trailhead.
Distance: 13.6 miles out and back to Big Heart Lake.
Difficulty: Moderate.
Best season: Summer through fall.
Traffic: Foot traffic only; heavy use.
Total climbing: About 2,900 feet.
High point: About 4,900 feet.

Fees and permits: A Northwest Forest Pass is required.
Maps: USGS Big Snow Mountain; Green Trails No. 175 (Skykomish).
Trail contacts: Mt. Baker-Snoqualmie National Forest, Skykomish Ranger District, 74920 NE Stevens Pass Highway, P.O. Box 305, Skykomish, WA 98288; (360) 677-2414; www.fs.fed.us/r6/mbs.

Finding the trailhead: West Fork Foss River Trail 1064 begins via Foss River Road from U.S. Highway 2 near Skykomish. Drive US 2 to Foss River Road (Forest Road 68), about 2 miles east of Skykomish (0.6 mile east of the Skykomish Ranger District Office). Follow Foss River Road 1.1 paved miles to a fork, where a sign points the way to various trailheads, including West Fork Foss River Trail 1064. Take the right fork, continuing 3.5 gravel miles on FR 68 to another fork, and take a hard left onto FR 6835, which curves and crosses two recently repaired bridges over the East Fork Foss River, then straightens out and continues to the trailhead at road's end, 5.5 miles from pavement's end.

The Hike

West Fork Foss River Trail is popularly known as Foss Lakes Trail, since it leads to five alpine lakes set among the granite ridges and peaks above West Fork Foss River. Whatever you call it, this is a popular hike, at least as far as Copper Lake. The crowds seem to thin exponentially as the views expand the farther up the trail you go. Too bad for those who stop at Trout or Copper Lakes; each lake in succession is more lovely than the last. Pity even those who stop at trail's end; there are many wild lakes beyond Big Heart Lake.

Get your permit at the trailhead register, and start hiking. The trail starts out flat and rocky, like a streambed for a few hundred yards, as you cross the wilderness boundary amid maples and hemlocks. Soon the trail climbs up a few feet and becomes more trail-like, through hemlock and alder forest, gaining very little elevation in the first 0.5 mile. Soon the trail nears and then crosses West Fork Foss River via footbridges and rock hopping. If the river is running high, footlogs bridge the gap. A slender, 150-foot ribbon waterfall drops over a cliff directly across the river just before you reach the crossing.

Logjam at the outlet of Little Heart Lake ▶

The trail climbs a bit beyond the river crossing, then levels out and passes a huge specimen of Douglas fir before resuming its gradual climb through open hemlock and silver fir forest. At 1.5 miles, the trail crosses a wide rocky wash, then descends a bit to a gravel bank, dropping into the now still river. A few steps beyond and you realize you are at Trout Lake, elevation 2,020 feet. Trout Lake is calm and quiet but eerie, mysteriously ringed by dead trees. This phenomenon is readily explained. Recall the rockslide you crossed just before the lake; a decade or so ago it dammed the river, raising the water level, which killed the trees and sent the hikers camped at Trout Lake scurrying for higher ground. Fishermen flock to Trout Lake but are often disappointed; there are trout here, sure, but the lake is overfished, so the usual catch is small fry. If it's fish you're after, keep going. Trout Lake has five designated campsites and a pit toilet. Restoration efforts are under way here, so stay on the trail and use only designated campsites.

The trail ascends from Trout Lake, gaining 400 feet in a long 0.5 mile. At a switchback, the trail comes within a few yards of Copper Creek, a noisy creek cascading down granite slabs. A side trail leads down to the creek; if you need water, get it here, as the trail doesn't get closer to the creek than this for another mile, the steepest, hottest section of the trail. Continue climbing via a series of switchbacks, at first through old-growth Douglas fir, hemlock, and cedar, then up lush slide alder and maple slopes overgrown with bracken fern, thimbleberry and huckleberry, tiger lily, pearly everlasting, and bleeding heart, always within sound or sight of the creek, including a 300-foot waterfall crashing down granite slabs that never quite comes into full view. This section of the trail is best done in the early morning, before it gets too hot, or late afternoon, when it slips into shade. After the last of the switchbacks, the trail traverses woodsy talus slopes and at 3.3 miles crosses a footbridge over Malachite Creek. Another switchback higher is the Lake Malachite Trail junction.

From the junction, the trail flattens out briefly through open hemlock and huckleberry forest, then switches back a couple of times, again coming tantalizingly close to a waterfall, only to veer away at the last moment. Finally, the trail levels out and crosses the outlet stream of Copper Lake via rock hopping and footlogs, soon arriving at the lakeshore, elevation 3,961 feet. Restoration work is in progress at Copper Lake, too, but there are several designated campsites near the outlet stream and farther up the east shore.

Most hikers turn around from Copper Lake, but the best part of the hike—and the worst—is farther on. Continue up the east shore, then contour hemlock and silver fir forest, paralleling and then crossing the inlet stream via boulder hopping. The next quarter mile is a boggy mess most of the hiking season. The trail devolves into a proliferation of muddy trenches. In early season or after rain, count on slipping and sliding your way up the trail. The Forest Service is planning on rerouting this section of trail in the near future. The bogginess has its rewards, though; wildflowers aplenty are found here, including shooting star. The ugliness is over soon enough, and before you know it, you're at Little Heart Lake, elevation 5,204 feet. This is an

West Fork Foss River to Foss Lakes

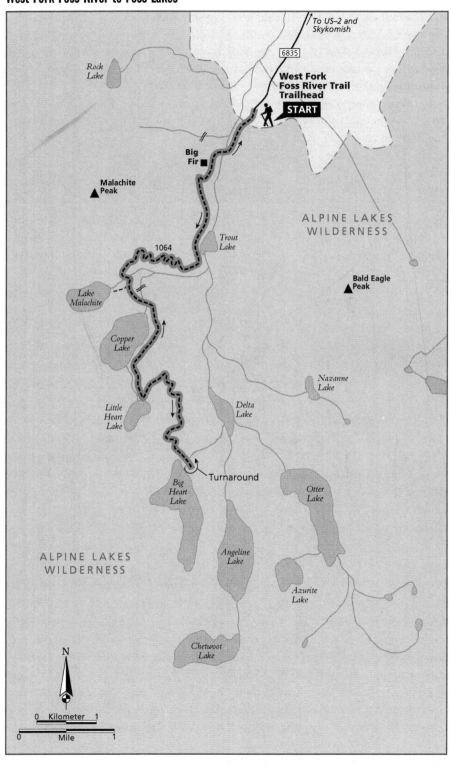

To US–2 and
Skykomish

6835

**West Fork
Foss River Trail
Trailhead**

START

*Rock
Lake*

**Big
Fir** ■

**Malachite
Peak** ▲

ALPINE LAKES
WILDERNESS

*Trout
Lake*

1064

**Bald Eagle
Peak** ▲

*Lake
Malachite*

*Copper
Lake*

*Nazanne
Lake*

*Little
Heart
Lake*

*Delta
Lake*

Turnaround

*Big
Heart
Lake*

*Otter
Lake*

ALPINE LAKES
WILDERNESS

*Angeline
Lake*

*Azurite
Lake*

*Chetwoot
Lake*

N

0   Kilometer   1

0   Mile   1

alpine lakes gem, a small jewel set in a talus-rimmed basin. There are a few campsites here, on the heather ridge just up and right from the trail.

If you turn around at Little Heart Lake, it's a 10-mile round-trip hike, still reasonable in a day for most hikers, but the trail leads on to Big Heart Lake. From Little Heart Lake the trail climbs up to and over a wooded ridge, traverses above tarns, and switches back up the open ridge above, with views back to Malachite Peak, Bald Eagle Peak across the canyon, and Glacier Peak in the distance. Once over the ridge, the trail descends mossy, fir-scented talus slopes into a lovely meadow basin. Watch and listen for pika scurrying in the talus. Two hundred yards beyond the basin is Big Heart Lake, elevation 4,545 feet, the crown jewel of the Foss Lakes, nestled in among wooded granite cliffs and snowy talus-strewn peaks. There are a few campsites along the trail, more hidden nearby. Even on a sunny summer weekend, you might have the lake all to yourself, except for an occasional day hiker or fisherman.

Options

The trail to Lake Malachite is steep and strenuous, but mercifully short, climbing a quick 300 feet in only 0.3 mile. Lake Malachite is set in a rocky cirque. The lake is about half the size of Copper Lake and has fewer campsites, making it a good alternative if you want some privacy. Some hikers camp at the little meadow where the trail reaches the lake, but there's a better spot on a wooded shelf above the lake just across the logjam.

If you have a map and are good at route finding, you can continue beyond Big Heart Lake to Angeline Lake and Chetwoot Lake. There's an old trail leading to Angeline Lake, although it doesn't show up on maps. The route to Chetwoot Lake is pure cross-country, up and over the ridge dividing Big Heart and Angeline Lakes. One could spend a week or more exploring these lakes and high ridges; actually, a week may not be long enough. Hikers without off-trail experience and proven route finding ability should stick to the trail.

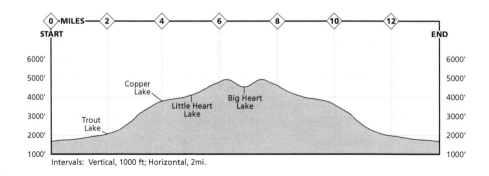

Intervals: Vertical, 1000 ft; Horizontal, 2mi.

Key Points

0.0 West Fork Foss River trailhead.

0.7 West Fork Foss River crossing.

0.9 A huge Douglas fir tree.

2.0 Trout Lake.

3.5 Lake Malachite Trail junction; stay left.

4.0 Copper Lake.

5.0 Little Heart Lake.

6.8 Big Heart Lake.

13.6 Back to West Fork Foss River trailhead.

43 Pacific Crest Trail–Stevens Pass to Snoqualmie Pass

A segment of the Pacific Crest Trail from Snoqualmie Pass to Stevens Pass, through the heart of the Alpine Lakes Wilderness.

Start: Pacific Crest Trail trailhead at Stevens Pass (south).
Distance: 68.4 miles one way from Stevens Pass to Snoqualmie Pass.
Difficulty: Mostly moderate, with some strenuous ups and downs.
Best season: Midsummer through fall.
Traffic: Foot and stock traffic; heavy use near Stevens and Snoqualmie Passes, moderate to light use elsewhere.
Total climbing: About 12,000 feet gain, 13,100 feet loss one way from Stevens to Snoqualmie Pass.
High point: About 6,100 feet.
Fees and permits: A Northwest Forest Pass is required.

Maps: USGS Stevens Pass, Scenic, Mount Daniel, Polallie Ridge, Chikamin Peak, Snoqualmie Pass; Green Trails No. 176 (Stevens Pass), 208 (Kachess Lake), 207 (Snoqualmie Pass).
Trail contacts: Mt. Baker-Snoqualmie National Forest, Skykomish Ranger District, 74920 NE Stevens Pass Highway, P.O. Box 305, Skykomish, WA 98288; (360) 677-2414.
Snoqualmie Ranger District, North Bend Office, 42404 SE North Bend Way, North Bend, WA 98045; (425) 888-1421; www.fs.fed.us/r6/mbs. Wenatchee National Forest, Cle Elum Ranger District, 803 West Second Street, Cle Elum, WA 98922; (509) 674-4411; www.fs.fed.us/r6/wenatchee.

Finding the trailhead: This description of the Pacific Crest Trail (PCT) begins at Stevens Pass and ends at Snoqualmie Pass, although it is just as feasible to hike it in the opposite direction. Take U.S. Highway 2 to Stevens Pass. Pull off into the southern parking lot, and find a service road leading up into the ski area. Signs point the way to the PCT trailhead.

The Hike

Very few hikers cover the entire 2,000-mile length of the Pacific Crest Trail (PCT) from Mexico to Canada. Of those who do, most do the trail in sections, hiking a few hundred miles one summer and so on until they have completed all or most of the trail. Likewise, few hikers cover the entire Washington section of the PCT in one go; more often they hike it in sections, from major highway to major highway, 60 miles here, 100 miles there. One of the most popular sections of the PCT traverses the Alpine Lakes Wilderness between Stevens and Snoqualmie Passes. This 68-mile hike takes between four and seven days for most hikers. A majority of hikers do this hike from north to south, starting at Stevens Pass and hiking to Snoqualmie Pass, to avoid an extra 1,000 feet of elevation gained when hiking south to north. Some follow the PCT faithfully, never straying far from this "superhighway" of Washington

Ridge Lake ▶

trails. However, there are many side trails and route variations leading to lakes, scenic meadows, and other points of interest all along the way.

From Stevens Pass, the trail climbs 1.5 miles up through the ski area into a wooded basin to a 5,100-foot saddle, then drops into a basin and passes below power lines, following the service road a short distance eastward before picking up the trail again. Once past the power lines, the trail contours forested slopes another mile to Lake Susan Jane, a small lake with a couple of campsites, then climbs briefly to a subalpine meadow bench and the Icicle Creek Trail junction above Lake Josephine, which is seen directly below. Some PCT hikers drop down to this large lake to camp, adding 2 miles to the overall hike distance; for those who don't want to increase the mileage, there are camps at the lakes farther along the trail. From this junction, the PCT leads southward, ascending the subalpine meadows and open forest over a ridge to a pass above Swimming Deer Lake, then descending to a gentle wooded ridge and along the ridge to Mig Lake. In another 0.5 mile is Hope Lake and the Tunnel Creek Trail junction. This area traverses open meadows renowned for their late summer berries. There are several campsites near the lakes. From Hope Lake, the trail climbs over a ridge into the Trapper Creek drainage and contours the slopes of Trapper Creek basin above Trap Lake, an inviting lake reached via a side trail. The trail continues up to Trap Pass, elevation 5,800 feet. The pass offers a brief break in the trees, allowing views down to Trapper and Surprise Creek basins.

From Trap Pass, the trail descends steeply down a wooded slope via switchbacks to a trail junction above Surprise Lake. The PCT stays high, contouring a long mile to another trail junction between Surprise and Glacier Lakes. At about 11 miles from Stevens Pass, many PCT hikers call it a day and find a campsite near one lake or the other. The lower trail (the old PCT) descends briefly to Surprise Lake, then leads up from the lake to rejoin the PCT just below Glacier Lake. The lower trail is just a bit longer, worth the extra 0.3 mile of hiking if you want to visit Surprise Lake, a good overnight stop. Either way, hike open forest past Glacier Lake into a talus basin below Surprise Mountain. An abandoned segment of the old Cascade Crest Trail leads directly up and over Surprise Gap from here, a shortcut to Deception Lakes. The new PCT stays right, switching back up the subalpine slope past a tarn set in a rocky basin, then climbing a bit more to Pieper Pass, a scenic 5,900-foot saddle in the ridge just north of Surprise Mountain, with a commanding view of Deception Pass and Mounts Daniel and Hinman. The trail drops over the ridge and descends the forested southern flank of Surprise Mountain about 1.5 miles to Deception Lakes. A few determined hikers cover the 16-odd miles to Deception Lakes on the first day, although taking two days is more common. There are several well-used campsites near the lakes. A side trip up Surprise Mountain is worth the extra effort; the views are spectacular.

From Deception Lakes, the trail contours up the eastern slope of Deception Creek basin some 3.5 woodsy miles to Deception Pass, elevation 4,470 feet. This pass forms the geographic center of the Alpine Lakes Wilderness, dividing north from south and east from west. The PCT continues southward from Deception Pass, contouring along the western slope of the upper Cle Elum River canyon, with good views down to Hyas Lakes and up to Tuck and Robin Lakes and Granite and Trico Mountains across the way, and ahead to craggy Cathedral Rock. This section of trail crosses several streams, including a couple that run high in early season. There are no bridges; you have to hop across rocks or ford the streams, which can be dangerous when the water is at peak flow. Check current conditions before undertaking this hike, lest you find the crossing too dangerous and have to turn back or take a lengthy detour down the Hyas Lake Trail and up the Cathedral Pass Trail. The Forest Service usually posts signs at key trailheads warning of dangerous crossings and recommending detours; pay heed.

Once past the creek crossings, the trail contours along talus basins and scenic meadow benches beneath Cathedral Rock and up to Cathedral Pass, elevation 5,610 feet. Views from the pass and adjacent ridgeline are some of the best so far on the hike, including mountains far and near and a look down to sparkling Deep Lake, your next stop. From the pass, the trail descends a series of rocky switchbacks, passing the Peggy's Pond Trail junction, then continuing down, down, down to Deep Lake. The side trail to Peggy's Pond is only 0.8 mile, close enough that some PCT hikers camp there, but most continue down to Deep Lake or Waptus Lake. Deep Lake is flanked by wide, grassy meadows, making it a popular spot to lie down for a rest before continuing on.

The PCT continues from Deep Lake, following the sound of Spinola Creek about 3.5 miles downstream to a trail junction, then rounding a ridge and contouring westward above Waptus Lake, one of the largest lakes in the Alpine Lakes Wilderness, set in a broad, forested valley below craggy peaks. In about 1.3 miles from the Spinola Creek Trail junction the PCT crosses Spade Lake Trail. The PCT does not drop down to Waptus Lake, but the lake is just 0.4 mile and a couple of hundred vertical feet down from this junction. If you do drop down to the lake, you can follow the old PCT along the lakeshore and rejoin the new PCT in about 0.6 mile. There are many campsites near the lake, which is a popular overnight stop among PCT hikers.

In about 0.8 mile upriver from Waptus Lake, the PCT forks off to the south and climbs a series of switchbacks up a steep, exposed slope to a ridge above Waptus Pass, a gain of 2,200 feet in about 4 miles, with impressive views of Bear's Breast Mountain and Mounts Daniel and Hinman across the valley as you climb higher. This is the most remote section of the trail, and the least maintained; there may be fallen trees blocking the trail in places. The trail continues up Escondido Ridge to a 5,600-foot saddle overlooking Escondido Lake, then contours southward to a subalpine meadow bench dotted with tarns, the Escondido Tarns. The trail continues around a ridge near a saddle, over which lie Vista Lakes, a few more tiny subalpine lakes set on a high shelf below Summit Chief Mountain. The entire traverse of Escondido Ridge is fantastically scenic, through lovely subalpine meadows with views of moun-

tains near and far, especially as you turn the corner and behold the Snoqualmie Crest peaks up close in all their sublime glory. Truly, this is one of the most beautiful spots on the entire PCT; take your time here. Some hikers camp in the vicinity of Escondido Tarns and Vista Lakes. Use existing sites only, away from the lakes; campfires are not allowed.

Beyond Vista Lakes, the trail descends 2,400 feet of switchbacks, first down open benches and later in forest, to Lemah Meadow and a trail junction. This trail leads 1.6 miles to Pete Lake, a very popular hike, which accounts for the appearance of so many hikers on the trail. The PCT continues through the meadows and old-growth forest, crossing Lemah Creek, to another trail junction at Delate Meadow. There are campsites at and near both Leman and Delate Meadows, although they are not the most scenic relative to the ridge views past and soon to come. The trail climbs from Delate Meadow to Spectacle Lake, one of the loveliest lakes along this section of the PCT. A side trail leads shortly to the lake, a popular place to pitch a tent, although some PCT hikers pass it by in favor of finishing the climb up to the ridge. Beyond Spectacle Lake, the trail climbs a series of switchbacks steeply up to Chikamin Ridge; this is the last brutal climb of the hike, nearly 3,000 feet from Delate Meadows, but it's worth it, because the views get better and better as you climb. From Chikamin Ridge you can see back into the Lemah Creek valley and down to Spectacle and Glacier Lakes, forward to Park Lakes, up to Chikamin and Lemah Peaks, and over to Three Queens and beyond. There is a campsite at the saddle, a popular spot for watching a sunset or sunrise, or both.

From the ridge, the trail drops briefly into a lovely subalpine meadow parkland above Park Lakes, with several campsites and a trail leading down to the lakes. From the Mineral Creek Trail junction, the trail climbs and then contours the head of the Mineral Creek basin to Chikamin Pass, another magnificent viewpoint. From the pass, the trail contours below the Four Brothers rock formation and continues across the upper meadows of Ptarmigan Park, just below the south face of 7,000-foot Chikamin Peak. The high point of the trail, about 6,100 feet elevation, is here where the trail climbs to a high ridge just west of Chikamin Peak. From a saddle you can look down to the Burnt Boot Creek basin, one of the truly wild places of the Alpine Lakes Wilderness. The trail curves southward along the ridge and the upper slopes of Gold Creek Basin, passing above Joe Lake and around Huckleberry Mountain, pausing at a saddle overlooking Edds Lake and Mount Thompson, then continuing around Alaska Mountain and above Alaska Lake. In a mile of gentle hiking above the Alaska Lake basin, the trail comes to Gravel Lake, on the right, and Ridge Lake, on the left. These lakes, just 7 miles from Snoqualmie Pass, mark the beginning of the end of the hike. Many PCT hikers spend their last night on the trail camped at one of these lakes, usually in the company of overnighters who hiked in from the pass.

◀ *Mount Daniel from the Pacific Crest Trail*

Pacific Crest Trail–Stevens Pass to Snoqualmie Pass

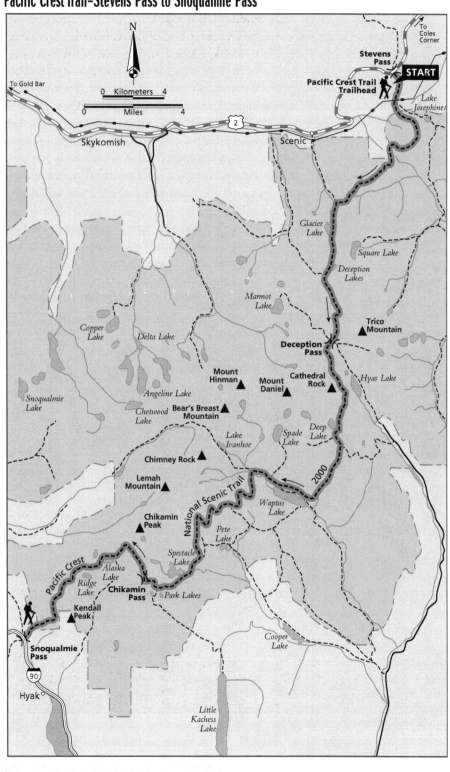

From Ridge Lake, the trail traverses open subalpine meadow slopes toward Kendall Peak, then crosses the famed Kendall Catwalk, a narrow, exposed ledge blasted out of the slabby cliffs. In early season, snow along the catwalk makes for dangerous going, another reason why most hikers wait until late summer or early fall to do this hike. Once across the catwalk, the trail continues along the rocky ridge to Kendall Pass. Cross over the pass and start down the final few miles, contouring along the rocky western slope of Kendall Peak, with views of the Snoqualmie Pass peaks, then descending into old-growth forest and switching back to the floor of Commonwealth Basin and a final trail junction. From the Commonwealth junction, the PCT crosses a talus slide, then climbs briefly into old-growth forest, and finally descends two long, lazy switchbacks through cool forest to the PCT trailhead at Snoqualmie Pass.

Many hikers are confused about the campfire rules along the PCT. On the eastern side of the crest, campfires are not allowed above 5,000 feet; on the western side, it's 4,000 feet. The trail crosses back and forth over the crest; hence the confusion. To clarify this, the Forest Service recommends no campfires at any lakes along the PCT, no matter what the elevation. Most of the popular lakes are no-campfire areas anyway. Definitely no campfires are allowed at any lake from Stevens Pass to Deep Lake, then from Escondido Tarns to Snoqualmie Pass. Use existing campsites at all lakes and trail junctions. If you bring a dog, it must be leashed.

Options

There are too many options to list here. Most of the side trails mentioned in the hike description are discussed in detail in one of the other hikes. Refer to your maps for trail data.

One could follow segments of the old Cascade Crest Trail, which leads up Commonwealth Creek to Red Pass and down the other side via an abandoned trail. This trail was abandoned because of a dangerous snow slope on the other side of Red Pass that didn't melt away until late summer most years, not at all in many years, forcing most PCT hikers to take a detour to Snow Lake and down Rock Creek. Wait until

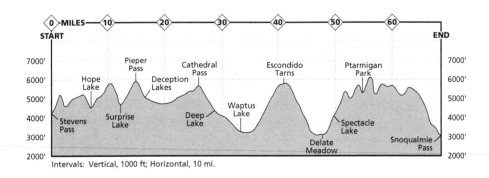

Intervals: Vertical, 1000 ft; Horizontal, 10 mi.

late summer of drought years to try it. The old crest trail continued up over Dutch Miller Gap to Waptus Lake, then up Spinola Creek to Deep Lake, then up and over Cathedral Pass to Cle Elum River, then up past Hyas Lakes to Deception Pass, then to Deception Lakes and over Surprise Gap to Glacier Lake and Surprise Lake, and finally up over Trap Pass and past Hope, Mig, and Susan Jane Lakes to Stevens Pass. This route would likely have less traffic than the new PCT, but it is much longer and not as well maintained (if maintained at all) in a few places. It's definitely more adventuresome, though, than the new trail.

Key Points

0.0   Pacific Crest Trail trailhead at Stevens Pass.

3.0   Lake Susan Jane.

3.3   Icicle Creek Trail junction; stay right.

6.5   Mig Lake.

7.0   Hope Lake.

10.5   Trap Pass.

12.0   Surprise Lake Trail junction; stay left.

16.5   Deception Lakes.

20.3   Deception Pass; stay on the PCT (southwest). If Daniel Creek is running high (Forest Service signs are usually posted), go down Deception Pass Trail and up Cathedral Pass Trail to rejoin the PCT past the trouble.

25.6   Cathedral Pass.

25.8   Peggy's Pond Trail junction; stay left.

28.8   Deep Lake.

32.4   Spinola Creek Trail junction; stay right.

33.4   Waptus Lake junction; stay right.

35.2   Dutch Miller Trail junction; stay left.

39.3   Waptus Pass Trail junction; stay right.

41.0   Escondido Tarns.

45.9   Lemah Meadow; stay right.

47.8   Delate Meadow; stay right.

49.6   Spectacle Lake.

52.6   Mineral Park and Park Lakes.

53.5   Chikamin Pass.

55.0   Ptarmigan Park.

61.1   Gravel Lake.

62.9   Kendall Peak divide.

66.0   Commonwealth Trail junction.

68.4   Snoqualmie Pass.

Appendix

Passes and Permits

Enchantment Lakes Wilderness Permit

Because of the overwhelming popularity of these areas, overnight hikers visiting the Enchantments, Nada and Snow Lakes, and Eightmile Lakes and Lake Caroline are required to obtain a Wilderness Permit prior to entry. The permit season is from June 15 to October 15, the prime season for visiting this area. Permits are available only from the Leavenworth Ranger Station, by mail or in person. Mail-in applications may be submitted on March 1; you may put them in the mail no sooner than February 21. In-person applications may be submitted after March 31. In-person reservations do not get priority, and reservations are filled at random starting on March 1, so you should mail in your application to improve your chances of getting a permit. The application process requires you to select three alternative entry dates and to choose the zone you want to camp in. If you get a permit, you may camp only in the designated zone. You may still day hike into another zone but may not camp anywhere except where your permit says you may camp. You must also submit an application fee equal to $3.00 per person, per day of your requested visit. So, if you are planning on taking a party of three into the Enchantments for four days, your fee would be $36.00. Permits must be picked up from the ranger station in person. Twenty-five percent of permits are given out in a daily lottery held at 7:45 A.M. each day at the Leavenworth Ranger Station.

Additional information is available from the Forest Service. Call the Leavenworth Ranger District for current permit information. If you ask nicely, they will mail you a permit application and informational brochure. Wilderness Permit information is also available on-line at www.fs.fed.us/r6/wenatchee.

Northwest Forest Pass

Ostensibly to provide a "simpler, easier way to support recreation" in the national forests, the USDA Forest Service implemented its Northwest Forest Pass program in May 2000. This program, like its predecessor, the Trail Park Pass, requires hikers and climbers using hiking trails and other designated "fee sites" in Pacific Northwest forests and parks to purchase and display a trailhead parking pass. An annual pass is $30.00; a daily pass is $5.00. The Northwest Forest Pass is available from the Forest Service and many outdoor retail stores throughout the Pacific Northwest region. For more information about ordering or purchasing a Northwest Forest Pass, contact your nearest ranger district office, or log on to the Forest Service's Web site at www.fs.fed.us/r6/mbs/nwpass/order.htm or www.fs.fed/us/mbs/nwpass/vendors.htm.

Other Parking Passes and Permits

Washington State Parks implemented a parking pass program effective January 1, 2003. Currently no other parking passes are required for hiking in the Alpine Lakes Wilderness and vicinity. The Washington Department of Natural Resources (DNR) does not have a permit system yet, but don't rule out the need to have a parking pass for DNR trails in the future.

Sno-Park Passes

The fees collected from the Winter Sports Sno-Park Permits pay for clearing and maintaining access to ski and snowshoe trailheads. A one-day pass costs $8.00 and allows one-day parking at all nonmotorized winter sports Sno-Parks, including special groomed trails areas. A seasonal pass costs $20.00 for a basic pass. Parking at groomed trails parks costs $40.00 per season. One-day, seasonal, and groomed site permits are available at several state park locations or may be purchased through the mail from the state parks' winter recreation program headquarters (P.O. Box 42650, Olympia, WA 98504). One-day Sno-Park permits may be purchased on-line from December 15 through April 30. Permits may also be purchased in person (for an extra dollar to cover handling fees) from more than 125 different retailers throughout the state. Log onto www.parks.wa.gov/winter/vender.asp for a list of vendors.

Local Contacts

Okanagan and Wenatchee
National Forests
Headquarters
215 Melody Lane
Wenatchee, WA 98801
(509) 664–9200
www.fs.fed.us/r6/wenatchee

Cle Elum Ranger District
803 West Second Street
Cle Elum, WA 98922
(509) 674–4411

Lake Wenatchee Ranger District
22976 Highway 207
Leavenworth, WA 98826
(509) 763–3103

Leavenworth Ranger District
600 Sherbourne Street
Leavenworth, WA 98826
(509) 548–6977

Mt. Baker–Snoqualmie National Forest
Supervisors Office
21905 Sixty-fourth Avenue West
Mountlake Terrace, WA 98043
(425) 775–9702
www.fs.fed.us/r6/mbs

North Bend Ranger District
42404 Southeast North Bend Way
North Bend, WA 98045
(425) 888–1421

Skykomish Ranger District
74920 NE Stevens Pass Highway
P.O. Box 305
Skykomish, WA 98288
(360) 677–2414

Northwest Avalanche Center
7600 Sand Point Way NE
P.O. Box 15700
Seattle, WA 98115
(206) 526–6164

Outdoor Recreation Information
Center
222 Yale Avenue North
Seattle, WA 98109-5429
(206) 470–4060

Snoqualmie Pass Visitor Center
P.O. Box 17
Snoqualmie Pass, WA 98068
(425) 434–6111

Washington Department of
Natural Resources
North Bend Office: (425) 888–1566

Washington State Parks
7150 Cleanwater Lane
P.O. Box 42650
Olympia, WA 98504-2650
(800) 452–5687
www.parks.wa.gov

Maps

Alpine Lakes Protection Society: The Alpine Lakes Wilderness and surrounding management unit, Central Cascade Mountains of Washington State (1:100,000-scale topographic map with trail data). Available from many outdoor retailers; somewhat outdated, but still useful.

USGS and Green Trails maps listed in each chapter. USGS maps may be viewed on-line via the Microsoft TerraServer at http://terraserver.microsoft.com; Green Trails maps may be previewed and ordered on-line at www.greentrails.com.

The North Central Cascades pictorial map, published by Richard A. Pargeter, P.O. Box 844, Kent, WA 98032.

TOPO! Interactive Maps on CD-ROM: North Cascades, Mount Baker, and Surrounding Wilderness Areas; Seattle, Mount Rainier, and Central Cascades; and Olympic Peninsula, San Juan Islands, and Puget Sound. Preview on-line at www.topo.com.

USDA Forest Service: Recreation Opportunity Guides (Skykomish, North Bend, and Cle Elum Ranger Districts); Trail Guide (Lake Wenatchee, Leavenworth, and North Bend Ranger Districts); Mount Baker–Snoqualmie National Forest 1:168,959-scale Forest Visitor Map, 1988; Leavenworth Ranger District and Cle Elum Ranger District topo maps. These and other maps available at all Forest Service offices.

Washington State Department of Natural Resources (1:100,000-scale planimetric maps): Snoqualmie Pass, Wenatchee, Chelan and Skykomish River. Available from DNR Photo & Map Sales, 1111 Washington Street SE, P.O. Box 47031, Olympia, WA 98504, (360) 902–1234.

Weather Information

Cascades Avalanche Report: (206) 526–6677.

Cascades Weather Report: (206) 464–2000 (category 9904 and 9908).

Washington State Department of Transportation Real Time Road and Weather Traveler Information ("Weather Beta"): test.wsdot.wa.gov/rwis/.

Washington Weather Web site: iwin.nws.noaa.gov/iwin/wa/wa.html.

Selected References

Beckey, Fred. *Cascade Alpine Guide, Climbing and High Routes, 1: Columbia River to Stevens Pass.* 2d ed. Seattle: The Mountaineers Books, 1997.

Manning, Harvey, Ira Spring, and Vicky Spring. *100 Hikes in Washington's Alpine Lakes.* 3d ed. Seattle: The Mountaineers Books, 2000.

Matthews, Daniel. *Cascade-Olympic Natural History.* 2d ed. Raven Editions, 1999.

Meyer, Kathleen. *How to Shit in the Woods.* Berkeley, Ca.: Ten Speed Press, 1994.

Smoot, Jeff. *Climbing Washington's Mountains.* Guilford, Conn.: The Globe Pequot Press, 2001.

About the Author

Jeff Smoot is a hiker, climber, and author based in Seattle, Washington. His other books include *Adventure Guide to Mount Rainier, Rock Climbing Washington,* and *Climbing Washington's Mountains.*